IMAGES
of America

CRESTON

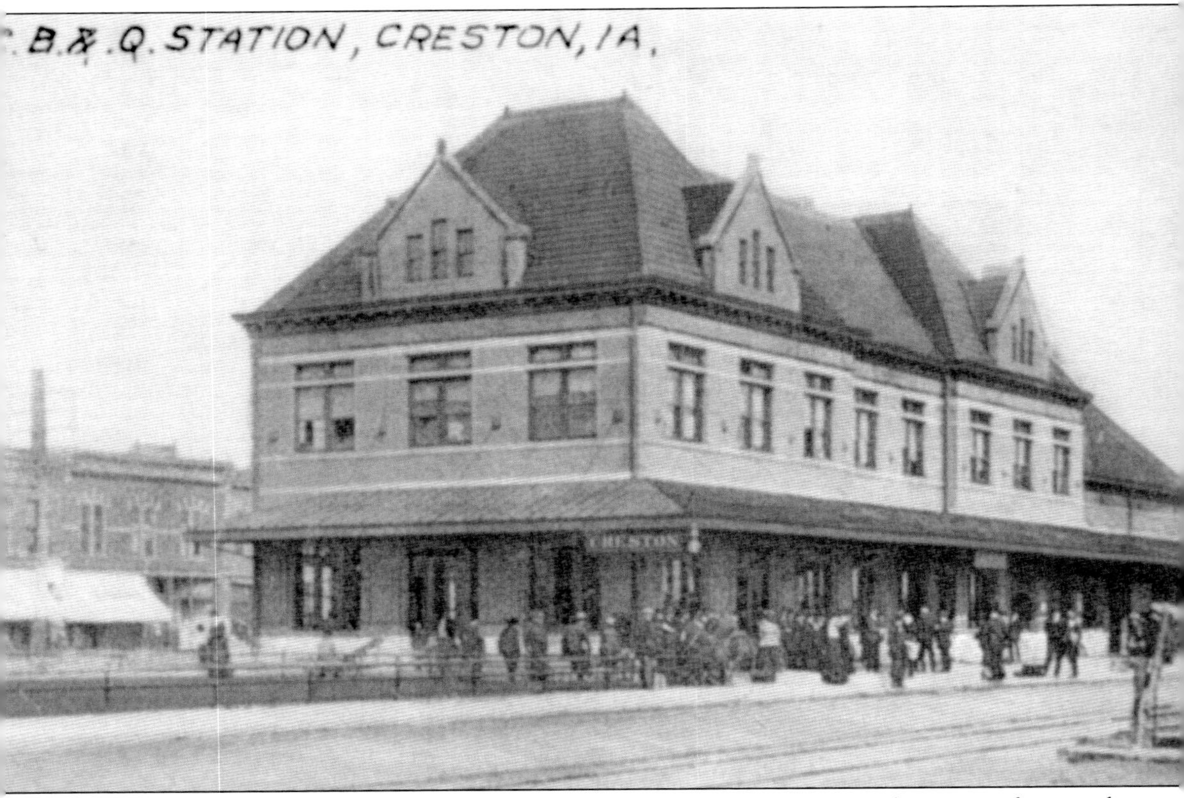

The Creston Railroad depot has long been a center of community life and a source of city pride. Built in 1899 for the Chicago, Burlington, and Quincy Railroad (CB&Q), the depot was described as the largest and finest depot in Iowa up to that point. The 2.5-story, yellow-pressed-brick structure was designed by renowned Chicago architects Burnham and Root in the Renaissance Revival style at a cost of $65,495. Originally, the canopy along the south and west sides was to be constructed of glass and copper to allow sunlight to illuminate the interior. (Union County Historical Society.)

On the Cover: This image shows the crew of engine No. 1550 shortly after a record-breaking mail run in 1899. From left to right are Jack Woods, conductor; Harry Smith, brakeman; Joe Knowles, conductor; Lon Abbott, fireman; and Pat Sweeney, engineer. Engine No. 1550 was brought to Creston after Chicago's 1893 Colombian Exposition to aid in faster mail service. Please see page 39 for more information. (Union County Historical Society.)

IMAGES
of America

CRESTON

Dianne R. Osmun

ARCADIA
PUBLISHING

ISBN 978-0-7385-8345-7

Published by Arcadia Publishing
Charleston, South Carolina

Printed in the United States of America

Library of Congress Control Number: 2010933315

For all general information, please contact Arcadia Publishing:
Telephone 843-853-2070
Fax 843-853-0044
E-mail sales@arcadiapublishing.com
For customer service and orders:
Toll-Free 1-888-313-2665

Visit us on the Internet at www.arcadiapublishing.com

This book is dedicated to Marcella Howe, who passed away on June 19, 2010. Marcella dedicated her life to educating the youth of the community and promoting the history of Union County. She taught for 50 years in the Creston area, including Lincoln No. 5 country school, a one-room schoolhouse. She volunteered for more than 40 years at the Union County Historical Society. Her tireless efforts to preserve the heritage of the one-room schoolhouse for future generations has been an inspiration to all who knew her. Her guidance and knowledge will be sorely missed.

Contents

ACKNOWLEDGMENTS

This book is a small slice of the rich and extensive history of Creston, gathered from a wide variety of sources, including memoirs, personal accounts, newspaper articles, and records of the period. I regret that I was not able to include the wealth of interesting and unique information available in its entirety. It is my hope that the breadth of this book serves to highlight and present with continuity the overall history of Creston.

There are several people and organizations that have helped made this book possible. I wish to thank the members of the Union County Historical Society who graciously allowed me access to their museum's research library, archives, and photographic collections. I specifically want to convey my gratitude to Brian Zachary, Dick Anderson, Steve Francis, and Brandon Cheers for aiding me in my search of the group's treasure trove of fascinating stories and information.

The many images appearing in this book were provided by a wide variety of sources. I want to thank the following for opening their collections to me and allowing me to use their images in this book: Lynne Schlaht, Hol Wagner, Dave Lotz, Steve Francis, Jane Briley, Dave Moffitt, Roger Nurnberg, Rosalie Denton, P. F. Allen, Norm Ridinger, Gary Wimmer, Dave Long of American Home Design Center, Walter Cunningham, Dr. Larry Tilley, John Robinson, Stephani Finley of the *Creston News Advertiser*, Ben Walter of KSIB Radio, Sarah Lane of St. Malachy School, Terri Higgins of Southwestern Community College, Maple Street Memories, Harvey Phillips Foundation, Roper Center for Public Opinion Research, and Jim Goss (director) of the Frank Phillips Home in Bartlesville, Oklahoma.

I also wish to express my appreciation to all those who offered their expertise in various areas, including editing, formatting, scanning, identifying images, taking pictures, and providing information. I specifically want to thank Dave Lotz, Ellen Gerharz, Warren Woods, Brian Zachary, Dale Liddocoat, Margaret Baker, Chris Coke, Bill Fastenow, Rose Osmun, Phyllis Allen, Barb Coenen, Linda Castillo, Nathan Hamilton, Norm Ridinger, Karl Knock, Joel Emerson, Jeff Emerson, Matt Thompson, Sharon Higgins, the Creston High School class of 1942, John Pearson, and Ted Gerstle.

INTRODUCTION

In the early 1800s, Iowa was considered a wild and inhospitable wilderness of undulating prairie grasses furrowed by wandering streams and dotted with dense groves of deciduous trees. The Sac and Fox people roamed freely, hunting wild game and fishing, until March 23, 1843, when the tribes were forced to relinquish their lands in southern Iowa to the federal government. The area was sparsely populated until 1846, when 3,000 Mormons reached the east banks of the Grand River in what would become the eastern part of Union County. Sickness forced the party to make a temporary settlement that the Mormon pioneers called Mount Pisgah. That same year, on December 28, Iowa became the 29th state admitted to the Union.

Marsh and Leech staked the township corners for Union County in 1848 and 1849. Union County was then legally created by the Third Iowa General Assembly in 1850. The Mormons remained the largest collection of inhabitants, until the group suffered an extremely harsh winter in which about one-tenth of the population perished. The remaining members moved on to the Promise Land in Utah in 1853. The journey westward took them to within a mile of what would later become Creston.

The next year, in 1854, surveyors returned to the region to create a wagon road from Burlington to Kanesville, now Council Bluffs. This route was a heavily traveled stage and freight road that roughly follows the present Highway 34. The 1850s saw great anticipation in the residents of Iowa about the prospect of the coming of the railroad. Excitement grew as the Burlington Railroad made connections with the Burlington and Missouri River Railroad (B&MR). This final link created the circumstances for the expansion of the route across southern Iowa. Unfortunately, the rails had only reached Ottumwa, 75 miles from its starting point in Burlington, when the Civil War broke out. Construction was halted until after the war in 1865, when work began again in July.

When contractors Wolf and Carpenter reached Union County with the B&MR rails in the summer of 1868, Petersville was the county seat of Union County. Petersville was located in the eastern part of the county, just west of the Grand River. In the early days of Union County, business was conducted in the log cabins that had sprung up around the gristmill Henry Peters acquired from the Mormons. District court was held in one of the log homes there. On one especially stormy day, torrents of rain collapsed a clay chimney, forcing court to be adjourned suddenly, as the people in the "courtroom" were literally smoked out.

The railroad bypassed Petersville to the north by a quarter-mile and continued west through Afton and on to the western edge of the county. Shortly after the railroad reached Union County in 1868, commissioners chose Afton, established in 1854, to be the next county seat and the site of a county courthouse. As Afton was more centrally located within the county, it was a logical choice. Union County's first courthouse, finished in November 1857, was a 20-foot-by-40-foot frame building located on the southwest corner of the Afton city square.

Initially railroad officials chose Cromwell as the division point between the Mississippi and Missouri Rivers. The town was platted out, a large reservoir was constructed to provide water for locomotives, and a substantial frame hotel was constructed in anticipation of the railroad's arrival. Cromwell, however, had one very distinct disadvantage: It was located 5 miles west of the watershed divide between the two great rivers. This meant that all eastbound trains would have to begin their runs with a 5-mile climb out of Cromwell.

Creston's destiny was sealed when Charles E. Perkins, superintendent of the railroad, decided to relocate the division point to higher ground, 5 miles east of Cromwell on the crest of the grade—at 1,318 feet above sea level. This was substantially higher than the beginning elevation of 533 feet at Burlington and the ending elevation of 978 feet in Council Bluffs. The spot selected was on the summit of the treeless, grass-covered prairie where a Burlington and Missouri River Railroad survey crew had camped in 1868.

On June 21, 1869, the first scheduled B&MR train arrived in Creston from the east, with the throttle manned by engineer Dan W. Scullen. The engine, called "J. C. Hall," was the railroad's second locomotive. It was an ancient engine that was scrapped soon after reaching Creston.

By the fall of 1869, the town was platted and construction began in earnest. The first house was hauled in on a flatcar by the railroad from Afton. Union Street became the first center of business, as it was located just south of the new tracks running through town. Shortly after the town was laid out, the first store was built by A. C. Rowell. Much of the tiny community of Cromwell literally packed up and moved to Creston, including the sizeable new hotel, which was loaded on flatcars and hauled to Creston. The hotel, the Revere House, was reassembled on the corner of Union and Maple Streets in the newly established business district.

While Creston was developing as a community, the railroad was busy establishing its division station; a roundhouse and machine shops were constructed around the recently built freight and stockyards. A large two-story frame depot was built along the north side of the tracks. Creston very rapidly became the industrial and transportation center for the area. The influx of laborers, including machinists, boilermakers, switchmen, firemen, and engineers, made Creston's workforce more like Chicago's than a small Iowa frontier town. Creston soon earned the reputation of "Little Chicago" because of the stockyards and railroad.

The railroad created Creston and gave it its character. It was the town's largest employer, drawing immigrants from all over to the fledgling community in search of jobs. Railroad employees made up much of Creston's early population, creating what was described as a "rough and ready" place. In 1876, Creston city marshal W. H. Hamilton wrote to a friend in Ohio: "This country has more life, more grit, more fun, more amusements of all kinds, and is far better for speculation than Ohio."

One

The Scream of a Steam Whistle

While founded by the railroad in 1869, it was not until April 1871 that Creston was incorporated. Three prominent citizens—Capt. H. M. Way, Col. S. D. Swan, and R. P. Smith—advanced their own money for the purpose. Swan was elected as Creston's first mayor. Soon commercial brick buildings and framed houses began to appear. The Town Company (the railroad) donated the land five blocks south of the railroad and between Birch and Vine Streets for Creston's first park, South Park.

A year later, in 1872, Afton proudly presented the county with a new brick-and-limestone courthouse, miles of plank sidewalks were constructed, and Swan was elected to a second term. That same year, Creston narrowly escaped a smallpox outbreak when a Dr. Lewis discovered an infected woman at the Kunath House Hotel when he went to deliver her baby. Luckily she was quarantined before exposing the whole town. Creston continued to grow and prosper. On December 31, 1872, the B&MR was leased to the Chicago, Burlington, and Quincy Railroad (CB&Q), which later purchased the line on July 31, 1875. This acquisition placed Creston on the mainline from Chicago to Denver.

In 1873, the CB&Q financed the building of the town's first library on the corner of Union and Maple Streets, across from the Revere House. Many churches and civic organizations utilized the second floor of the structure for meetings until their own buildings were constructed. That fall, frequent grass fires demonstrated the need for a fire department. Always active in civic matters, several railroad employees became some of the first members of Creston's volunteer fire department.

By 1875, the roundhouse was complete, giving Creston the privilege of possessing the largest roundhouse west of Chicago. Yet this was an age when towns that were not county seats usually did not fair well. The railroad began advocating for the transfer of the county seat from Afton to Creston. The plot went as far as railroad officials and local merchants financing the construction of a new 72-foot-square courthouse, with the intention of donating it to the county in an effort to influence the transfer.

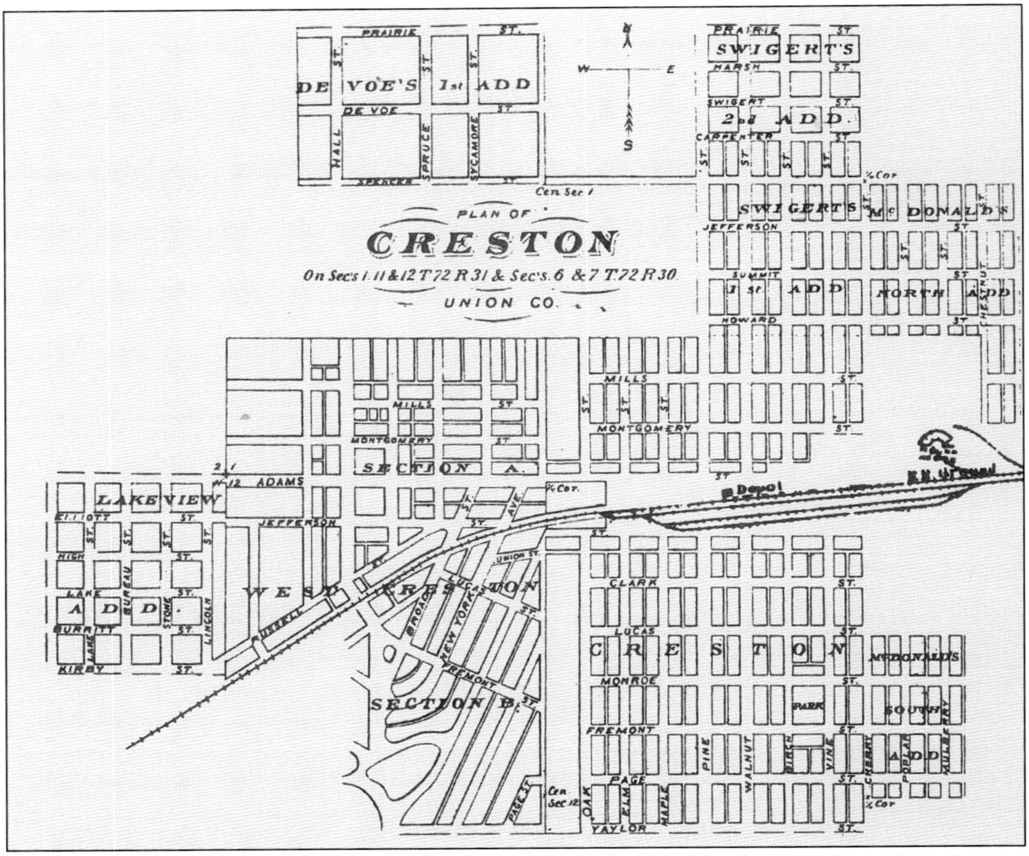

This map shows Creston as it appeared around 1875. When originally platted in 1869, the city was intended to be primarily on the south side of the tracks. The plot labeled "park," between Birch and Vine Streets in the lower right corner, was to be the town square; however, even at this early date, the town's growth was beginning to concentrate on the north side of the tracks. (Union County Historical Society.)

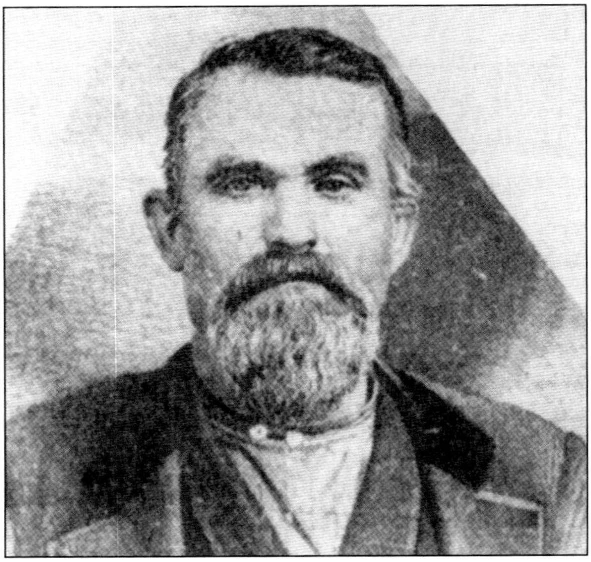

The first scheduled BM&R train arrived in Creston on June 21, 1869, with engineer Dan W. Scullen at the throttle. The Scullen family lived in a portable house on a railroad flatcar for several years as the construction of the railroad progressed across the state. In 1872, after the railroad's completion in Council Bluffs, the family returned to live in Creston. (*Creston News Advertiser.*)

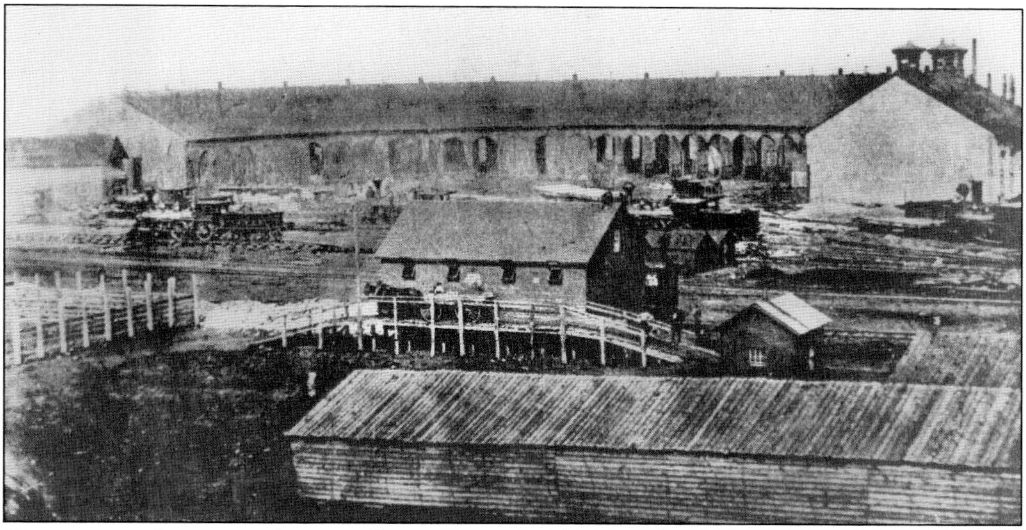

Construction began on the roundhouse immediately after the division point was established in 1869. Shown in the background are the 25 stalls that were completed by 1873. The original stockyards are at the far left. The ramp in the foreground served George A. Blackwell's granary. (Corbin-Wagner Collection.)

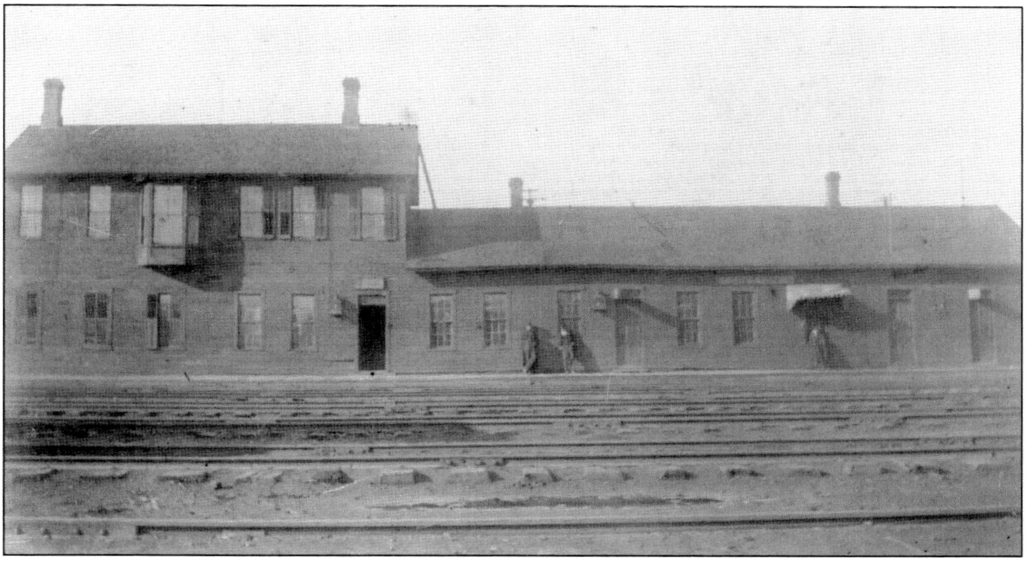

Creston's first permanent depot was built shortly after the city was founded. It was a fairly simple frame structure that was painted red. The entire one- and two-story construction is believed to be the original design, although the shuttered windows and bay window on the second story are unusual for a station of this type. This depot served Creston until 1899, when the more elaborate brick structure replaced it. (Corbin-Wagner Collection.)

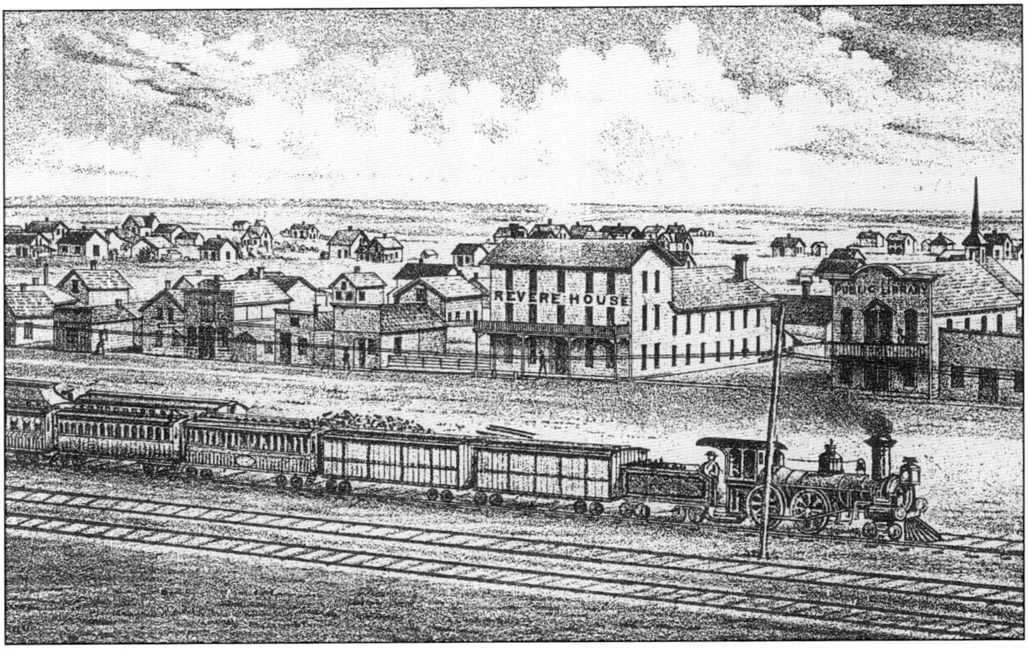

The first business district was along Union Street on the south side of the tracks, shown above in 1875. The Revere House was reassembled on the corner of Union and Maple Streets after being brought to Creston from Cromwell. The CB&Q built the first library at the same intersection, across the street to the west. Lake Park was developed in west Creston to provide water for the railroad. Shown below looking north from Union Street, the completed roundhouse and shops can be seen. When the railroad donated the land for South Park, it was intended to serve as a town square. But as the new town grew, businesses began to emerge on the north side of the tracks instead. Eventually, the uptown business district overtook Union Street as the commercial center for Creston. (Both, Union County Historical Society.)

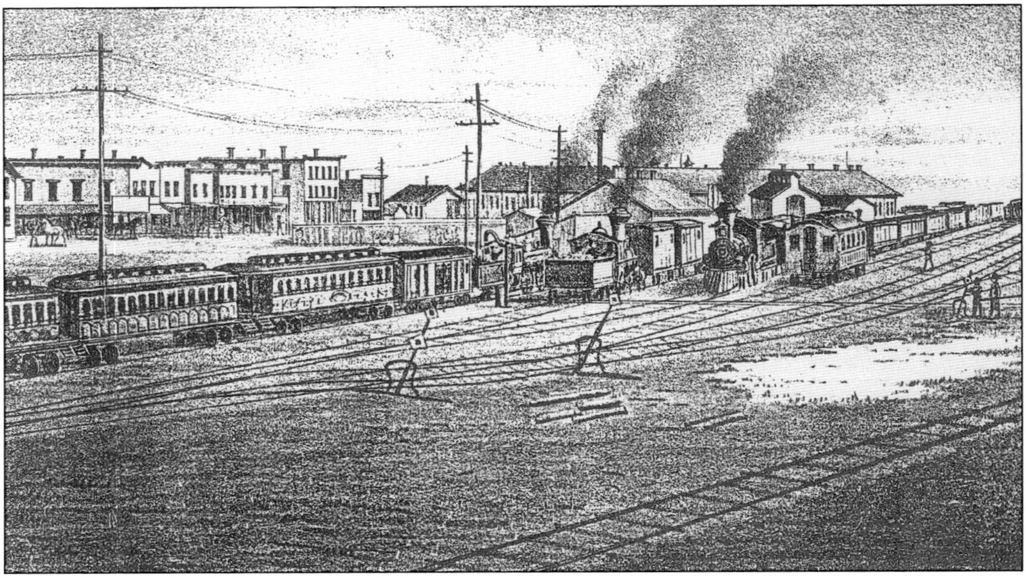

Col. S. D. Swan was elected as Creston's first mayor in 1871. He was the proprietor of the Summit House Hotel, located on the corner of Adams and Elm Streets. Summit House Restaurant was considered to be the finest eating establishment in Creston until it burned in January 1896. Swan's home was a stately Italianate-style structure located in the 700 block of West Adams Street. The home was originally decorated and furnished by Marshall Fields of Chicago. The ceilings were trimmed in gold leaf, and there were two beautiful fireplaces, one with a black-marble mantel and the other with cinnamon marble. Swan's house was featured in the 1892 *Souvenir of Creston* lithograph collection. The house still remains standing, though it has been altered considerably. (Right, *Creston News Advertiser*; below, Union County Historical Society.)

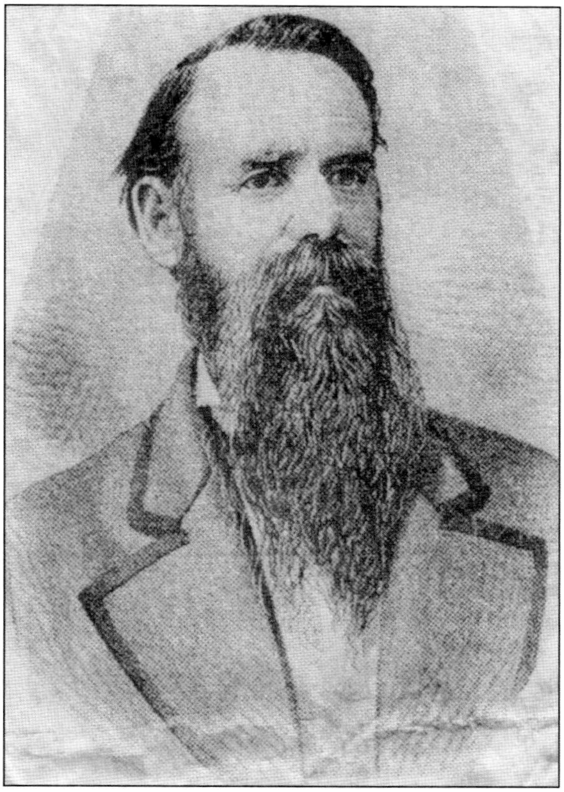

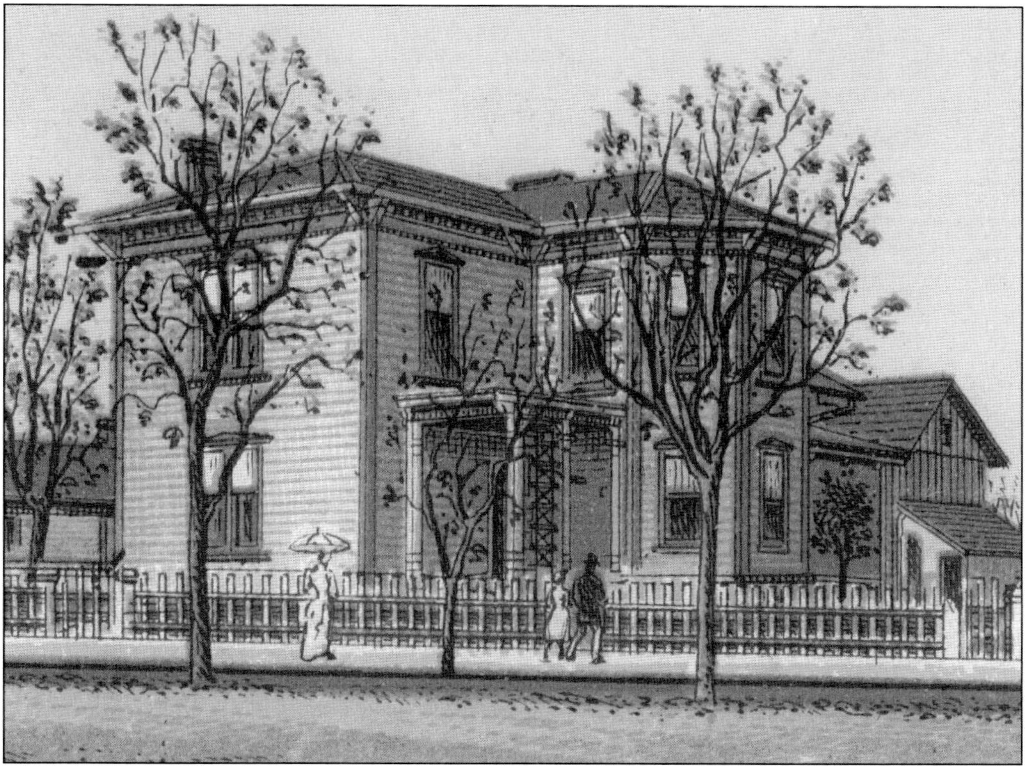

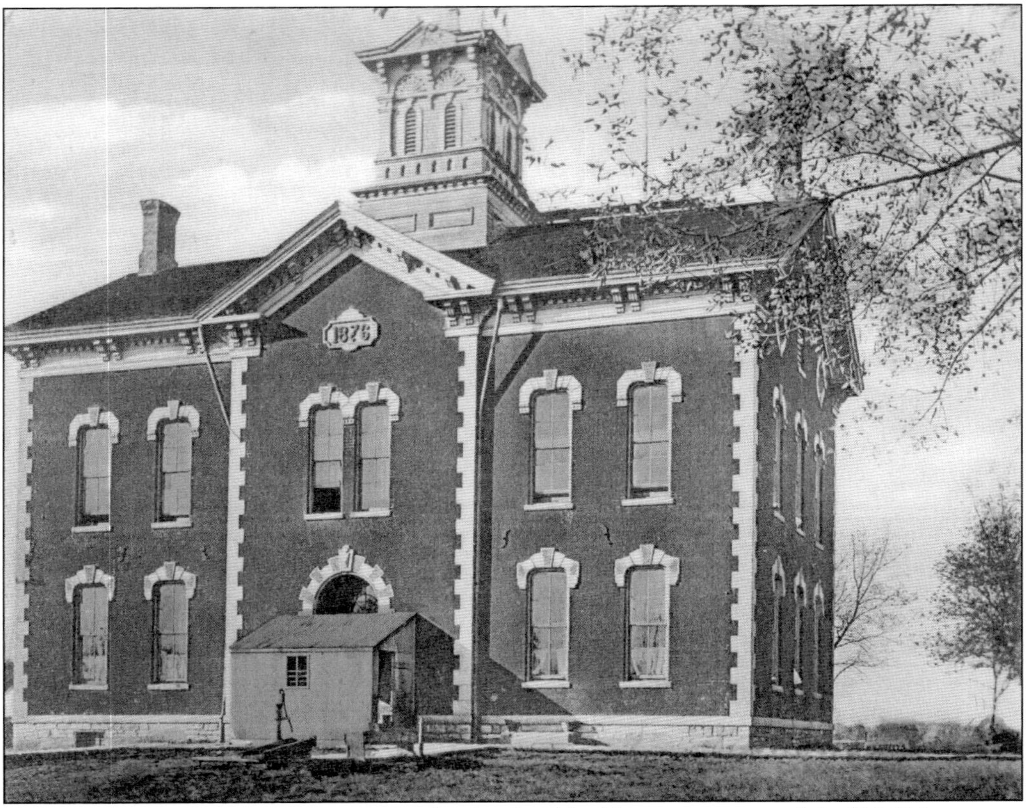

In 1876, two brick school buildings were erected for $18,998: Irving School (above) on the north side and Franklin School on the south side. The identical structures were two-story edifices that consisted of four rooms each. Irving School was located on the corner of Maple and Irving Streets. It was later replaced with the high school at the same location in 1925 (see page 74). Franklin School was on South Pine Street. (Lynne Schlaht.)

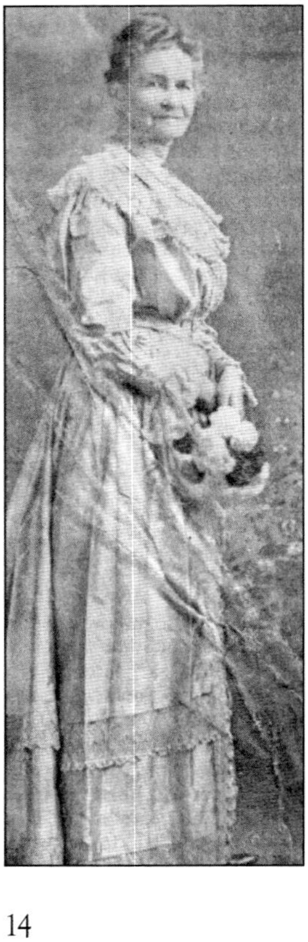

Sarah Elizabeth Joiner Sawyer, the high school's second principal, taught in Creston for 30 years. She provided the following description of her experience: "In 1872, I landed in a little hamlet on the vast, rolling prairie, where the wild flowers grew close up to the door. Churches and school were still in their infancy, the former bravely holding the forces against intemperance, vice, and immorality, and the latter not even graded." (*Creston News Advertiser.*)

St. John's United Church of Christ, dedicated in 1878, was originally St. John's German Evangelical Lutheran Church. In 1879, the east wing was built for a school. It is now a fellowship hall. The parsonage, just south of the church, was built in 1907. There were still some services held in German at the church until the early 1970s. It is still located on the corner of Maple and Fremont Streets. (Lynne Schlaht.)

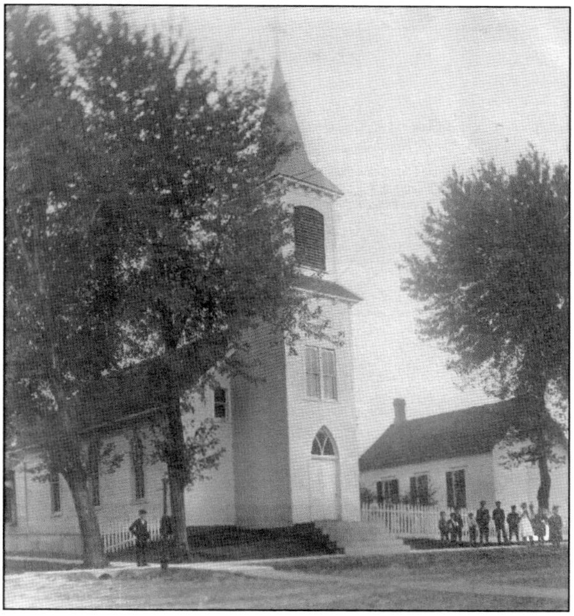

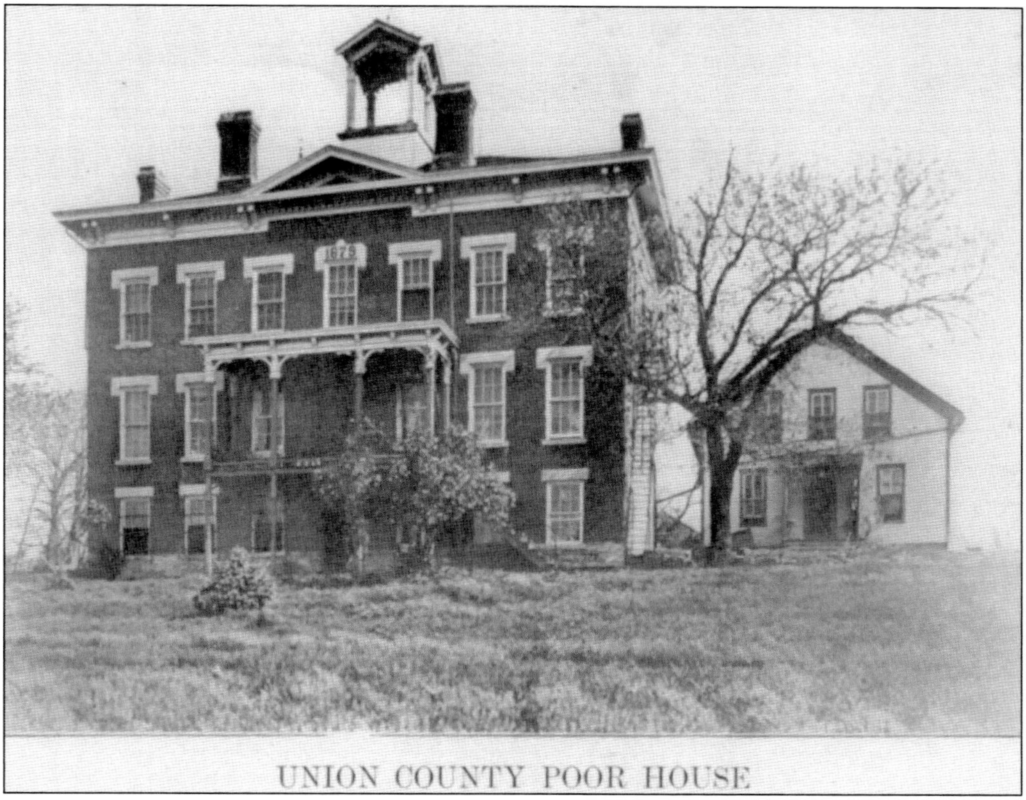

The Union County Farm (Poor House) was located just east of Creston along Highway 34 on the 160 acres purchased in 1874 for the original home (right). In 1879, a three-story brick structure with 27 rooms (left) replaced this home. Its purpose was to provide relief for those needing aid. As late as 1981, it was still in operation. The brick building was torn down in July 2010. (Union County Historical Society.)

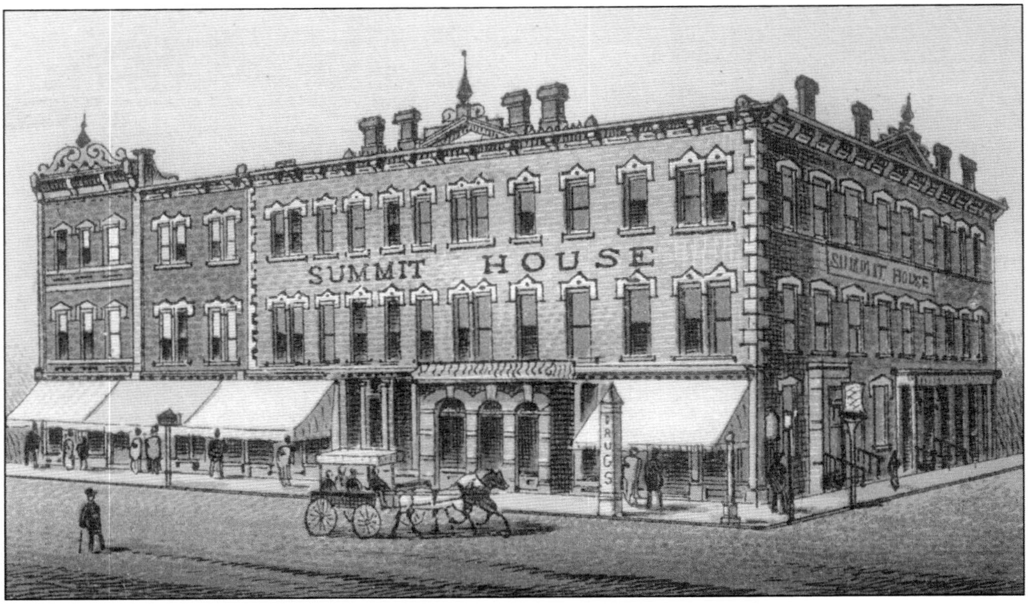

In 1880, the Summit House was built by S. D. Swan and John Becker Jr. on the corner of Elm and Adams Streets. The imposing three-story structure, shown in the above picture as a lithograph drawing from the *Souvenir of Creston* booklet from 1892, was the most popular hotel in the city at that time. The elegant lobby welcomed travelers with an impressive, broad stairway that led to a beautiful dining room on the second floor. The unsurpassed restaurant had a reputation for serving excellent food. (Above, Union County Historical Society; below, *Creston News Advertiser.*)

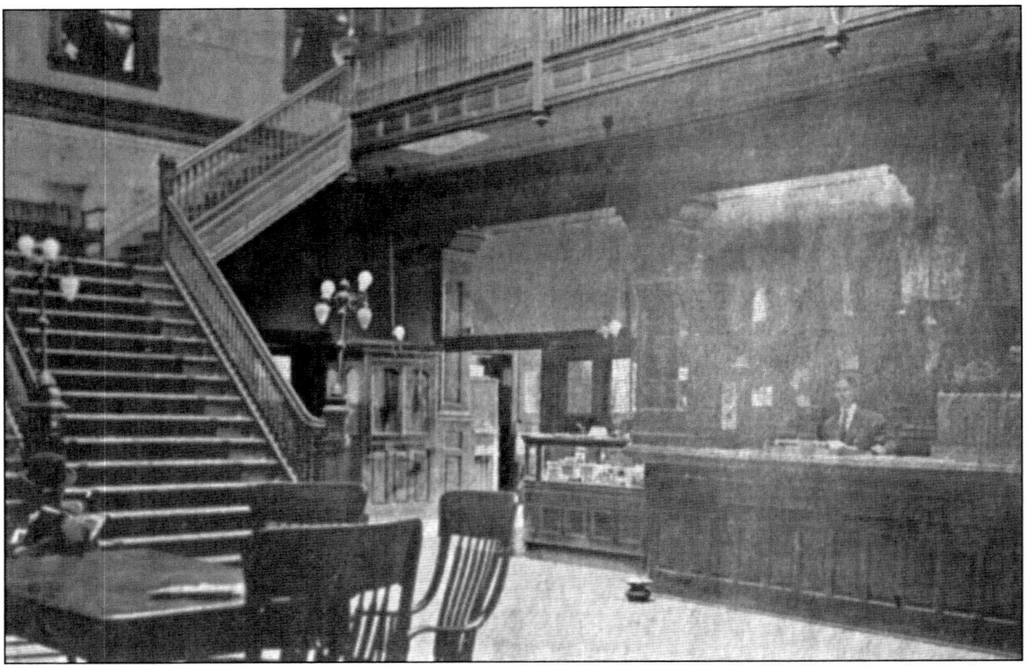

In the late 1860s, the rapidly growing Catholic parish saw a need for parochial school education for Catholic children. Fr. B. P. McMenomy opened the first private Catholic school in 1870. By 1880, a new two-story brick Catholic school was built near St. Malachy's Church on Clark Street. This school was staffed by the Benedictine Sisters, who taught the 170 pupils enrolled. (St. Malachy School.)

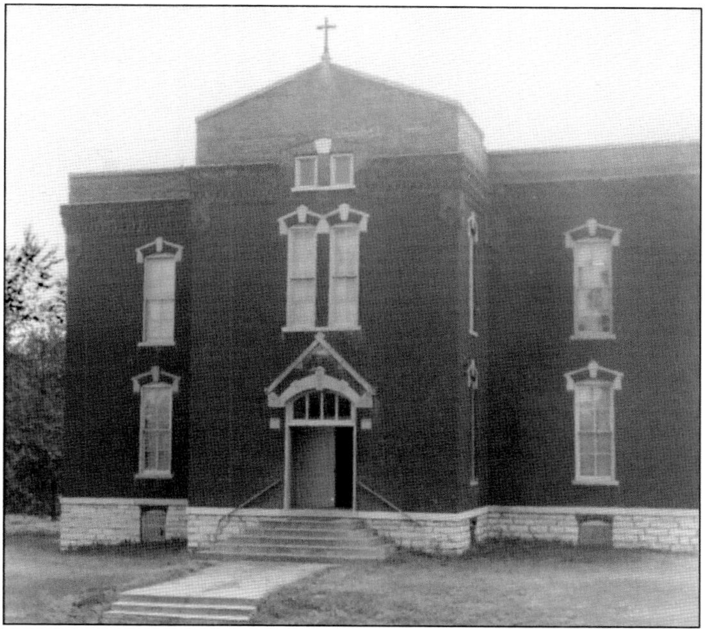

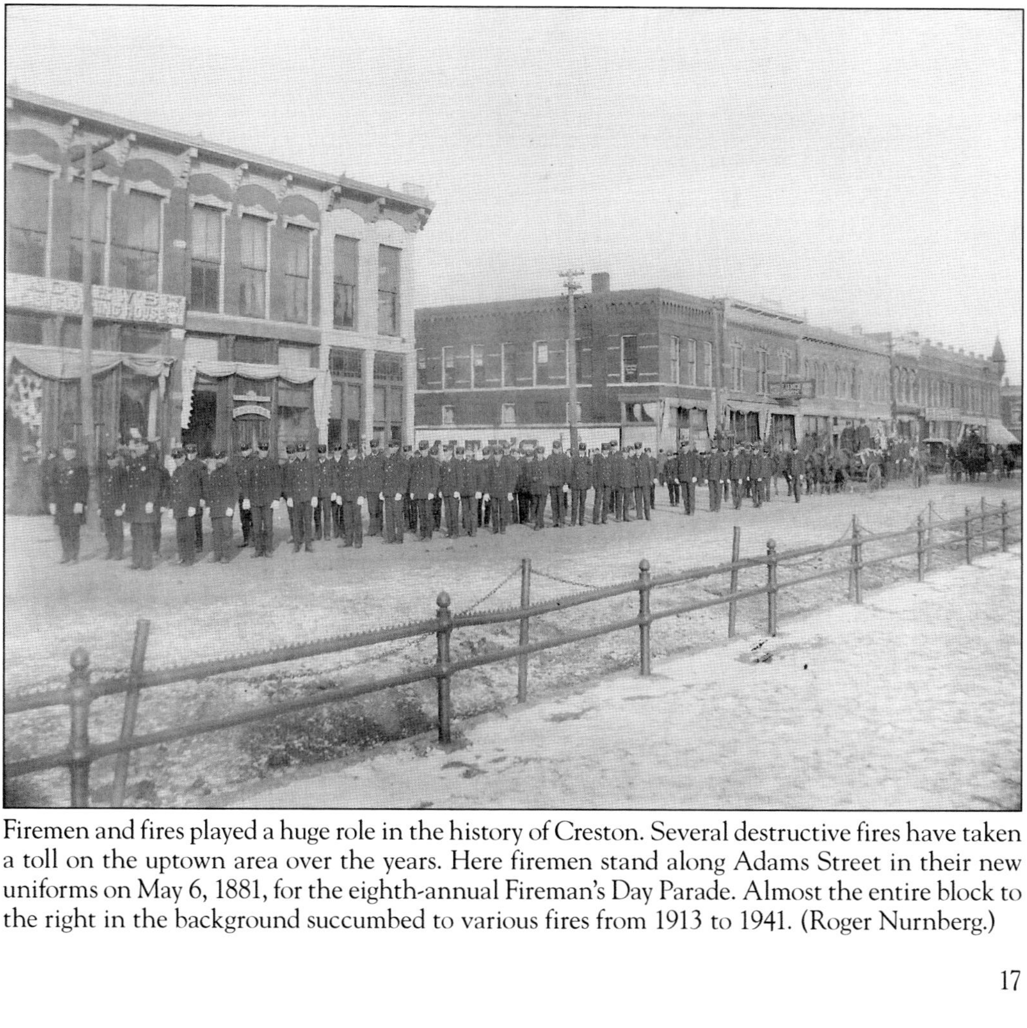

Firemen and fires played a huge role in the history of Creston. Several destructive fires have taken a toll on the uptown area over the years. Here firemen stand along Adams Street in their new uniforms on May 6, 1881, for the eighth-annual Fireman's Day Parade. Almost the entire block to the right in the background succumbed to various fires from 1913 to 1941. (Roger Nurnberg.)

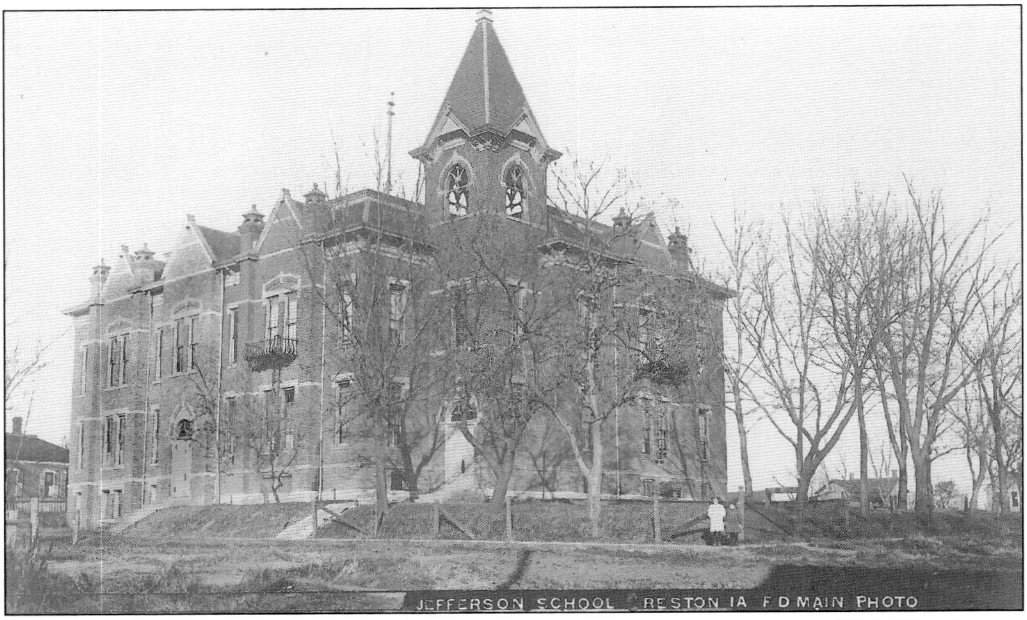

In 1883, two new school buildings, with six rooms each, were erected at a cost of $23,550. The one shown here on North Cherry Street was first known as East Brick and was later called Jefferson School. In 1903, four rooms and a basement were added to Jefferson School. (Steve Francis.)

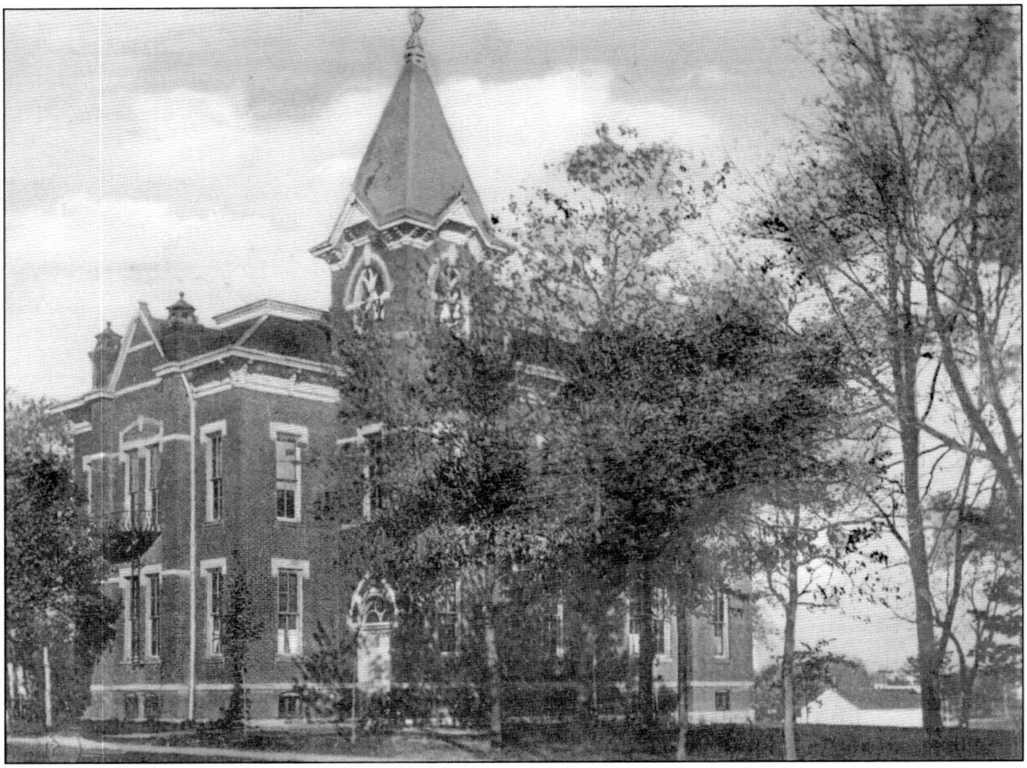

The second school, known as West Brick, was built on West Jefferson Street and later changed its name to Lincoln School. Both buildings were designed with generous closets and steam heat. The two schools were ready to be occupied on January 3, 1884. (Lynne Schlaht.)

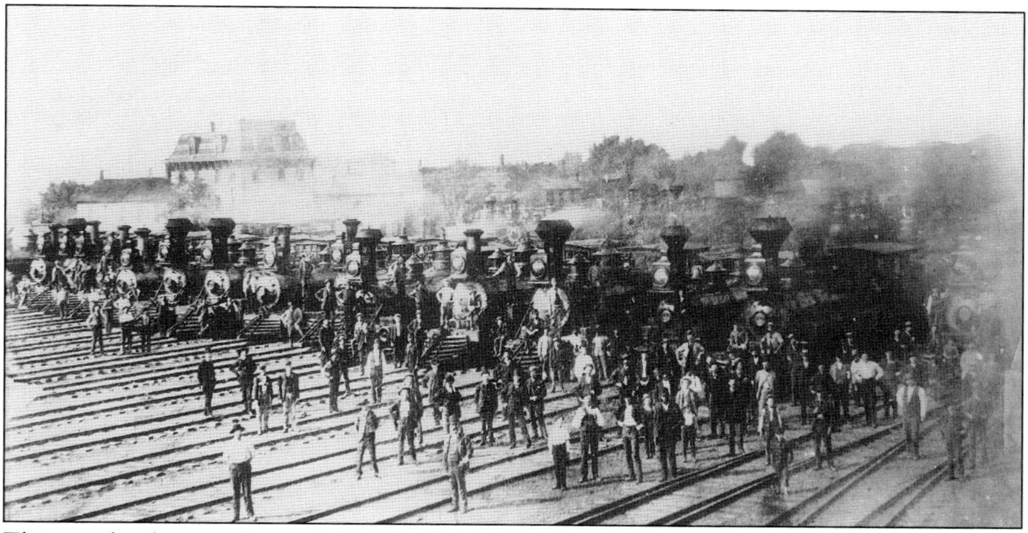

This may be the most famous photograph ever taken in Creston. Twenty-five locomotives lined up to blow their whistles at noon on November 12, 1883, to announce the nationwide adoption of standard time. The sheer magnitude of the Creston freight yards is evident in this view from near the roundhouse looking southwest toward Union Street. (Corbin-Wagner Collection.)

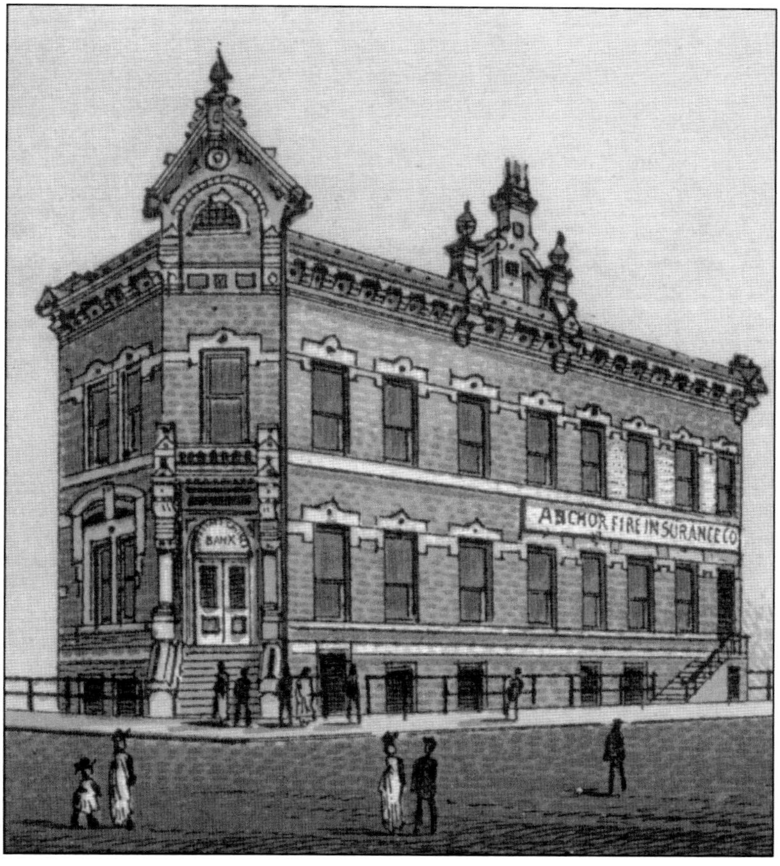

Iowa State Savings Bank was incorporated in 1883. It was located on the northeast corner of Pine and Montgomery Streets in 1892, when this drawing was done for the *Souvenir of Creston* booklet. By 1895, the bank moved across the intersection to the southwest corner. It later moved to 125 North Maple Street, where it remained until 1981. The bank is still in existence as of 2011. (Union County Historical Society.)

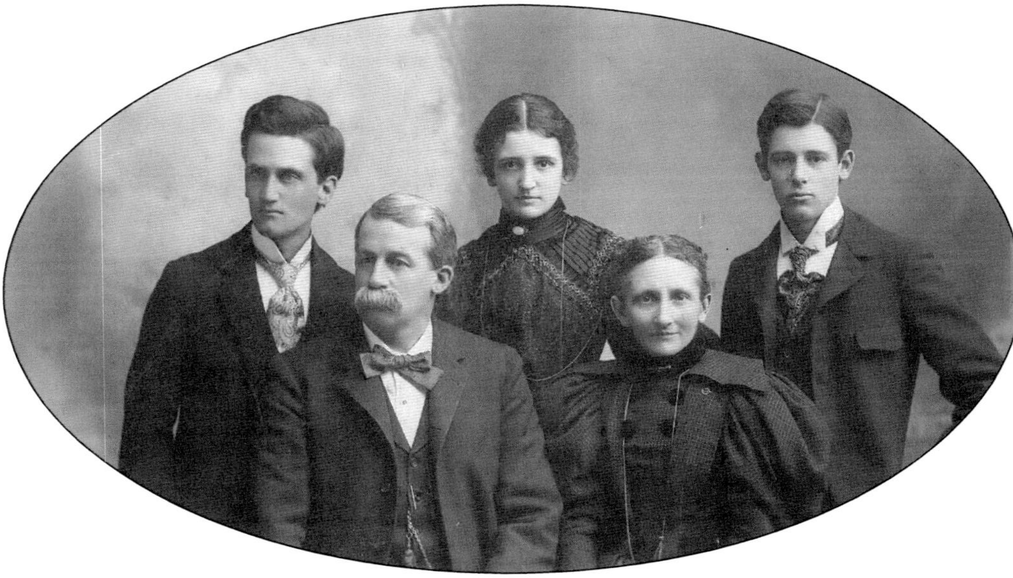

In 1872, John and Matilda Gibson moved to Creston, where they built a beautiful Italianate-style home (below) at 906 North Sycamore Street. The Gibson children—John, Jane (who later took the last name Phillips), and Josiah—were born in Creston. In 1886, John Gibson Sr. took over as president of Iowa State Savings Bank, which quickly grew under his guidance. Gibson possessed a keen eye for business, so when Jane decided to wed an up-and-coming young businessman named Frank Phillips, he saw an opportunity to recruit her ambitious new husband into the banking business. Frank Phillips and Jane Gibson were married in a simple ceremony at the Methodist Episcopal Church on February 18, 1897. A quiet wedding supper followed at the Gibson home. Frank Phillips later went on to found Phillips Petroleum. (Both, Frank Phillips Home, Bartlesville, Oklahoma/Oklahoma Historical Society.)

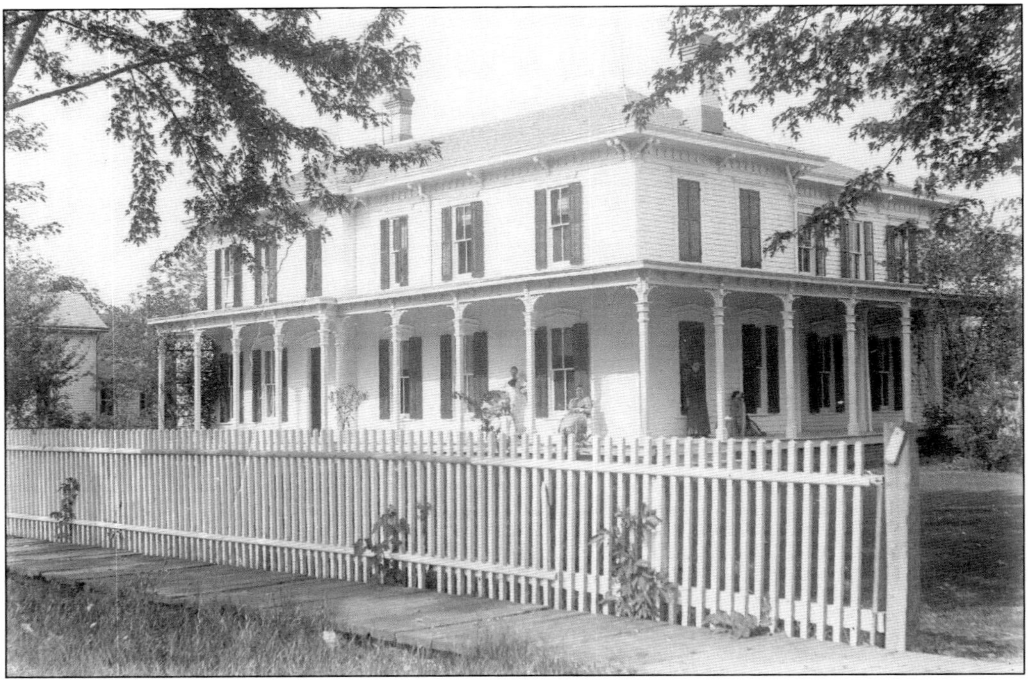

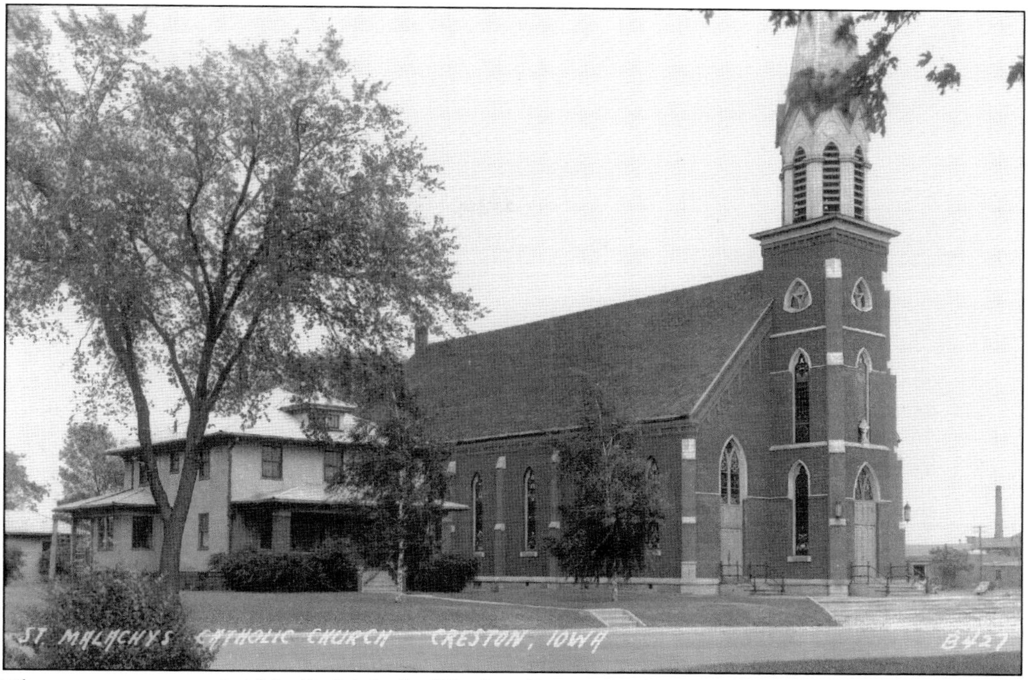

The cornerstone was laid for St. Malachy Worship Center on August 30, 1886. It was not until June 23, 1889, that the $25,000 church was dedicated by Bishop Henry Cosgrove. St. Malachy Church was celebrated for its well-preserved tracker organ, which was built in 1892 by the A. B. Flegemacker Company of Erie, Pennsylvania. The lovely wooden case housed 774 pipes. (Lynne Schlaht.)

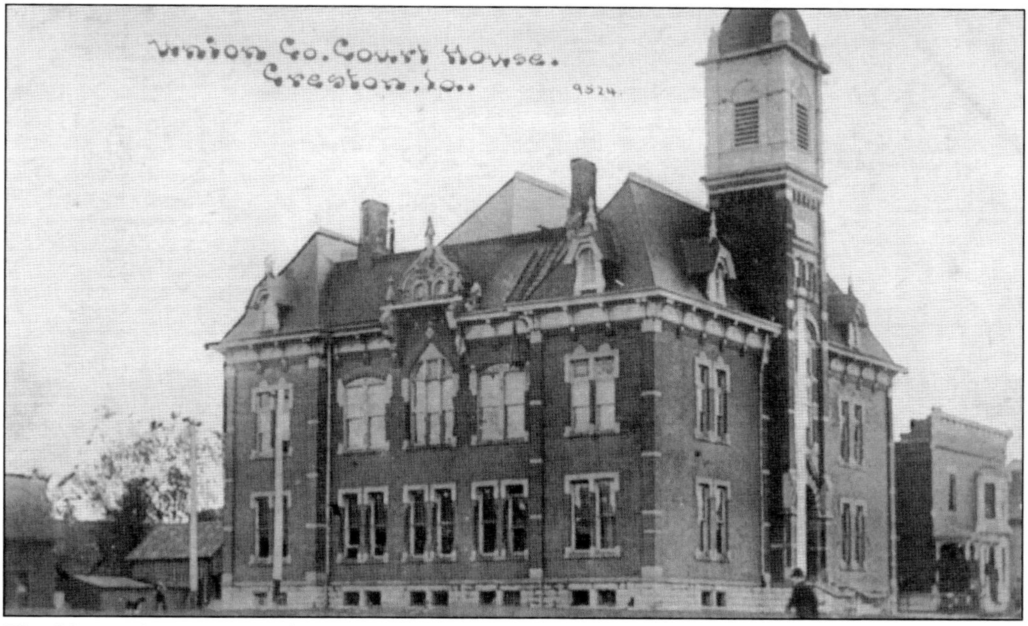

The Union County Courthouse was built in 1887–1888 by local citizens and the CB&Q in an effort to influence the transfer of the county seat. Creston finally secured the county seat through a somewhat underhanded effort on November 25, 1890, when the railroad moved a large force of workers into Creston just before the vote of a special election. The extra workers just as quickly left town. (Lynne Schlaht.)

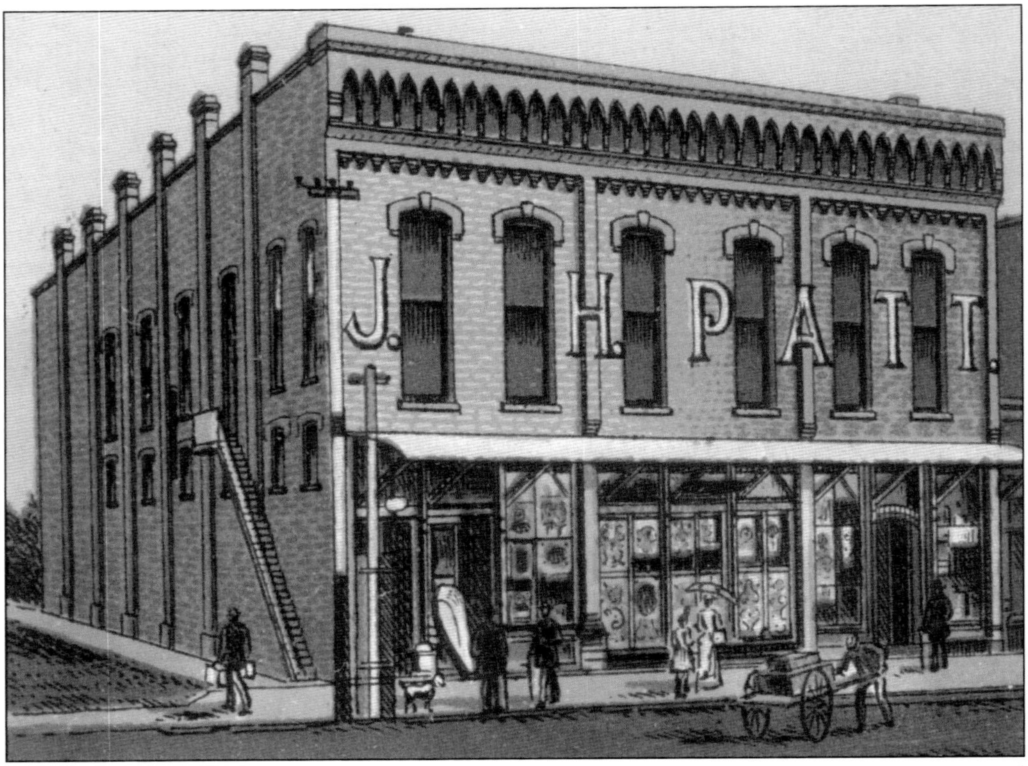

The Patt Opera House, built between 1889 and 1892, was located on the corner of Adams and Oak Streets. It was considered one of the finest opera houses in the state, with a seating capacity of 1,000 and the largest assortment of scenery seen in a city that size. J. H. Patt, proprietor of the opera house, was also a dealer of hardware, agricultural implements, and bicycles. (Union County Historical Society.)

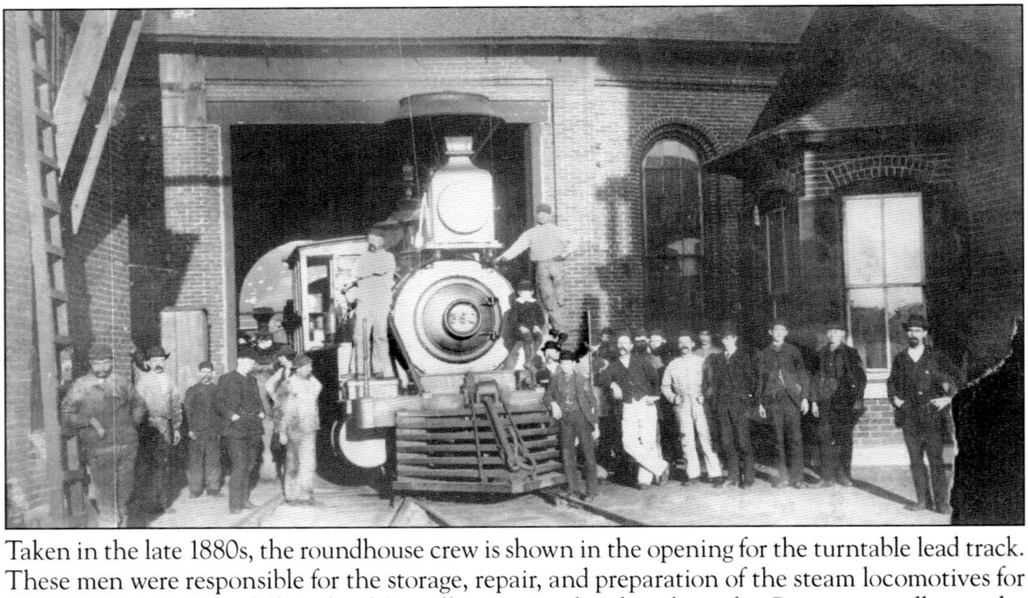

Taken in the late 1880s, the roundhouse crew is shown in the opening for the turntable lead track. These men were responsible for the storage, repair, and preparation of the steam locomotives for daily use. By 1883, the full circle of 60 stalls was completed, making the Creston roundhouse the largest west of Chicago. (Corbin-Wagner Collection.)

Two

Palace City

By the late 1880s, Creston had a booming economy due primarily to the railroad. Railroad employees were nearing 1,000 in number, and the town was growing into a cultural mecca. Creston boasted several fine hotels and opera houses. A growing number of impressive residences were being built daily, so much so that a collection of drawings of prominent businesses and homes was produced into a booklet of lithographs called *Souvenir of Creston*.

The rich soil of the area was ideal for agriculture, particularly lush stands of bluegrass. In 1889, eighteen counties of southwest Iowa cooperated to create the Blue Grass League of Southwest Iowa. In an effort to promote the agricultural wealth of the area, an 18-day exposition was planned for later that year. Creston, considered the "Queen City" of the region, was the ideal location for the event to take place. In addition to a district agricultural fair, there were horse races, exhibits, entertainment, and political speeches. The centerpiece of the festivities was a palace—an elaborate exhibition hall faced with bales of bluegrass. The exposition was held annually for a total of three years, with each palace evolving and becoming more ornate than the previous year. The exposition ended in 1891.

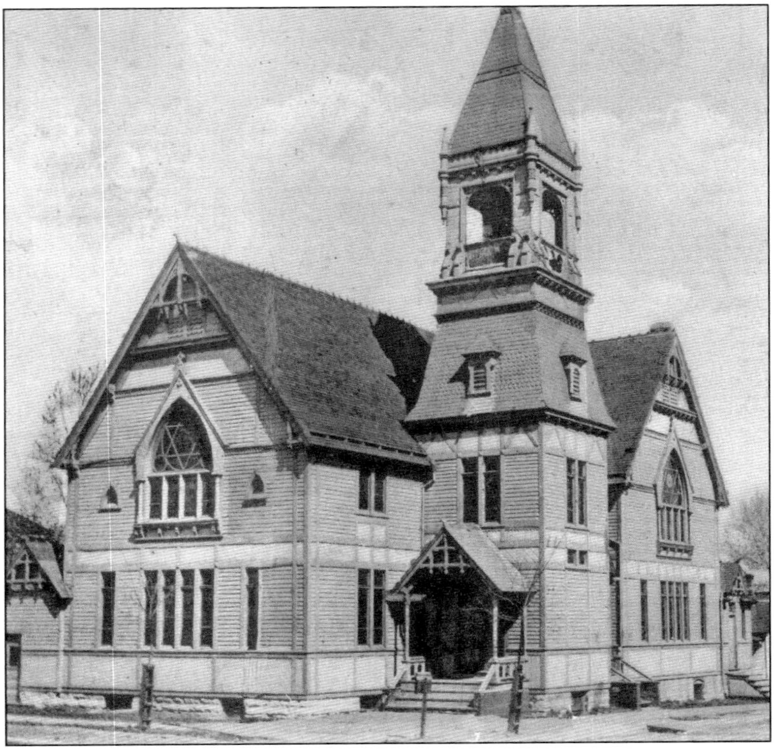

The First Congregational Church was organized on January 28, 1873, with seven members. A small chapel was built on South Maple Street. By 1887, the membership outgrew the capacity of the chapel, and plans were made for a new church building on the corner of Montgomery and Division Streets. On September 2, 1888, the Gothic Revival–style church was dedicated at a cost of $13,000. (Union County Historical Society.)

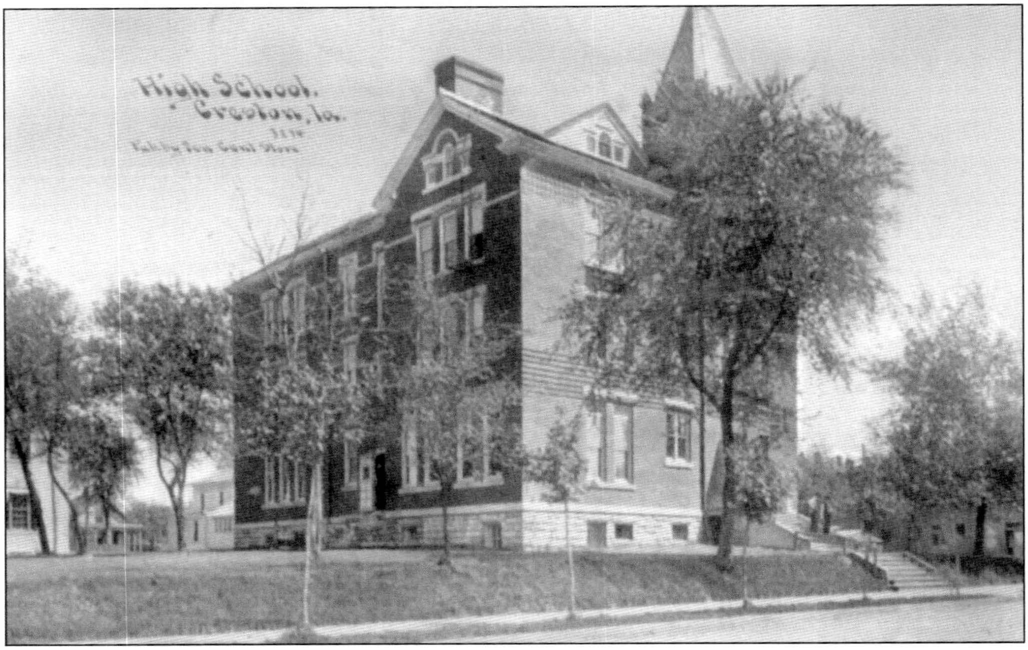

A new high school built on the corner of Elm and Mills Streets replaced the original two-story frame high school built at the same location in 1873. Occupied on April 8, 1889, the estimated value of the building, grounds, and furniture was $35,000. It contained eight classrooms on three floors, an assembly room, and offices for the superintendent and board of education. (Lynne Schlaht.)

The Blue Grass League of Southwestern Iowa was formed on March 1, 1889, by 18 counties. Creston was chosen as the league headquarters. The main objective of the league was to advertise and promote the excellent advantage of the bluegrass production of southwestern Iowa. The committee decided to present an agricultural exposition, the highlight of which would be the elaborate Blue Grass Palace Exposition Hall. Each county was given space within the palace to exhibit products. The Creston district fairgrounds were selected for the location of the Blue Grass Palace, the current site of the high school football field. The planning committee settled on a design submitted by Louis Syberkrop. The impressive palace was one 100 feet square with towers on each of the four corners. The thatching was completed by I. H. Steddom of Oskaloosa, who held a patent for a thatching machine. He furnished more than a dozen machines and oversaw the work of thatching the palace. (Both, Union County Historical Society.)

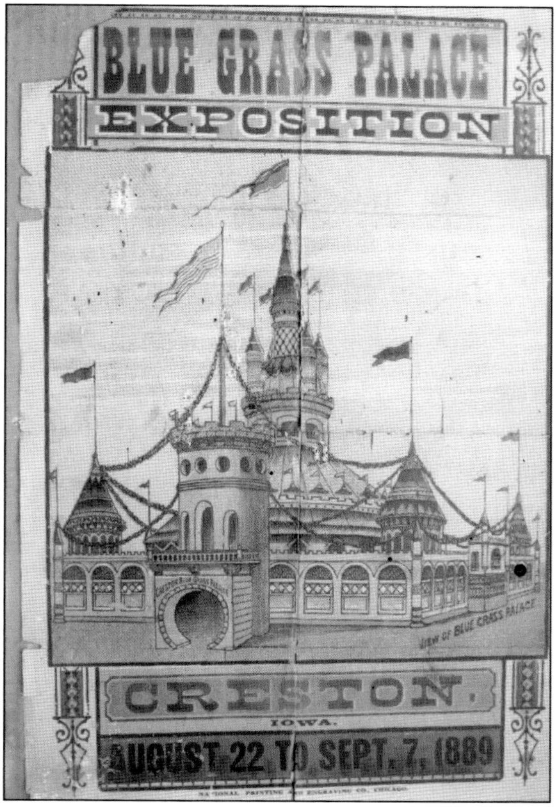

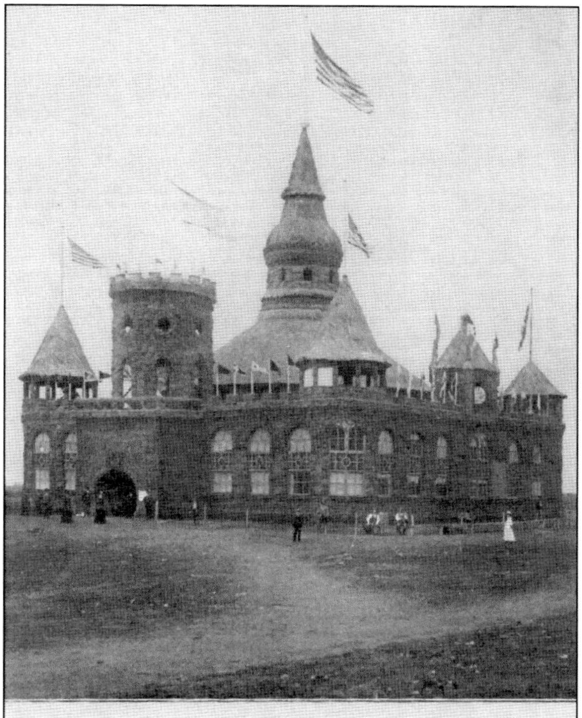

CRESTON'S BLUE GRASS PALACE, 1889

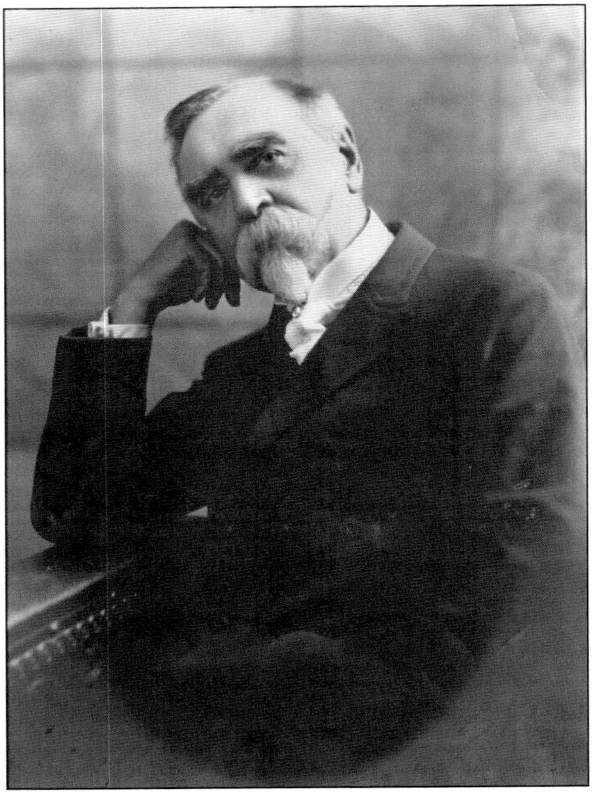

Louis Syberkrop Sr., decorator and artist, came to Creston in 1881. He soon became associated with the Creston Opera House Company and managed it for seven years. He was known primarily as a decorator of churches and theaters. He painted a large mural in the Temple Grand Opera House, the first Masonic Lodge. He is most famous for designing the first Blue Grass Palace of 1889. (Union County Historical Society.)

The Blue Grass Palace of 1890 was the best known and most ornate of the three palaces. The original palace was enlarged, with wings added to the north and south, making the overall size 260 feet by 130 feet. A 12-foot-wide bridge connected the 120-foot main tower to the 90-foot towers on the wings. The total area of exposition space was 30,724 square feet. (Lynne Schlaht.)

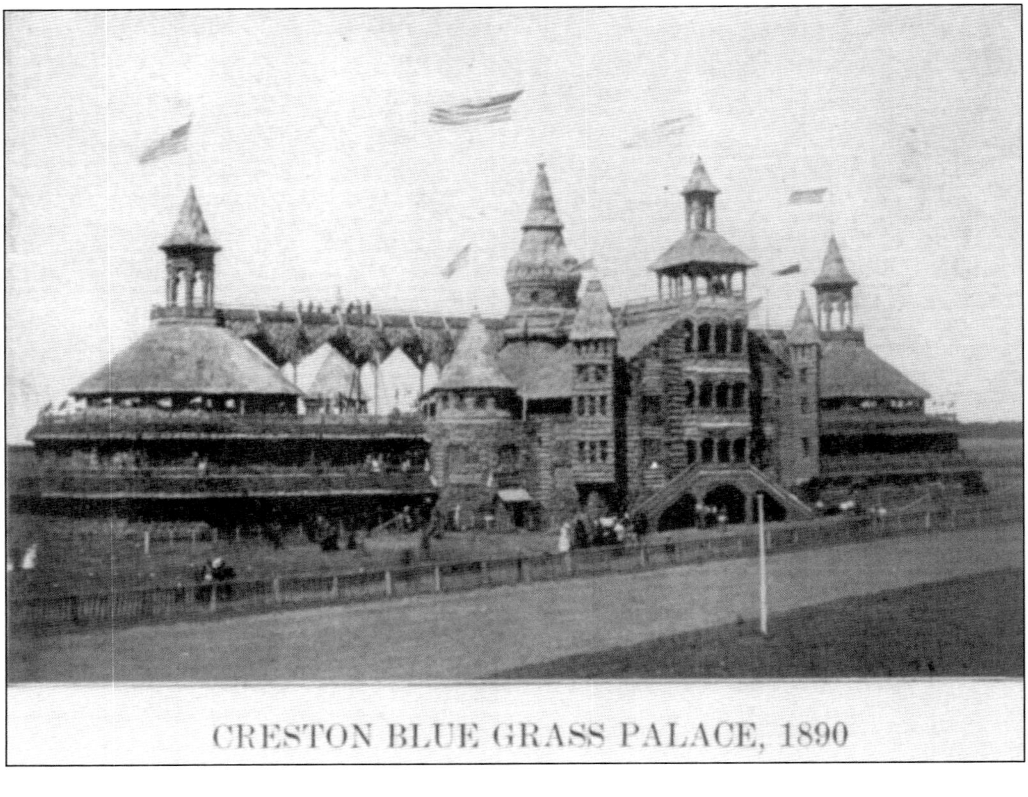

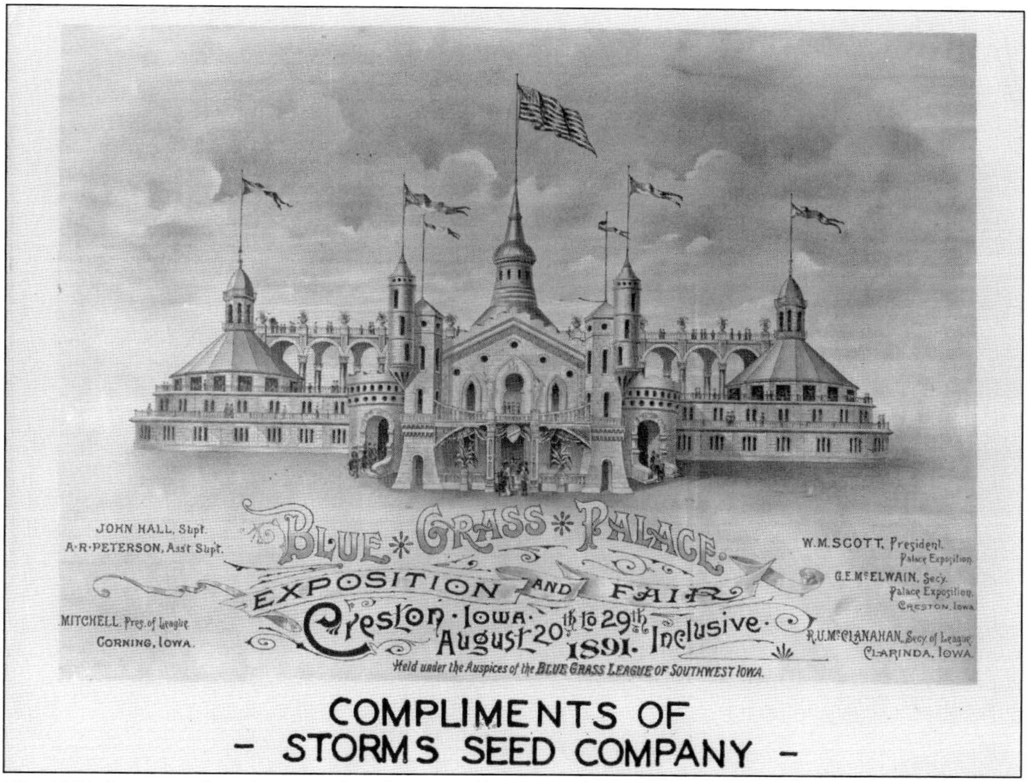

The 1891 fair opened on August 20 with minor changes and repairs to the 1890 palace. Louis Syberkrop, designer of the 1889 palace, created a display of 100 paintings made from pictures taken in each of the 18 participating counties. This was the final year for the Blue Grass Palace, as the exposition grounds were surrendered to the district fair association in 1892. (Union County Historical Society.)

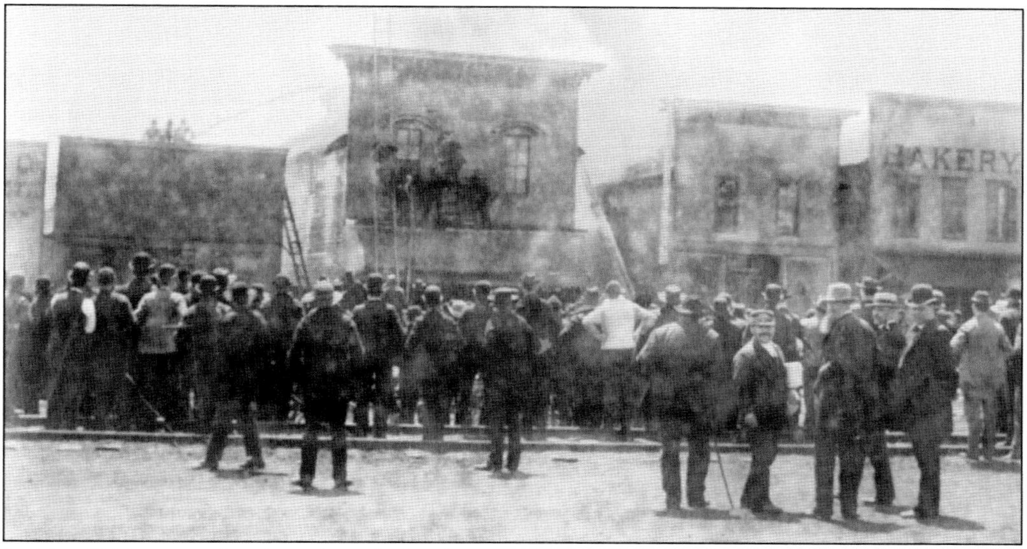

In May 1891, a crowd gathered on the Burlington Railroad tracks to watch firemen battle a blaze at Waterman's Grocery Store, located on Union Street. The men used ladders to climb the front of the building and the roof of an adjacent structure in an effort to contain the flames. The store was rebuilt in the same location. (Jane Briley.)

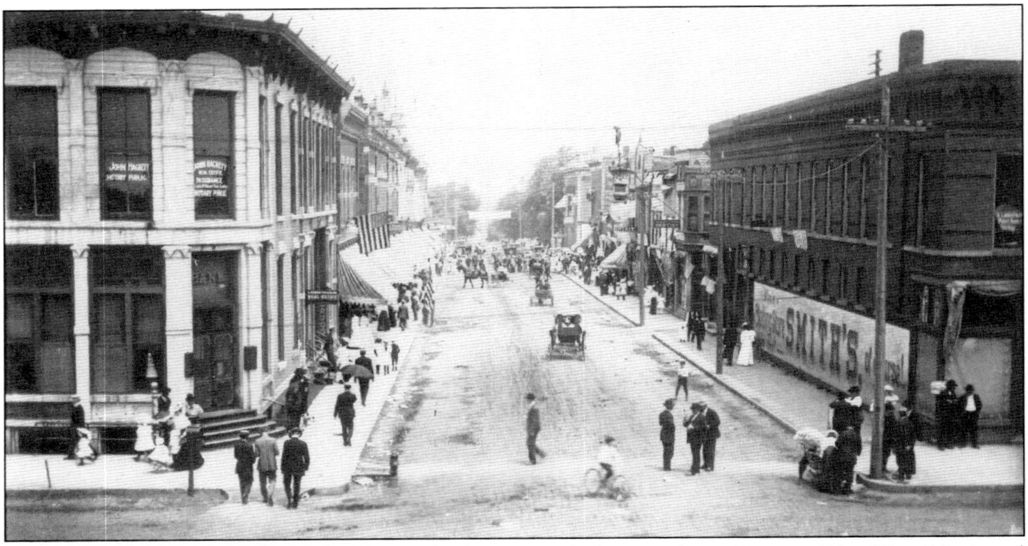

This is an early view of Maple Street, looking north from Adams Street. The First National Bank (left) was first founded in 1871 as the S. H. Mallory and Company Bank. In 1881, it was reorganized as the First National Bank. The bank moved into the location shown here in 1876. It remained in this location until 1967. At the time of this photograph, Adams Street was paved with bricks. Notice the storm drain at the corner on the left side of the street and the fire hydrant in the street next to it. A streetlight is suspended from a cable over Maple Street. The large banner strung across the street at the Montgomery Street intersection, the significant number of American flags hung along the street, and the large crowd indicate that this photograph was taken during a holiday celebration. (Union County Historical Society.)

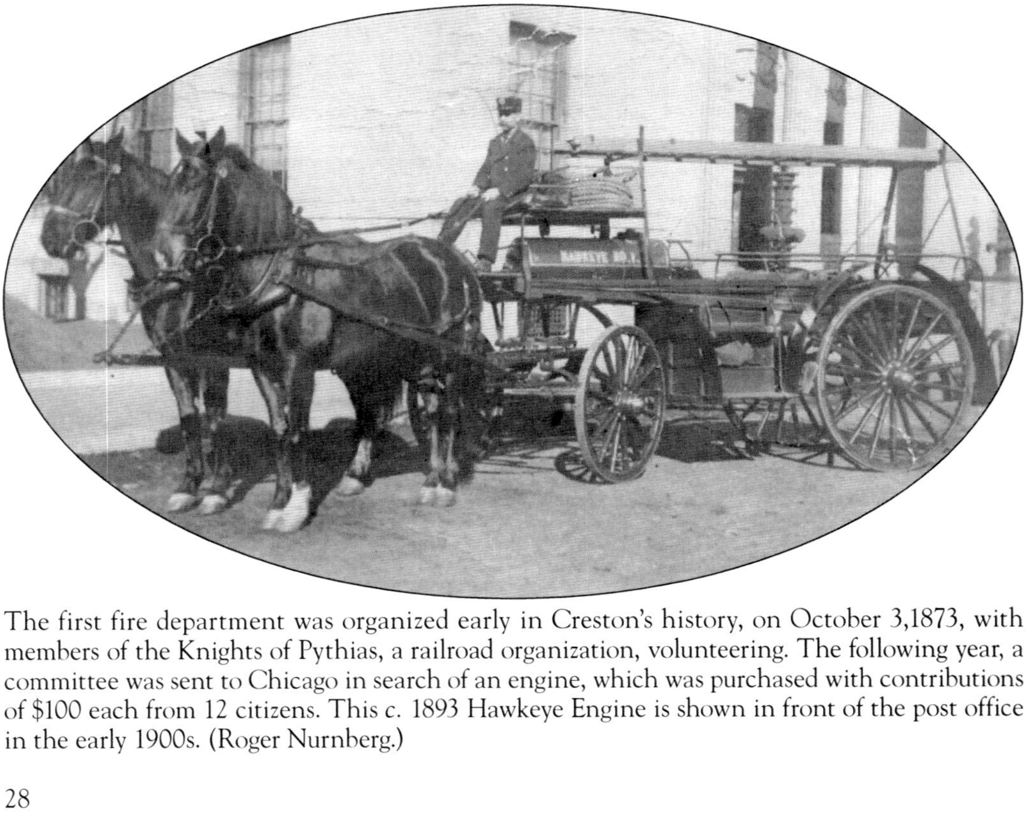

The first fire department was organized early in Creston's history, on October 3,1873, with members of the Knights of Pythias, a railroad organization, volunteering. The following year, a committee was sent to Chicago in search of an engine, which was purchased with contributions of $100 each from 12 citizens. This c. 1893 Hawkeye Engine is shown in front of the post office in the early 1900s. (Roger Nurnberg.)

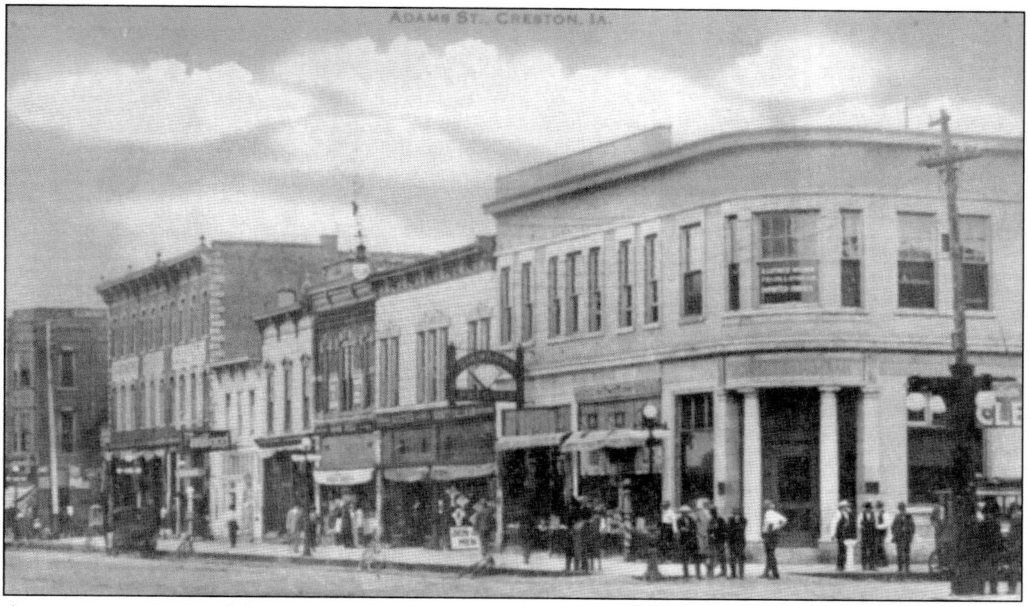

A major renovation of the First National Bank was undertaken in 1911. The building was completely refaced with granite, stone, and brick. The end result is seen in this photograph taken of Adams Street, looking west from Maple Street, sometime after 1916. Additional remodeling was done in 1939 and 1951. The second Summit House, built in 1916, can be seen at the far left edge of the picture. The same type of suspended streetlight as the picture on the opposite page can be seen hanging over Adams Street. On the corner of the Summit House is the sign for Newcomb's Drug Store. Several bicycles lay against the curb along the street, and at least two of the buildings appear to be frame structures. (Lynne Schlaht.)

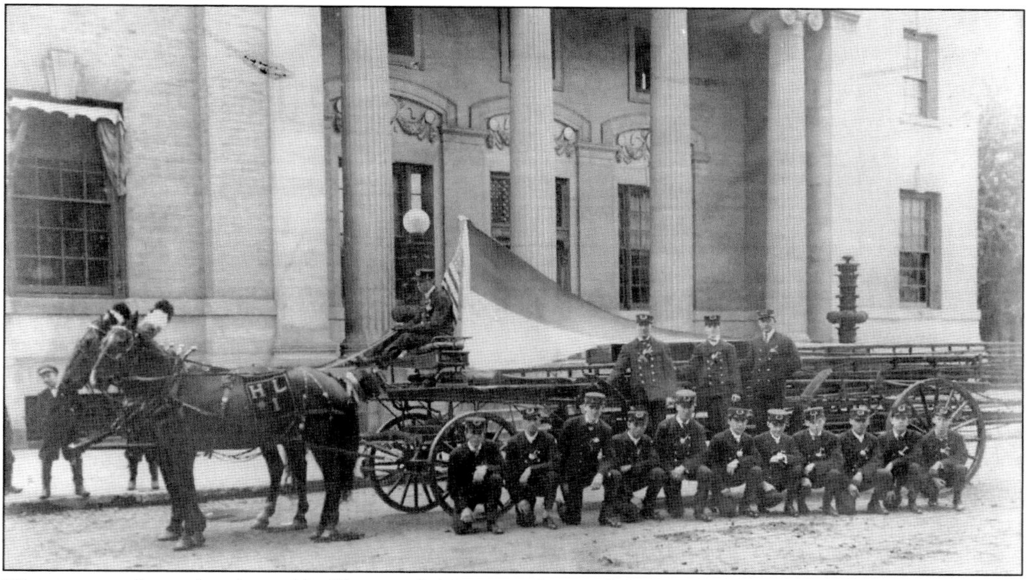

This image shows hook-and-ladder truck No. 1 in front of the post office just after 1900. Though the emergency apparatus consisted of what were called trucks, engines, and wagons, they were all horse drawn at this time. The new engine house built in 1902 (see page 47) was designed with three arched doorways across the front to house this truck, the engine on the previous page, and a hose wagon, all side by side. (Roger Nurnberg.)

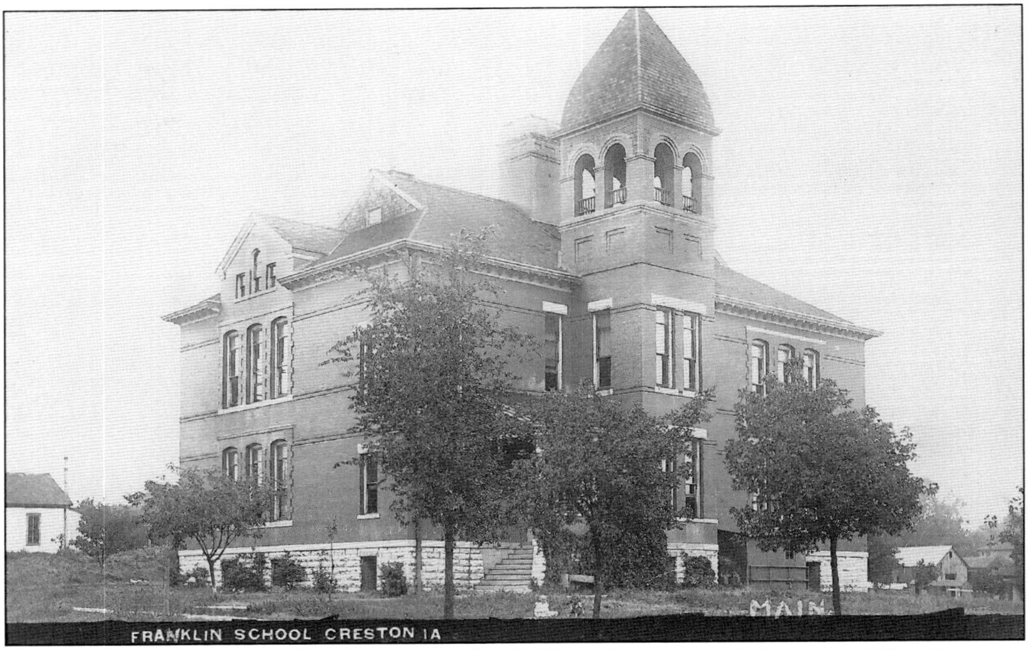

A new six-room Franklin School was erected in 1893 on the corner of Monroe and Elm Streets to replace the original Franklin School that was condemned due to safety issues. Classes continued uninterrupted during the construction process, as the new building was only a few blocks away. A south addition was added before 1915. The building continued to be used for educational purposes and was known as Franklin School until 1958. (Steve Francis.)

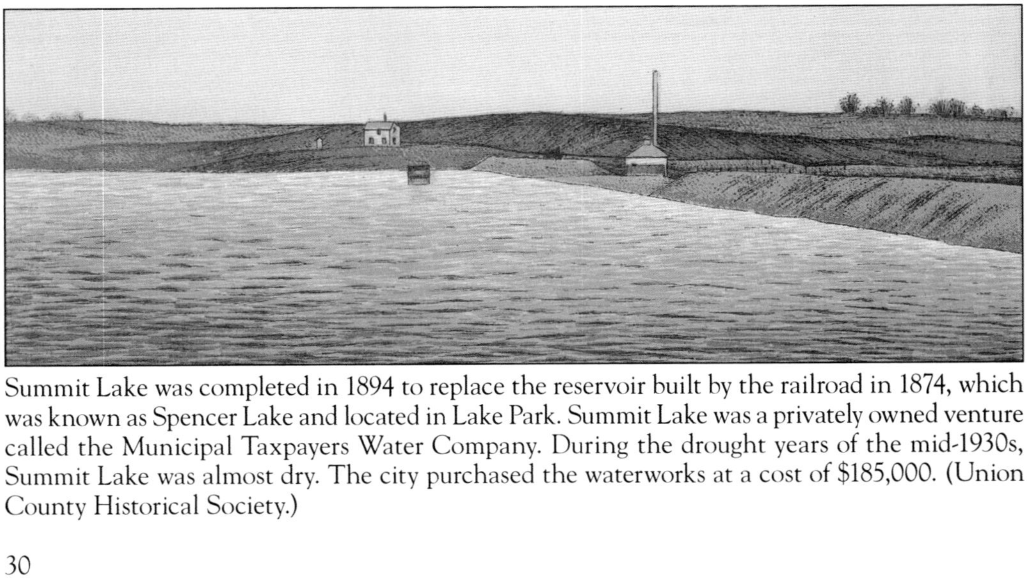

Summit Lake was completed in 1894 to replace the reservoir built by the railroad in 1874, which was known as Spencer Lake and located in Lake Park. Summit Lake was a privately owned venture called the Municipal Taxpayers Water Company. During the drought years of the mid-1930s, Summit Lake was almost dry. The city purchased the waterworks at a cost of $185,000. (Union County Historical Society.)

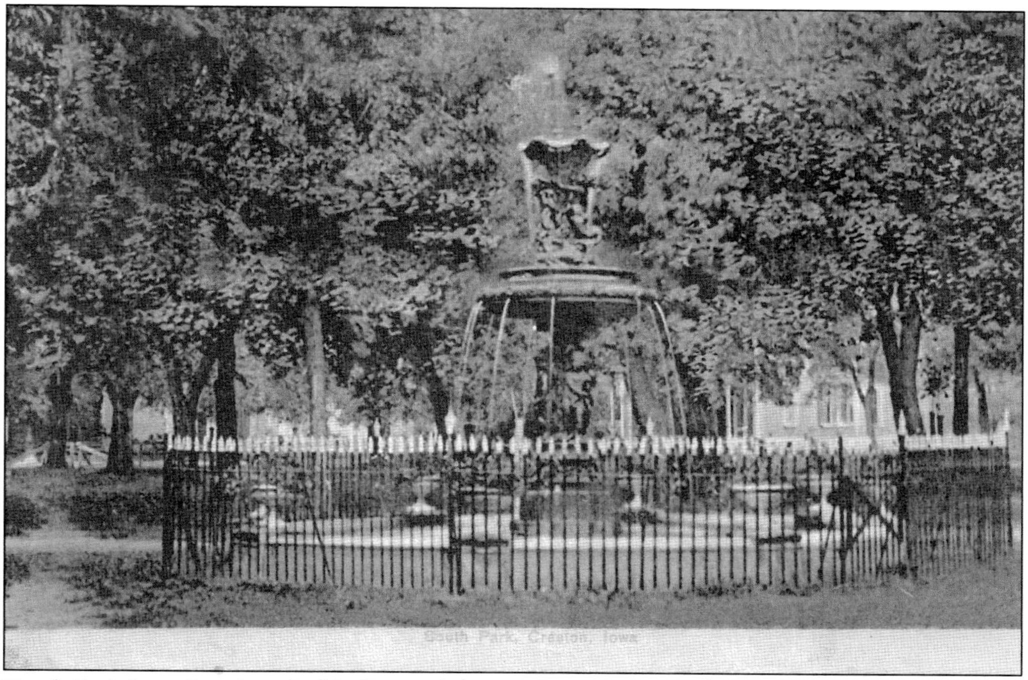

South Park (now Rainbow Park), Creston's first park, was given to the city by the Town Company when the city was platted with the intention of it becoming a city square. Initially, shade trees were planted and a decorative fence enclosed the park, but little else was done. In 1895, the Parlor Circle (a ladies' literary society) raised funds to erect a 20-foot-tall round fountain, rebuild the bandstand, and plant flowers. (Lynne Schlaht.)

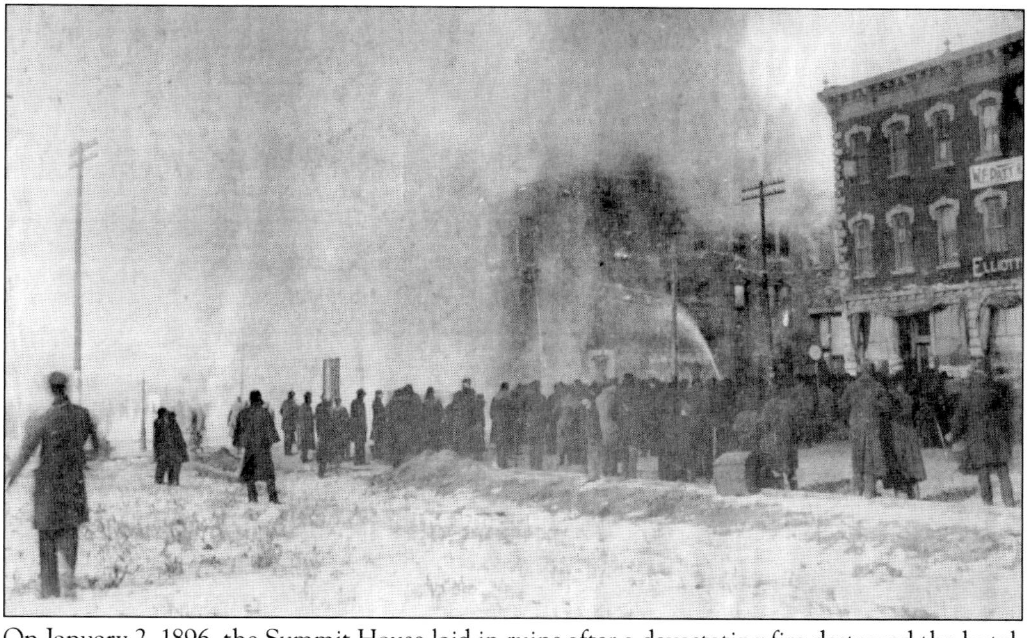

On January 2, 1896, the Summit House laid in ruins after a devastating fire destroyed the hotel. It was the worst fire in Creston history up to that point. The Summit House was immediately rebuilt in the same location on the corner of Adams and Elm Streets. It reopened later that same year. (*Creston News Advertiser.*)

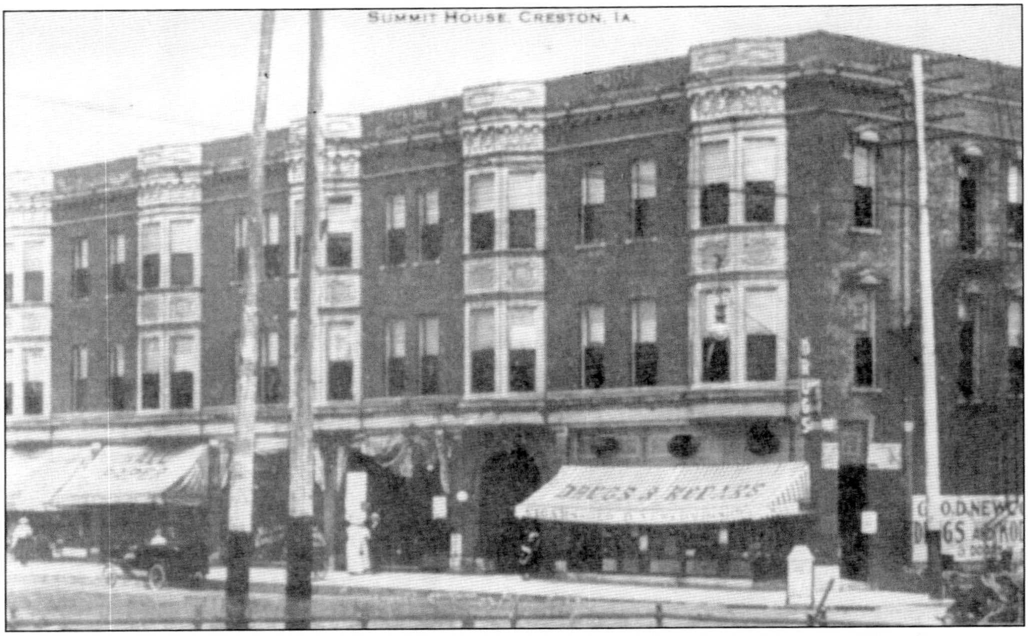

The second Summit House was considered one of the finest hotels in the state. The three-story structure was an impressive sight with its five "columns" of bay windows lining Adams Street. It quickly became one of Creston's most iconic structures until it, too, succumbed to fire in 1916. To make matters worse, a new fire engine sat on a flatcar in the rail yard waiting to be unloaded. (Lynne Schlaht.)

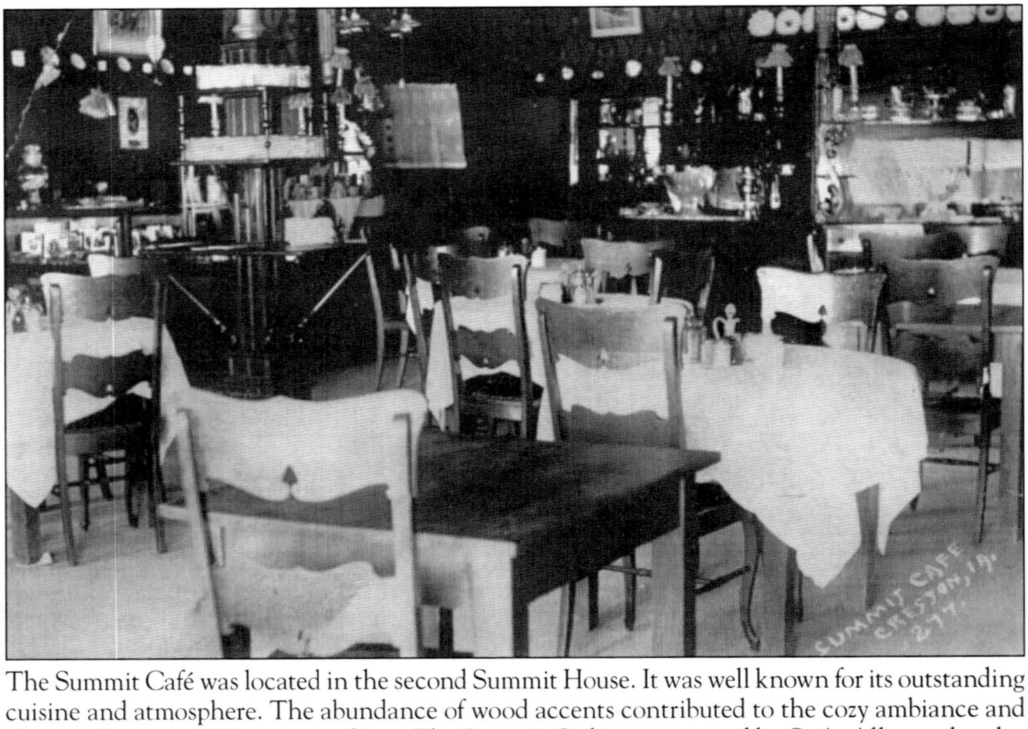

The Summit Café was located in the second Summit House. It was well known for its outstanding cuisine and atmosphere. The abundance of wood accents contributed to the cozy ambiance and elegant character of the surroundings. The Summit Café was managed by C. A. Allens, who also managed the lunchroom located in the depot. (Jane Briley.)

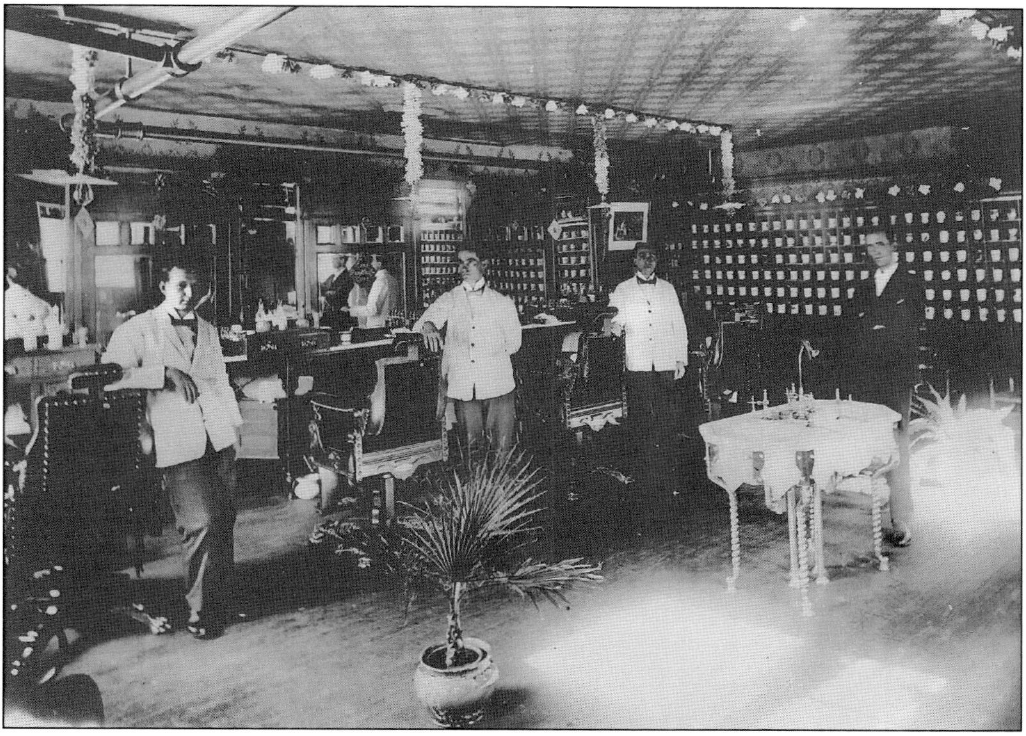

Frank Phillips (1873–1950), founder of Phillips Petroleum, possessed an entrepreneurial spirit and the drive to get off the family farm. He found his opportunity when he spotted a Creston barber wearing flashy striped pants. He wanted to afford such a luxury, so he approached a stylish barber for apprenticeship, and the man agreed. By 1897, Phillips, shown in one of his barbershops, owned all three shops in Creston. Banker John Gibson was one of Phillips's best customers. Phillips soon began courting Gibson's daughter, Jane. Gibson had no room in his life for a son-in-law who was a barber. He told Phillips he would consent to their marriage if Phillips gave up barbering to work at his bank. Frank Phillips and Jane Gibson (below) were married on February 18, 1897. (Both, Frank Phillips Home, Bartlesville, Oklahoma/Oklahoma Historical Society.)

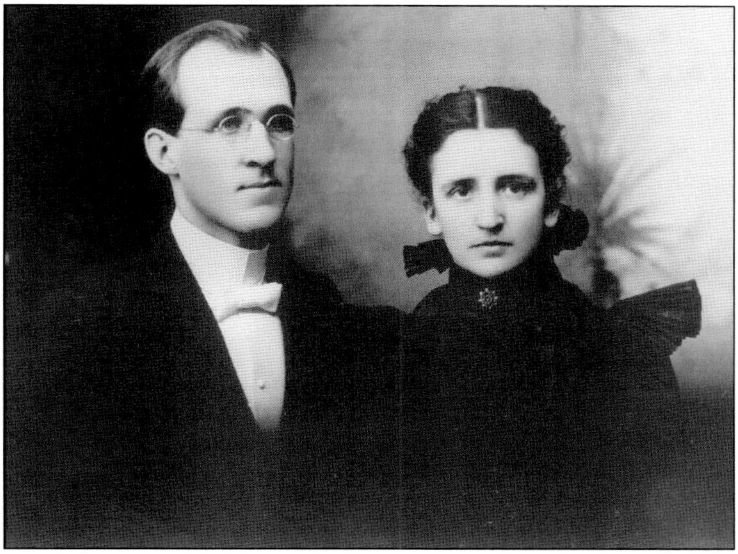

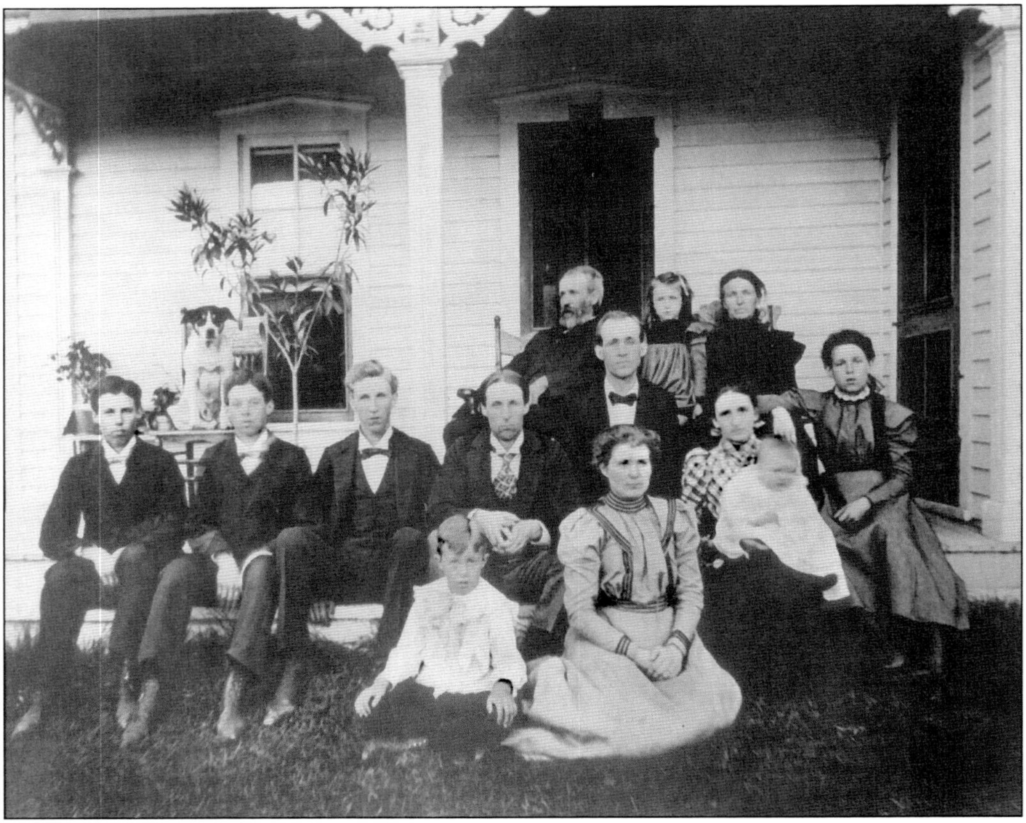

This Phillips family photograph was taken in the summer of 1899 on Lewis Phillips's farm near Conway, Iowa. Pictured, from left to right, are (first row) Fred Phillips and Jenn Phillips; (second row) Waite Phillips, Wiate Phillips, Edd Phillips, Lee Eldas Phillips, Frank Phillips, Jane (Gibson) Phillips holding John Gibson Phillips, and Nell Phillips; (third row) father Lewis Phillips, Lura Phillips, and mother Lucinda Phillips. (Frank Phillips Home, Bartlesville, Oklahoma/Oklahoma Historical Society.)

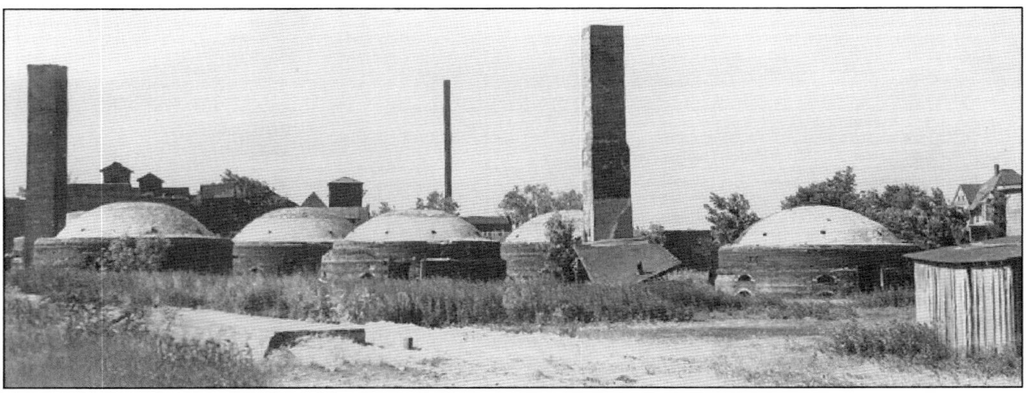

In 1896, Harry and Bid Tramp establish the Tramp Brick Yard, a manufacturing facility that turned out brick and tile into the 1930s. The plant operated 11 kilns at one time and serviced an area within a 75-mile radius of Creston. The site of the brickyard can still be seen in northeast Creston, just south of Townline Road. (Jane Briley.)

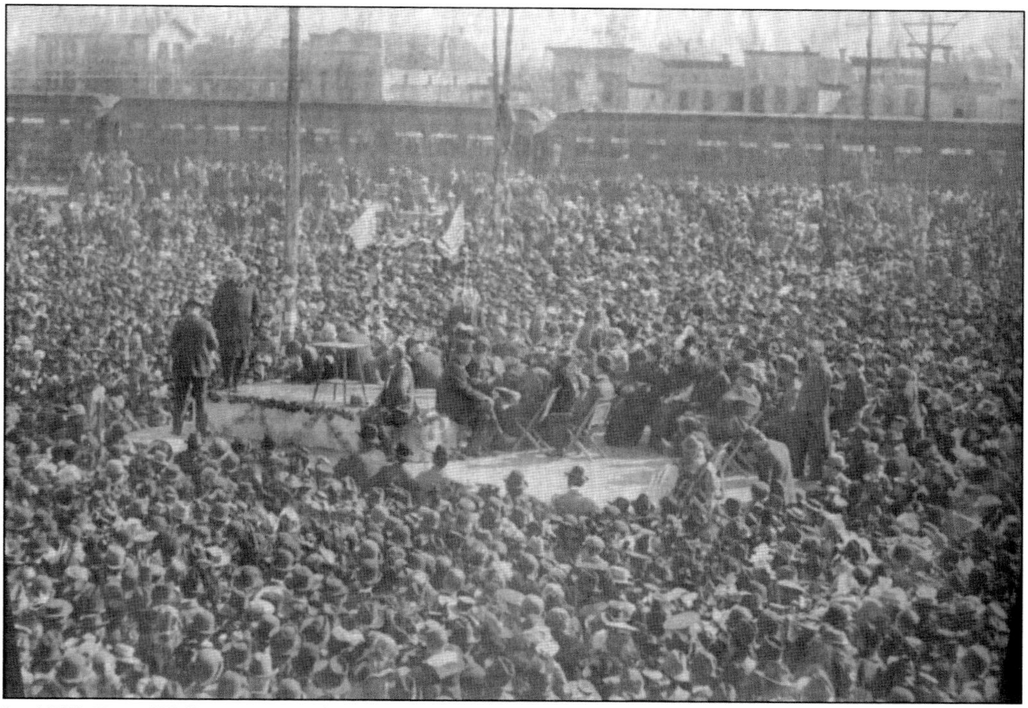

In 1897, Pres. William McKinley, standing on the platform facing the camera, addressed a large crowd at Creston in the block between Elm and Maple Streets. The camera is looking south, across the Burlington tracks, toward Union Street. McKinley was the second president to visit Creston. The first was Ulysses S. Grant in 1879. (*Creston News Advertiser.*)

Company C of the 3rd Regiment of the Iowa National Guard was mustered into federal service when the Spanish-American War broke out after the sinking of battleship *Maine*. The troops prepared to depart the Creston depot on April 26, 1898, after a hearty farewell ceremony. Businesses closed, schools dismissed early, and the city was decorated with flags and bunting in honor of the 47 men of the company. (Corbin-Wagner Collection.)

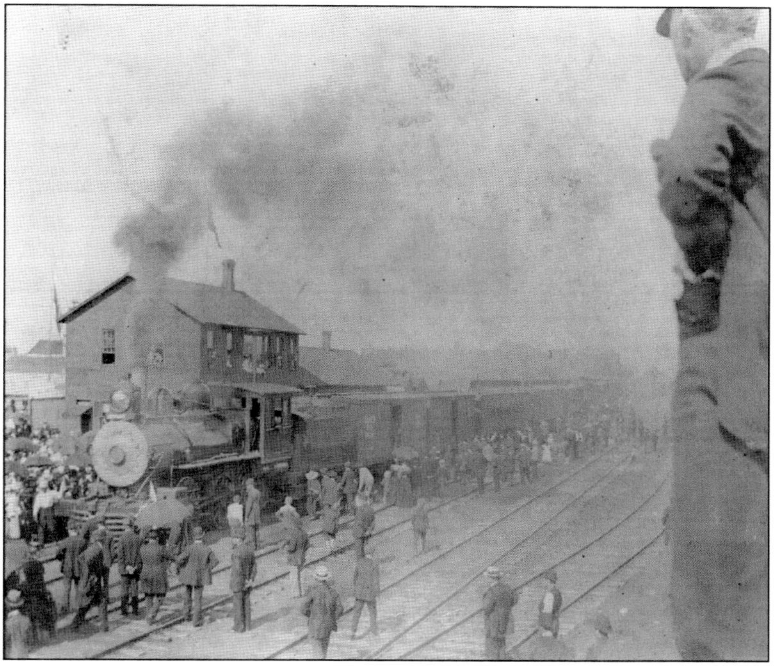

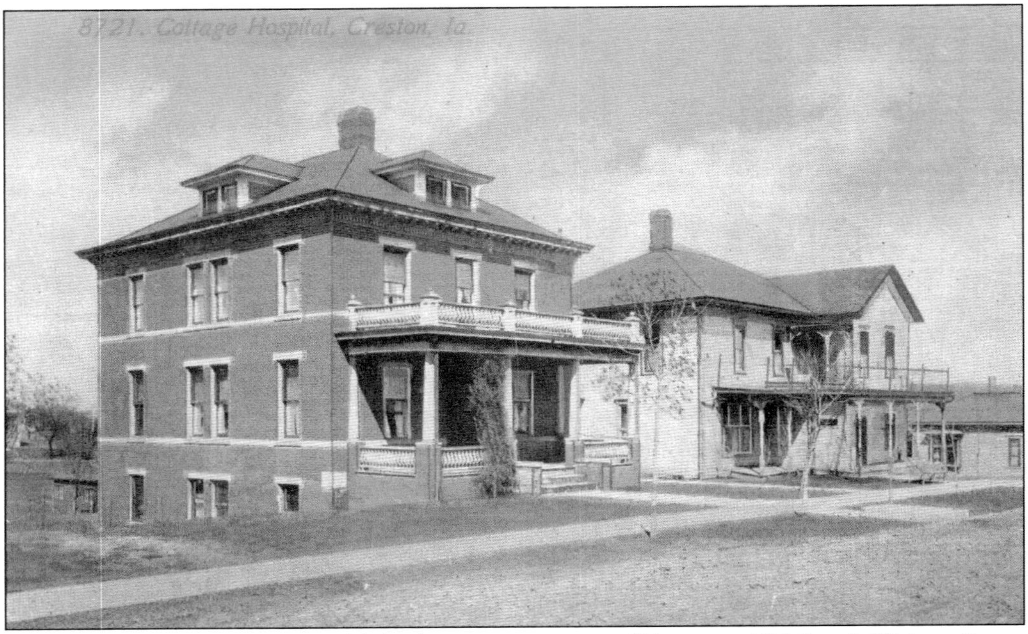

The first Cottage Hospital, established in 1894, was a small house at 500 South Walnut Street with one trained nurse, a housekeeper, and five patient beds. Two years later, in 1896, the hospital purchased and remodeled a residence at 404 North Oak Street (above left). A two-year nurses' college, associated with Cottage Hospital from 1898 to 1932, had its dormitory in the frame house next door (below). Various remodeling and additions took place from 1900 to 1917. In 1917–1918, a four-story brick building replaced the frame house (see page 87). (Above, Lynne Schlaht; below, Union County Historical Society.)

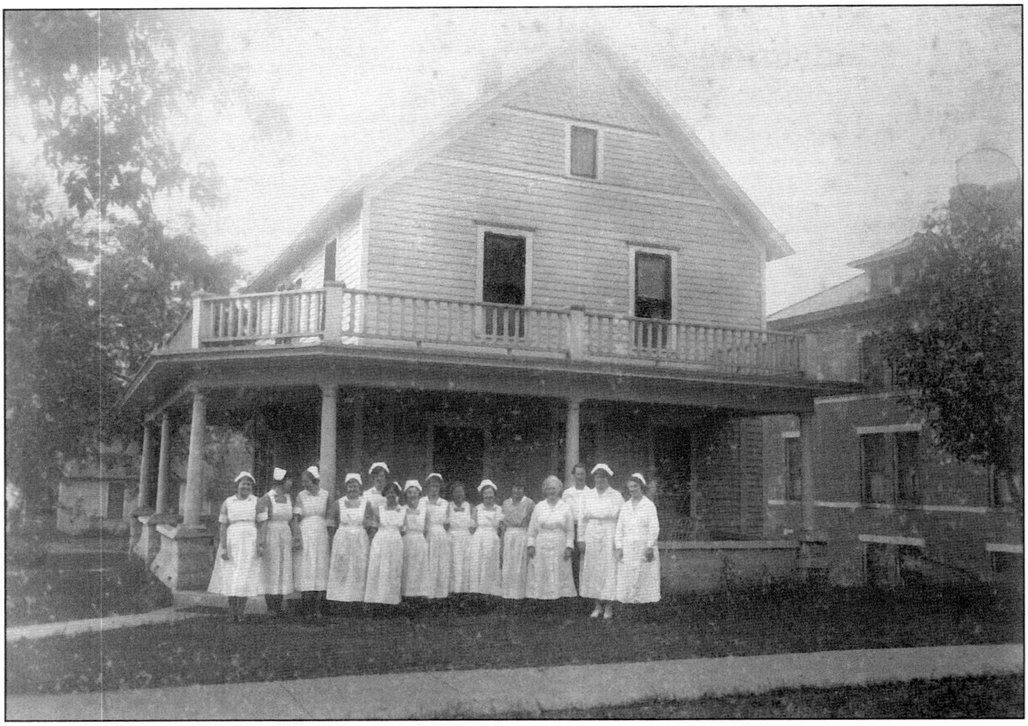

Three

Cigars, Saloons, and an Amusement Park

Creston was coming into her own at the beginning of the 20th century, with a new passenger depot gracing the north edge of the tracks. The impressive structure rose from what was once a grass-strewn prairie to welcome travelers with a warmth and elegance not seen before in the area. Increased passenger service meant more passenger trains, and by 1910, there were 24 passenger trains scheduled through Creston daily.

Early in the 20th century, Creston became a major crossroads when the Iowa State Highway Commission passed the 1913 Road Law, which recognized historical routes throughout the state. Two such highways pass through Creston: The Wilson Highway runs north and south, and the Bluegrass Road runs east and west.

The opening decades of the 20th century proved to be ideal for the manufacture of cigars, as nearly all men smoked. At least three companies existed at that time in Creston, all operating in a similar manner. Bales of dried tobacco leaves were shipped by train to the establishment, where the leaves were hand-rolled into cigars. The companies were rather small, with only a few employees.

In addition to cigars, another big business in Creston was alcohol. In 1871, the city council adopted regulations and assessments on saloons. By 1908, an annual fee of $1,500 was levied against each of the 10 saloons located within city limits. Of this, $3,000 went to the county, while Creston reserved $12,000 for itself.

In 1914, Creston became home to "The White City," an amusement park, possibly named after the famed White City of Chicago's 1893 Columbian Exposition. The park was located just east of Walnut Street, between Montgomery and Mills Streets. The entire complex was enclosed by a white board fence. Though the venture only lasted a few years, it was quite complex. There was a dance hall and roller-skating rink. Later an air dome (an outdoor stage with seating) was added for outdoor movies. In the concession area, the usual amusement rides were present, with a bathhouse and swimming pool completing the facilities. During the winter months, the concession area was converted to an ice rink.

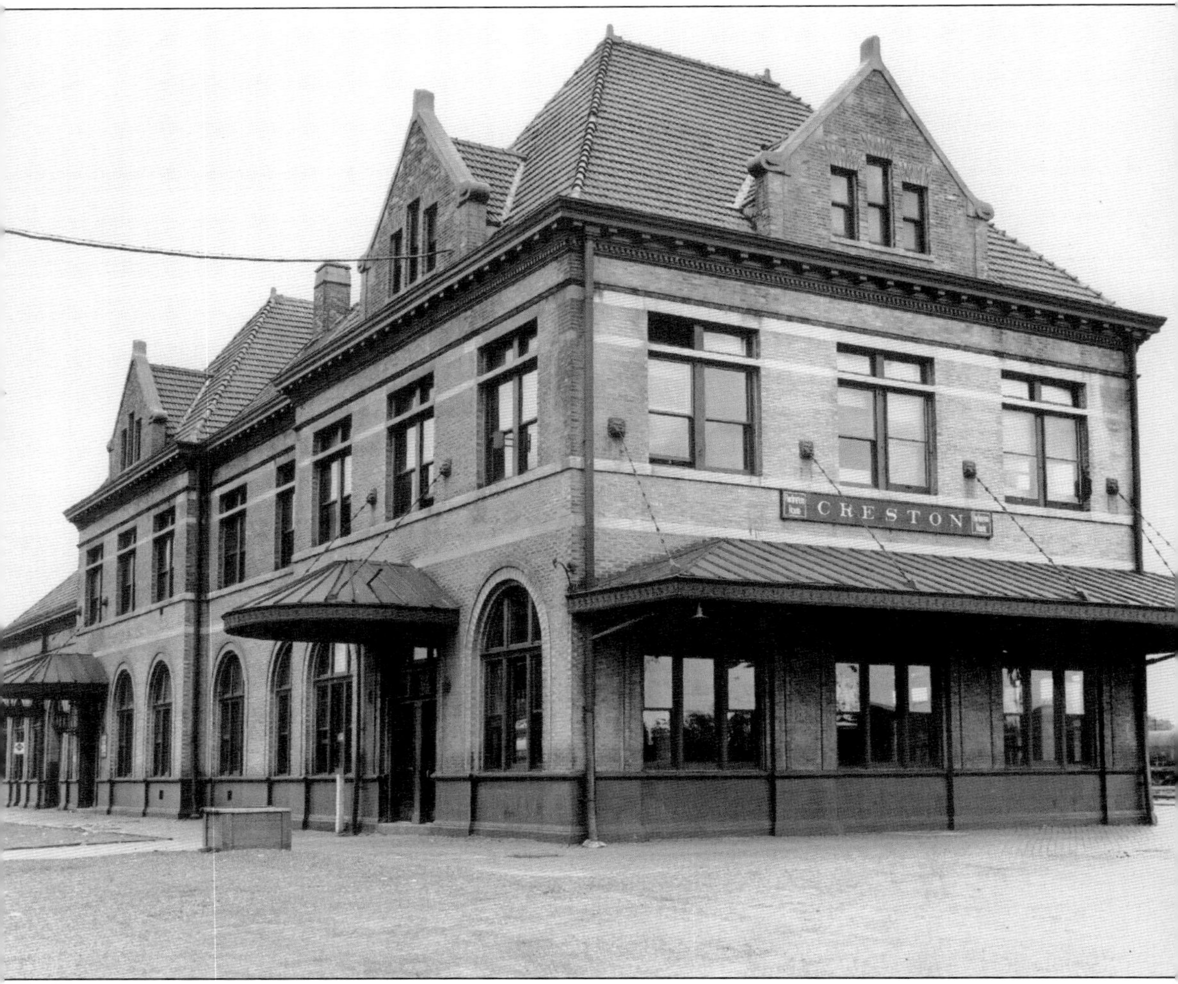

In 1899, the CB&Q built a magnificent new passenger depot designed by prominent Chicago architects Daniel Burnham and John Wellborn Root. Burnham and Root were famous for planning Chicago's 1893 Columbian Exposition. Shown from the Adams Street side, the original copper canopies can be seen over the doors and windows. The interior was illuminated by 236 electric incandescent bulbs. The first floor of the structure included a large waiting room, ticket office, and lunch counter, which was under the management of C. A. Allen of the Summit House. It was popular at the time for passenger orders to be sent ahead by the train personnel. Young boys would deliver the meals to passengers on board the train as it arrived at the depot. In addition to serving rail passengers, the depot was home to the Burlington Line division headquarters, which included rail offices and a telegraph room. (Corbin-Wagner Collection.)

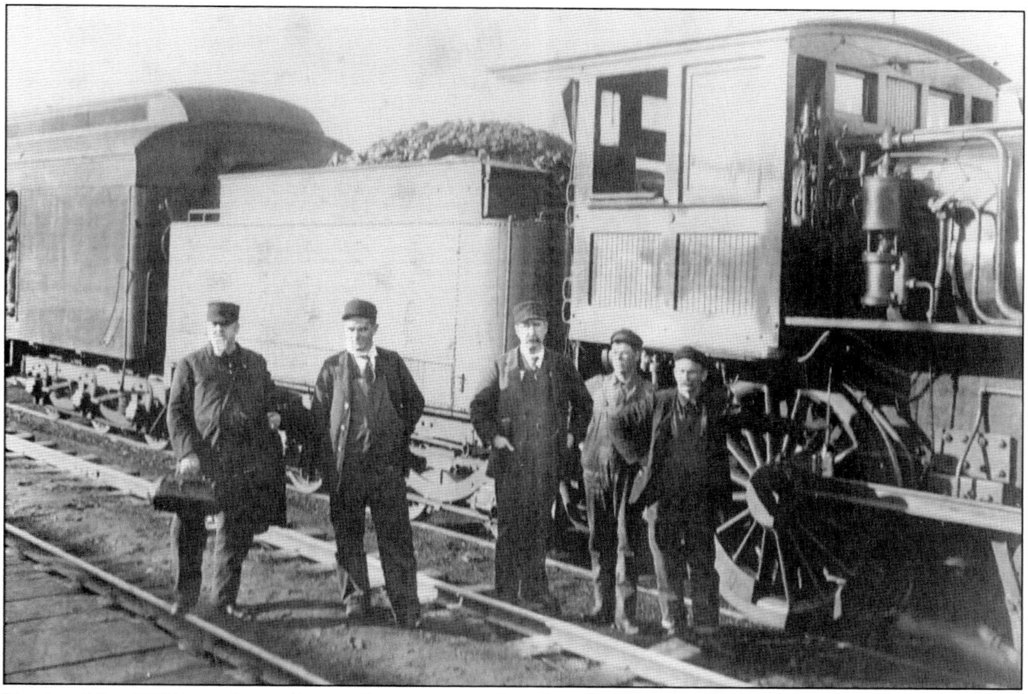

Engine No. 1550 was brought to Creston to aid in faster mail service. In May 1899, the crew left Creston behind schedule for Council Bluffs with an unusually heavy load of government supplies. By the end of the 104-mile ride, not a single window on the locomotive was left intact due to the engine reaching speeds of 90.2 miles per hour. Whether the record-breaking trip took 102 or 104 minutes, either way it was a terrific run. (Union County Historical Society.)

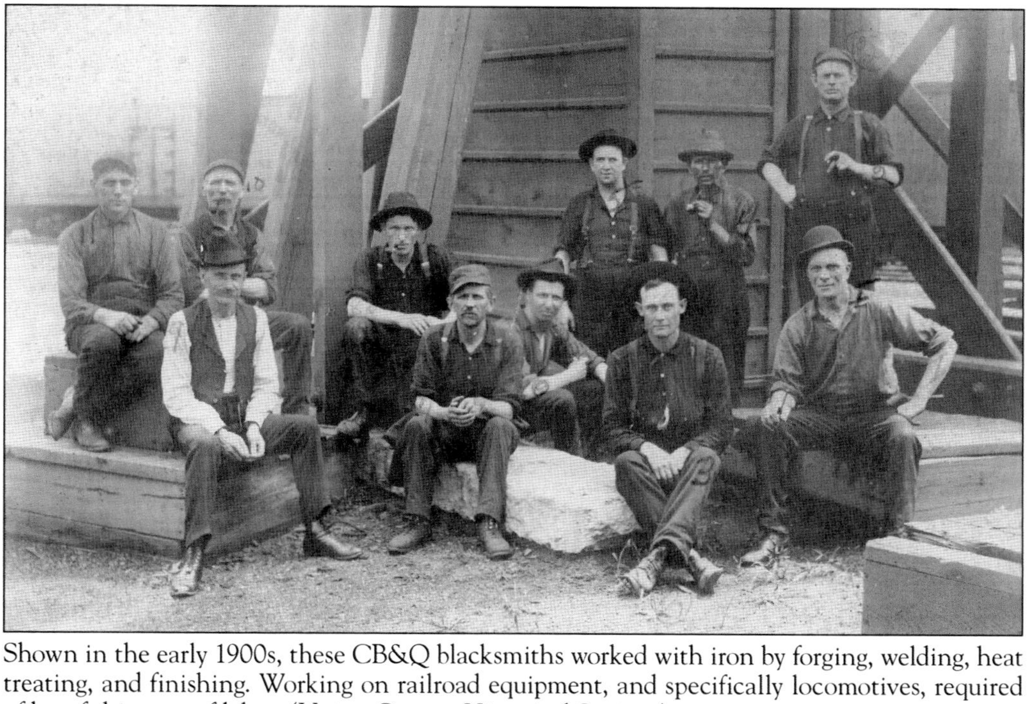

Shown in the early 1900s, these CB&Q blacksmiths worked with iron by forging, welding, heat treating, and finishing. Working on railroad equipment, and specifically locomotives, required of lot of this type of labor. (Union County Historical Society.)

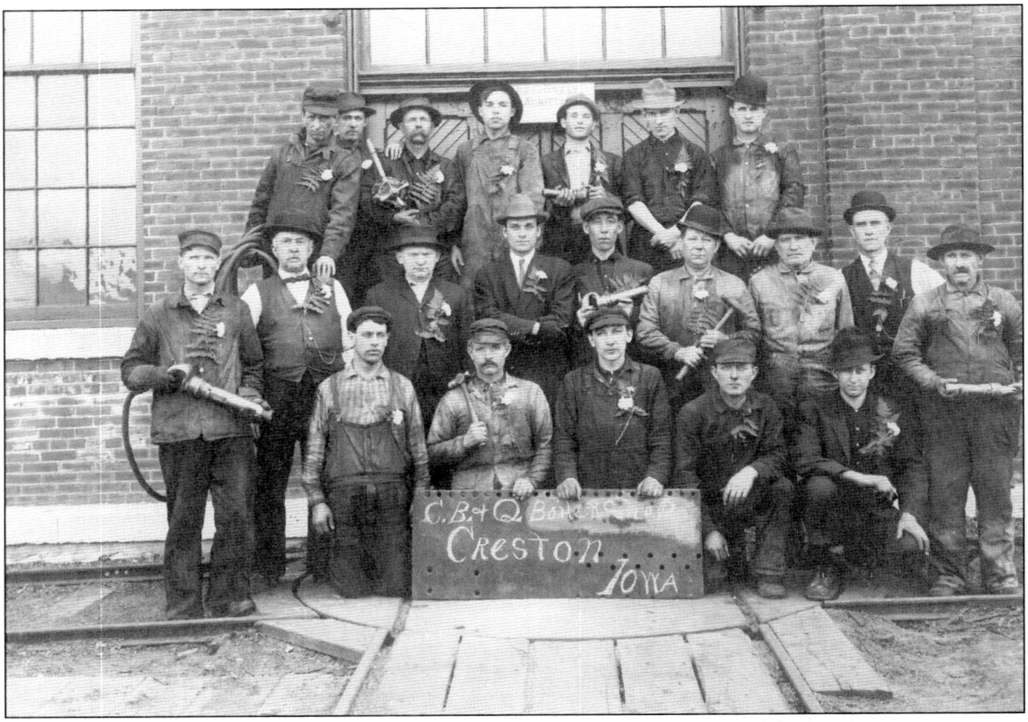

Shown sometime after 1900, the boiler shop employees were responsible for the maintenance and repair of the boilers on steam locomotives as well as most of the sheet metal work. (Maple Street Memories.)

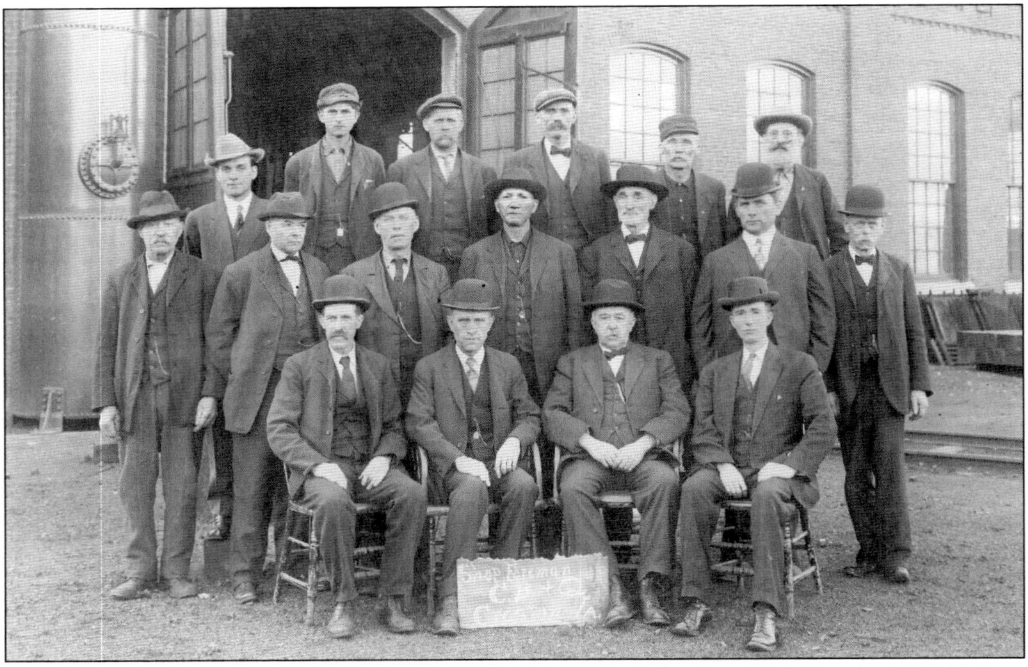

Taken in front of the Back Shop sometime after 1900, this photograph shows the CB&Q shop foremen. The foremen were the supervisors of the laborers, including machinists, boilermakers, and blacksmiths. (Maple Street Memories.)

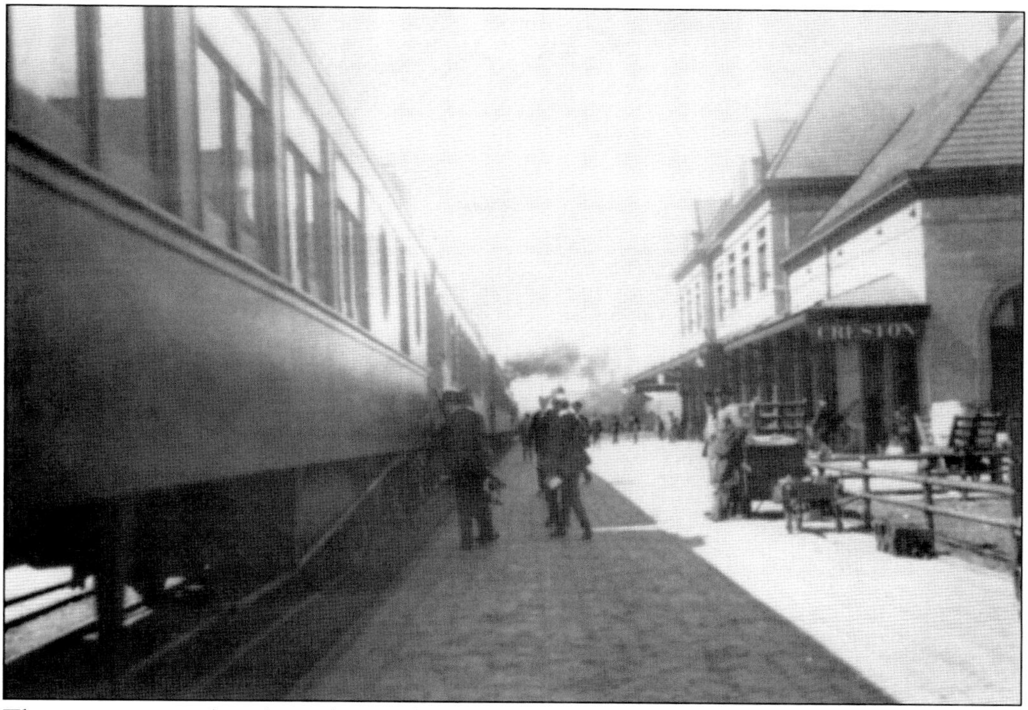

This image was taken from the southeast corner of the depot, shortly after it was built in the early 20th century. Several travelers are walking across the platform of Purington pavers to board a passenger train to Denver, probably the No. 3 train. In the distance, the freight station, which was built the same year as the passenger depot, can be seen across Elm Street. (Corbin-Wagner Collection.)

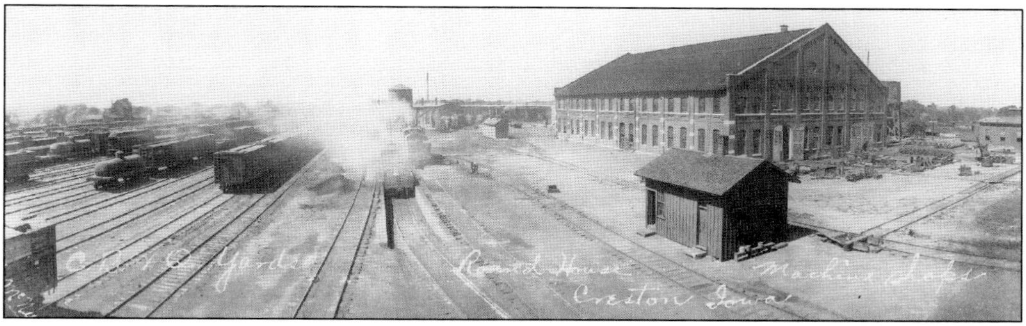

Looking west from the new coaling station, in 1905, is the freight yard, engine-servicing facilities, and machine shop. The large brick edifice, known as the Back Shop, was constructed in 1884 and served as the prototype for the larger shop constructed in West Burlington in 1886. A wheel-set turntable can be seen beside the small frame building in the foreground. (Corbin-Wagner Collection.)

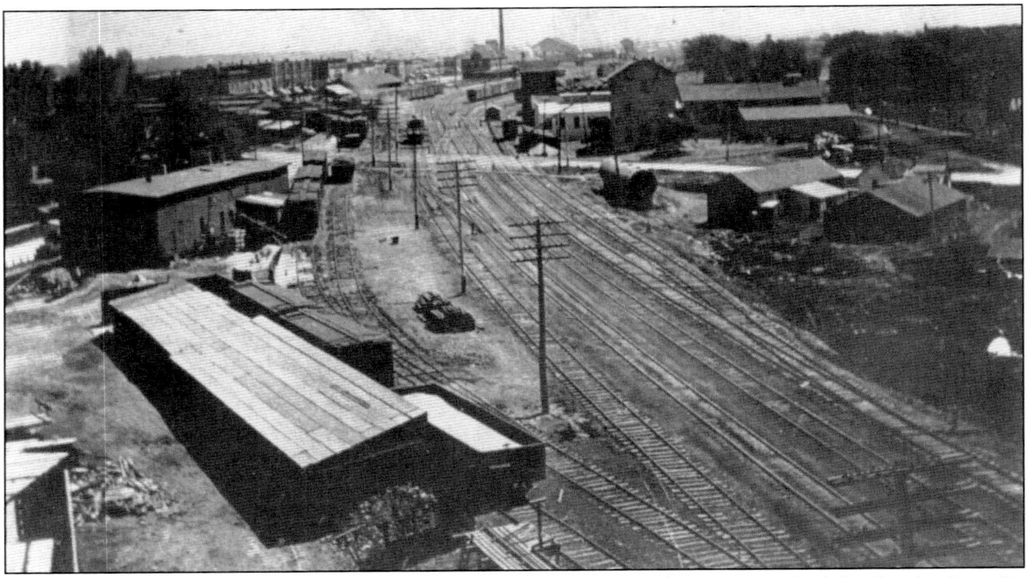

This photograph was taken sometime between 1900 and 1913 from the roof of the Swift plant. In the foreground are the coal sheds for the Rex brothers, with the Whipple egg house just behind. The 1899 depot, with the smokestack for the power plant, is at the back center. The railroad's Back Shop can be seen beyond that. The uptown area, with the Summit House, is to the left of the depot. (Rosalie Denton.)

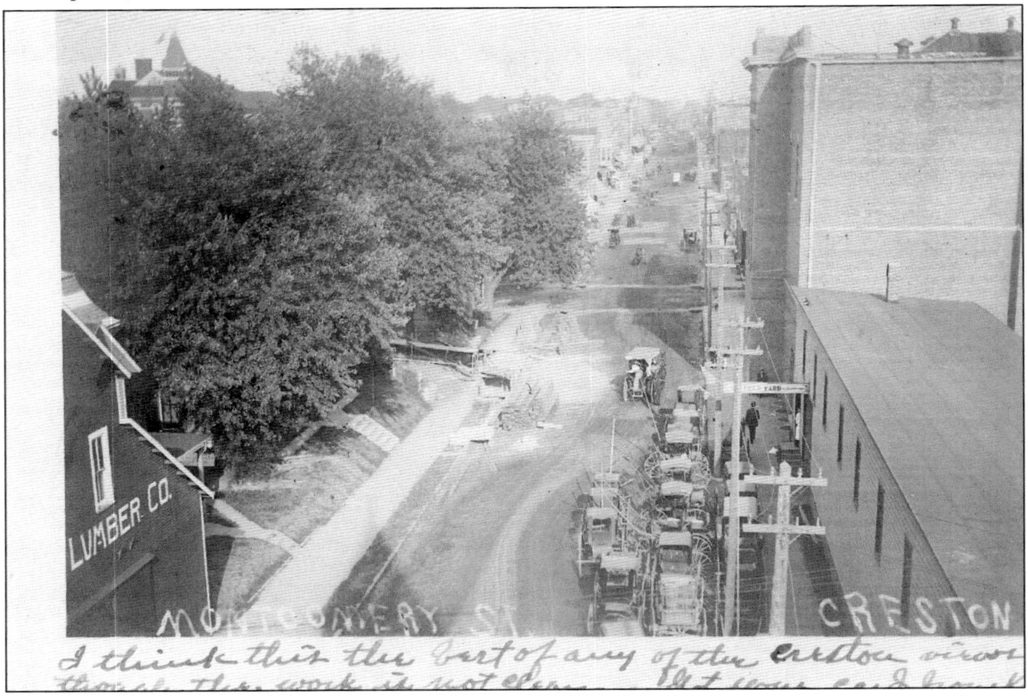

Looking east down Montgomery Street, this view was taken from the Congregational Church around 1906. The tall building on the right is the back of the Temple Grand Masonic Lodge. Building materials lie in the dirt street in front of the Elks Lodge site, which was under construction at that time. The tower protruding above the trees is the Union County Courthouse on Pine Street. (Union County Historical Society.)

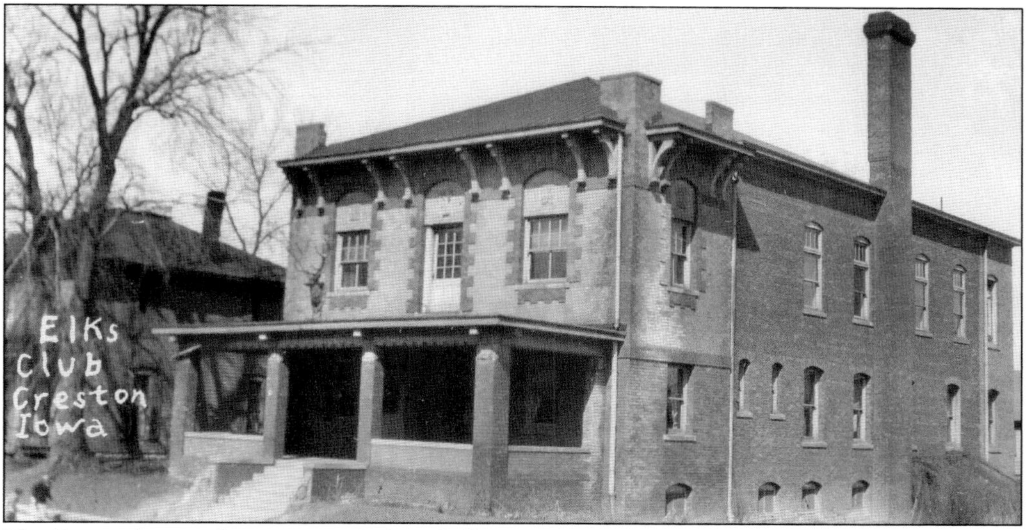

The Benevolent and Protective Order of Elks was organized in Creston on July 12, 1900, with 13 founding members. The lodge home, built in 1906, is still located at 403 West Montgomery Street. In the early 1920s, an addition was added to the back of the building. A major renovation followed in 1962. (Union County Historical Society.)

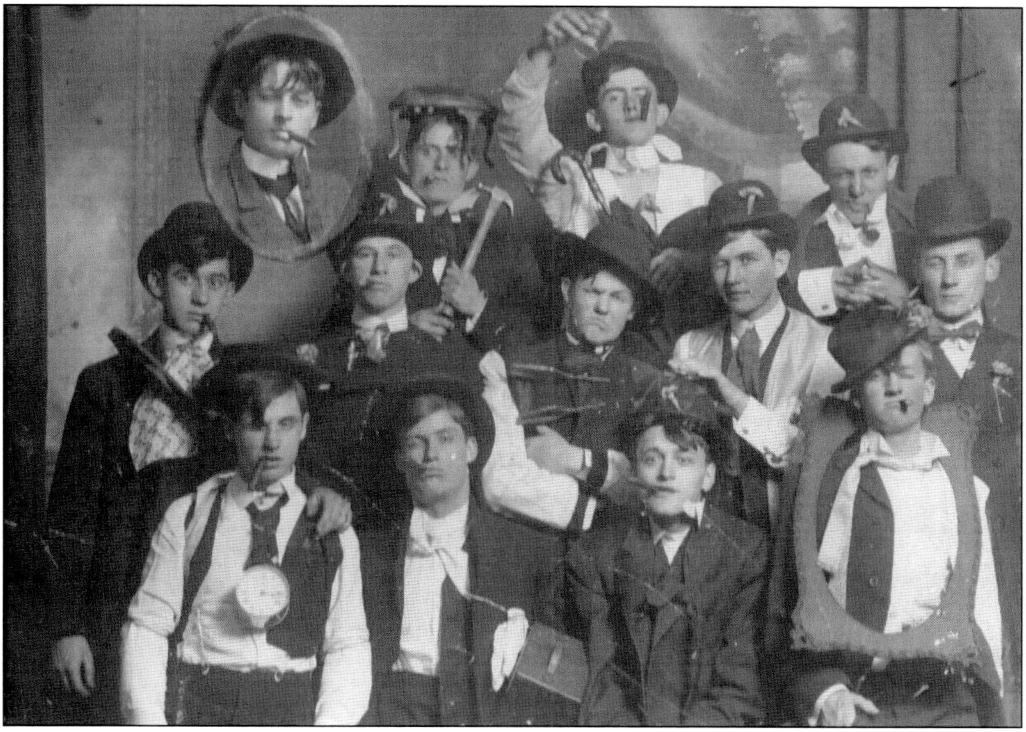

In the first year, the Elks' membership grew to 205. By Creston's centennial in 1969, there were nearly 600 members. This group of Elks initiates shown sometime between 1903–1906 are, from left to right, (first row) George Gentle, Lucien Wilson, Neil or Ernest Landsburg, and John Porter; (second row) Arthur "Beetle" Braunberger, Warren Royce, Ed Farrell, George Gault, and Ralph Tallman; (third row) Glen Morrison (inset), unidentified, John Sullivan, and Harry Archer. (Union County Historical Society.)

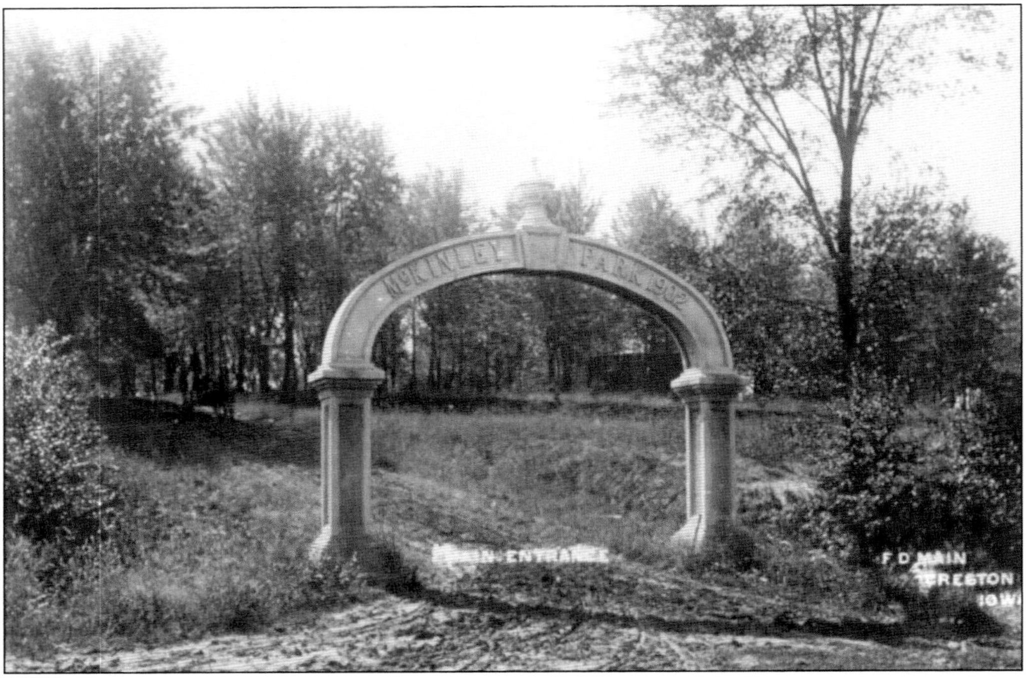

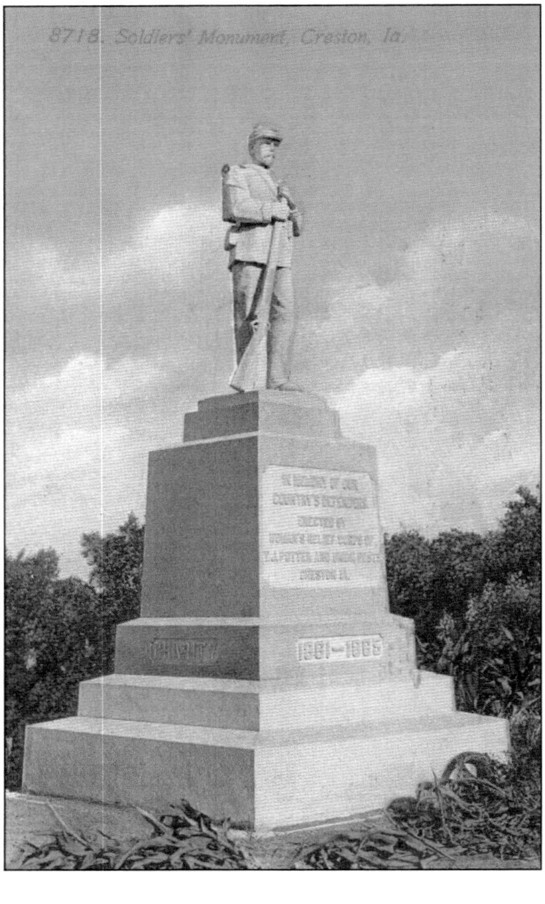

Lake Park and Spencer Lake were constructed by the Creston Ice Company, which was indirectly associated with the railroad, to supply water and ice to the city and railroad. When Summit Lake—a new, larger water supply system—was completed in 1894, Spencer Lake was drained. In 1901, the city purchased 30 acres of the old Lake Park to create McKinley Park (above) in honor of the assassinated president. A park commission was formed, and many improvements were made, such as restoring the lake, establishing a beach, and building shelter houses. A monument to pay tribute to Union County's war veterans was erected at the east edge of the park. A restoration of Soldiers' Monument (left) was completed in 2009. (Above, Jane Briley; left, Lynne Schlaht.)

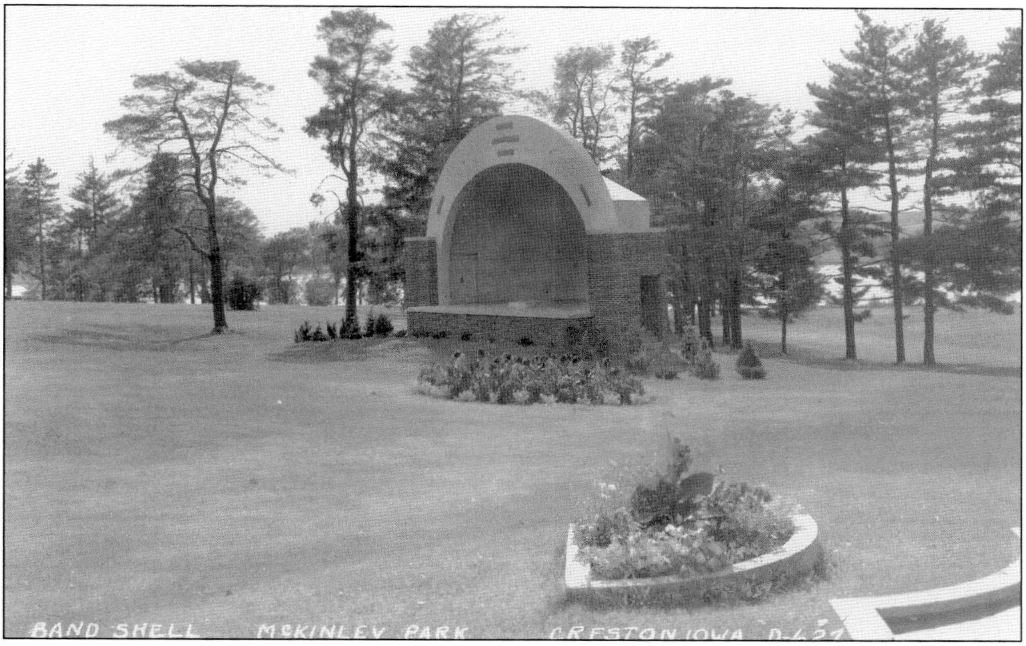

The McKinley Park Band Shell was constructed by Emerson Construction (see page 78) during the early years of the park's existence. Over the years, many bands and performers have graced the stage with their performances. In recent years, the stage has been an integral part of Creston's Independence Day Celebration, which includes the annual talent show held there each year. (Lynne Schlaht.)

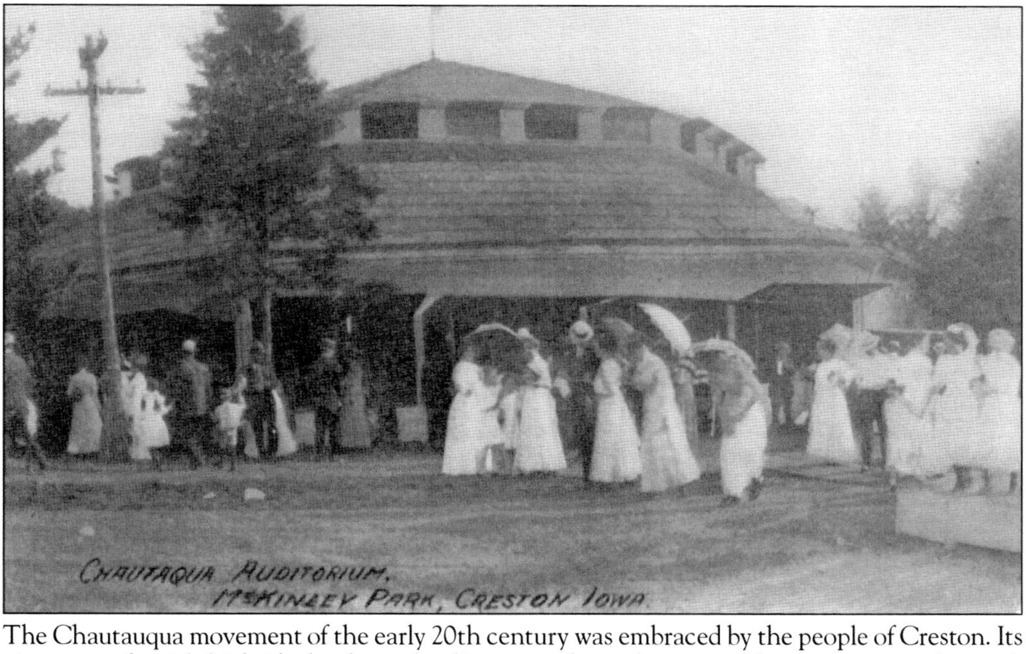

The Chautauqua movement of the early 20th century was embraced by the people of Creston. Its aim was to furnish high ideals of moral, religious, and social action and to give a mental, moral, social, and spiritual uplift by bringing the people in contact with educators, reformers, preachers, musicians, and orators. The Creston Chautauqua Association was organized in the spring of 1914, and an auditorium was constructed in McKinley Park. (Lynne Schlaht.)

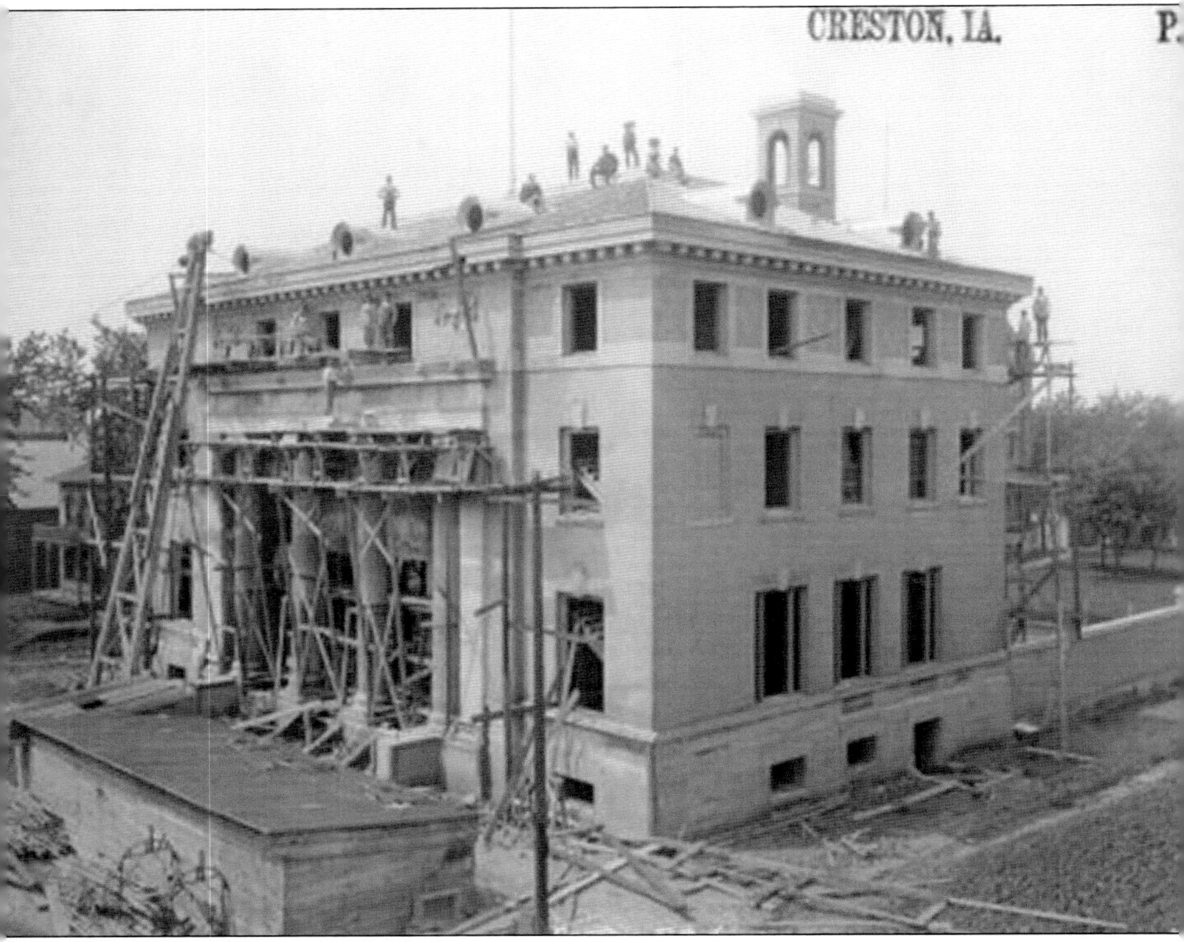

The post office was established in Creston in 1869. Initially it was located in the grocery store of E. L. Thompson, the first postmaster, but was moved from place to place. In 1903, the post office found a permanent home on North Maple Street when the government building was constructed. The first floor functioned as the city post office, where the large mail sorting room dominated the space. There were peepholes at the ceiling of the sorting room for supervisors to monitor postal employees (see page 125). Post office boxes were available for individuals in the main lobby. The second floor housed the U.S. federal and district courts, with an impressive courtroom, judge's chambers, jury room, and various offices. District court continues to be held in Creston in 2011, but federal court ended before Creston celebrated its centennial in 1969. As early as 1908, the graduating high school class has had its picture taken on the steps of the post office, and this tradition continues into the present. The classic architecture and Corinthian columns make for an ideal photo backdrop. (P. F. Allen.)

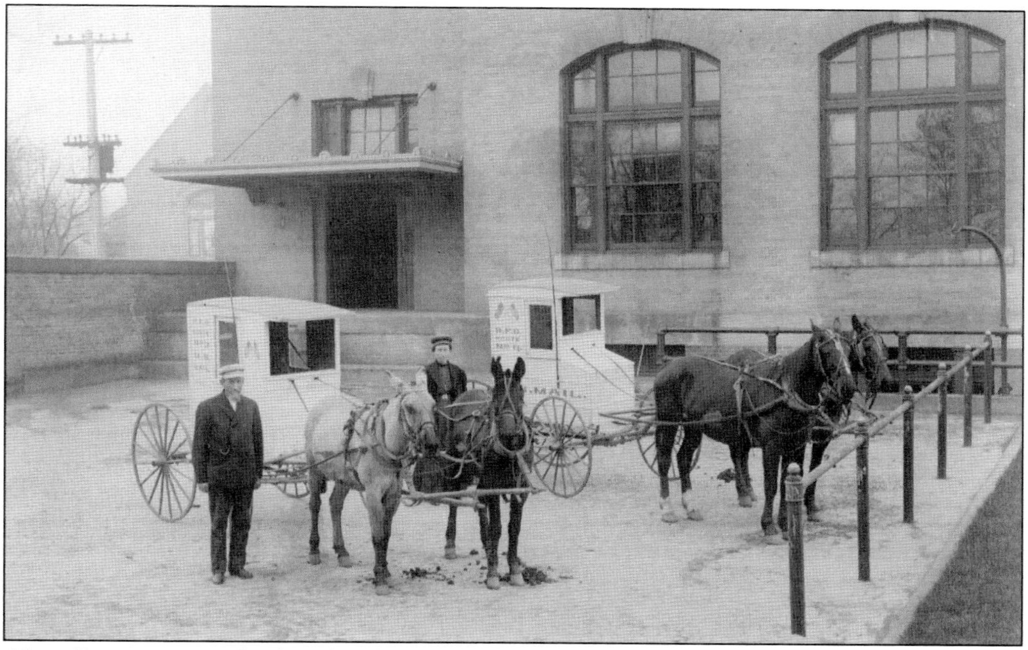

Alice Gummere was the first female postal carrier in the state of Iowa. She served the Creston Post Office from 1900 until her retirement in December 1933. She covered Rural Route No. 6 in a horse-drawn cart. She is shown, along with her father, at the back of the post office with their delivery wagons and horses in 1910. (Maple Street Memories.)

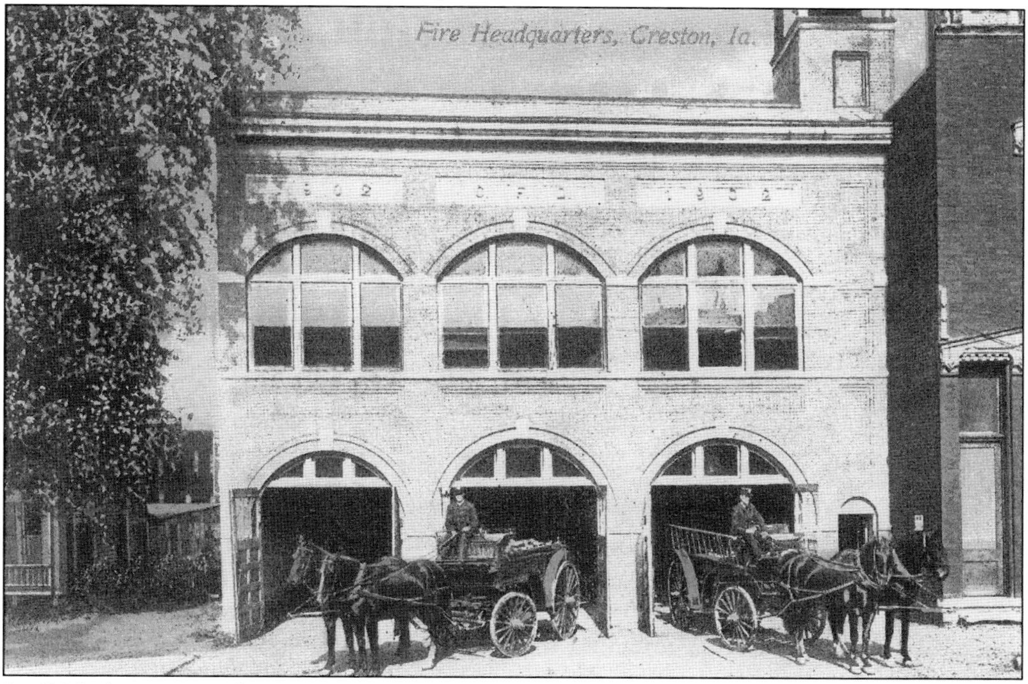

In 1886, the separate fire companies were organized into a single fire department. A new engine house was built in 1902 at 205 North Maple Street to serve as fire headquarters and to house the chemical engine, hose wagon, and hook-and-ladder truck. A stable for the horses was in the rear, while the second story functioned as a haymow. (Roger Nurnberg.)

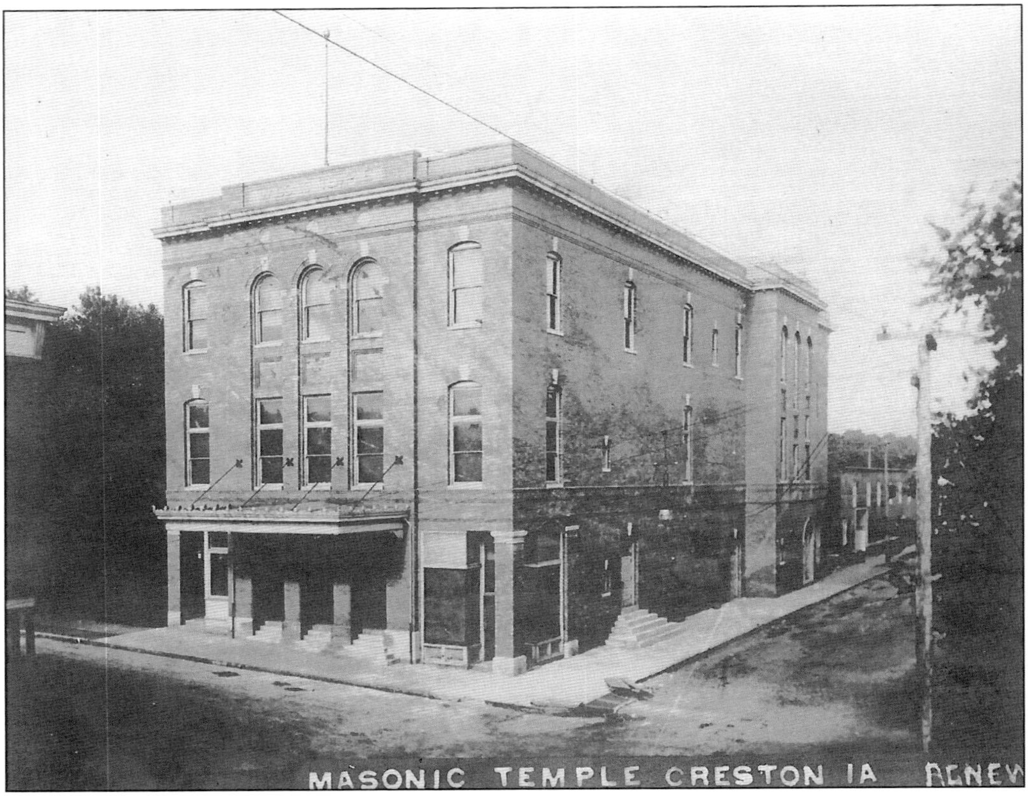

The Crest City Lodge was established in 1892. The first Masonic Temple and Temple Grand Theater were located on the corner of Montgomery and Oak Streets. There were elaborate murals painted on the walls of the opera house by Louis Syberkrop, a local artist and designer of the 1889 Blue Grass Palace. The building was lost to a fire on July 3, 1920. It was rebuilt in 1926. (Steve Francis.)

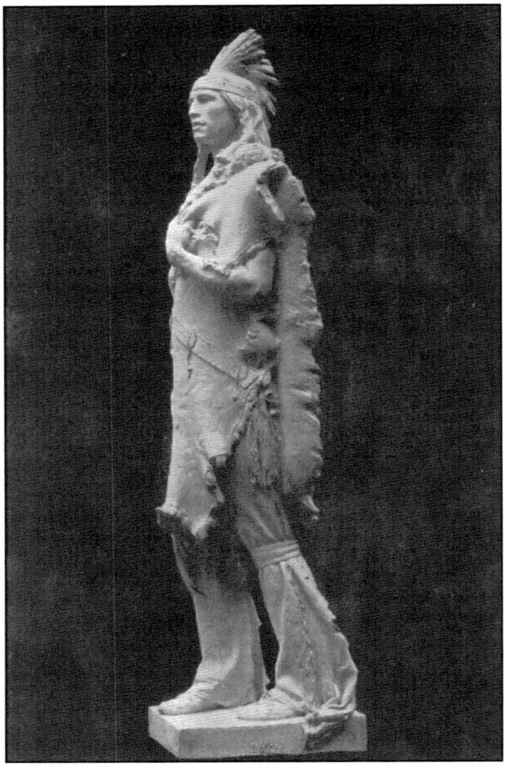

Sherry Edmundson Fry (1879–1966) was born in Creston on September 29, 1879. He was a well-known American sculptor who played a prominent role in the establishment of an American camouflage unit during World War I. One of his most significant commissions, completed in 1907, was a bronze statue of Chief Mahaska, which now stands in the town square of Oskaloosa, Iowa. (Union County Historical Society.)

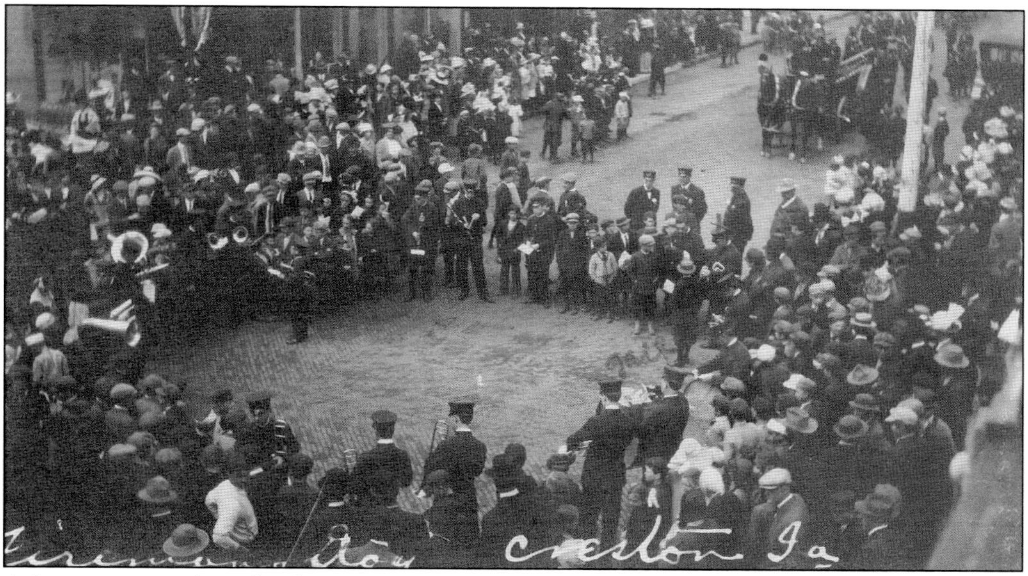

A large group gathers for the Fireman's Day Parade in 1912. In the upper right corner, horses lead a wagon with a ladder. In the center, members of the Fireman's Band form a circle, with the crowd surrounding them. They seem to be between numbers, as many of the musicians are flipping through their music. (Roger Nurnberg.)

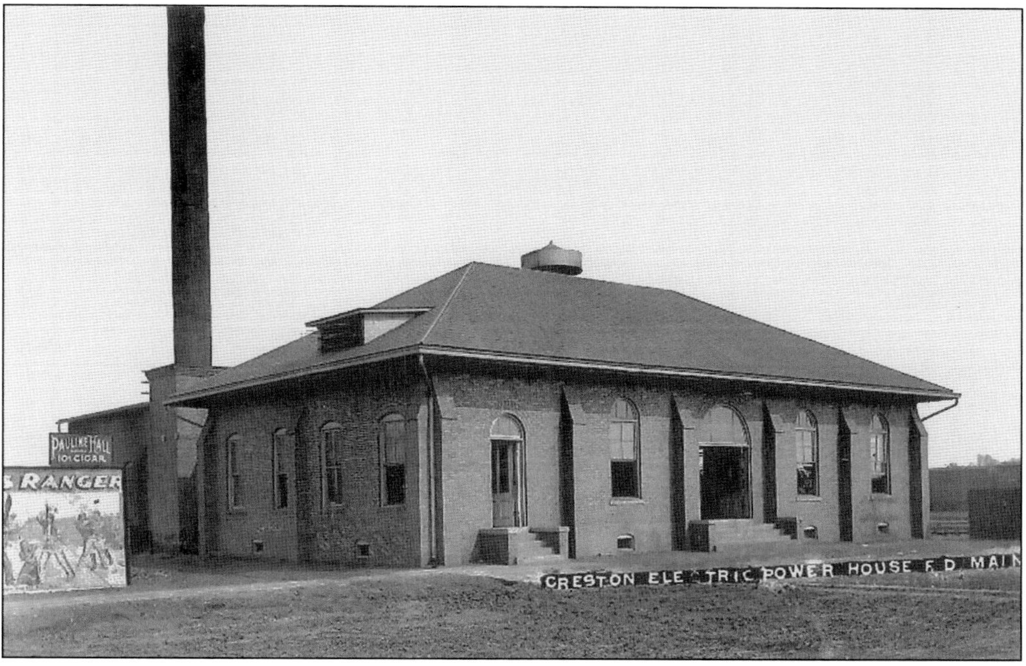

Creston was first supplied with electric power in 1905, when the Creston Mutual Electric Light, Heat and Power Company was organized. A progressive power plant was constructed at the east end of Adams Street, and modern equipment was installed. On April 1, 1923, the Creston plant was purchased by the Iowa Southern Utilities Company of Centerville, and it became a district office for the company. (Dave Long.)

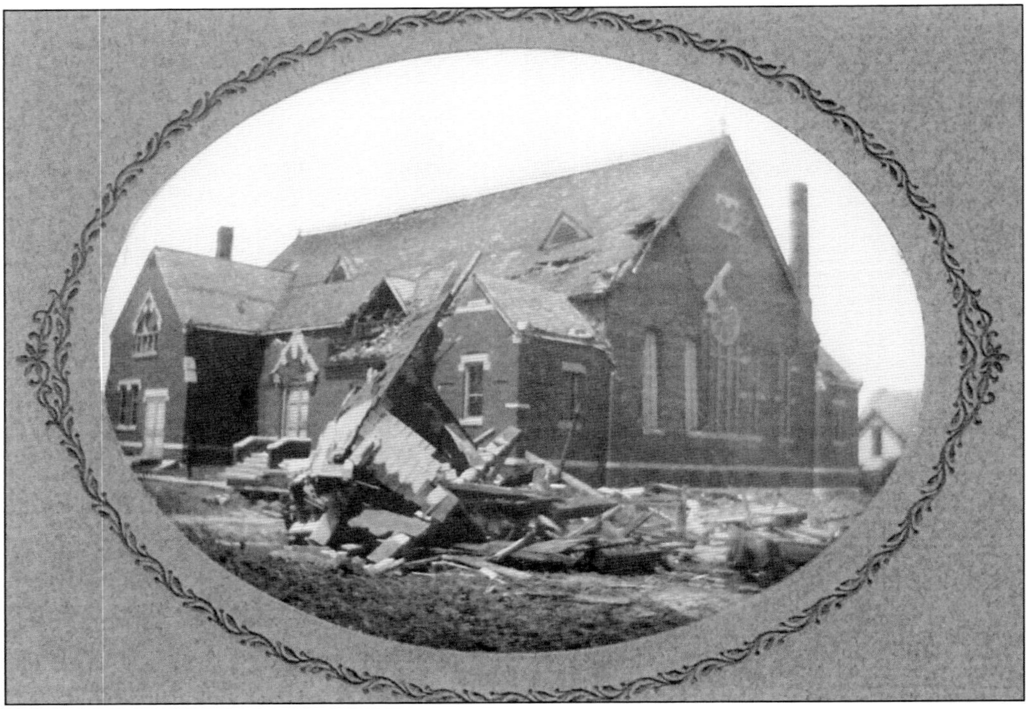

In the fall of 1871, a Methodist congregation was organized under the ministry of Rev. W. H. W. Rees. By 1887, the parish elected to expand, and a building lot on the corner of Elm and Howard Streets was purchased. The Methodist Episcopal Church, a brick veneer building costing $17,000, was built that same year. On May 17, 1903, a tornado ripped through the town of Creston, severely damaging the church. The cupola and spire were hurled to the south and east, embedding the bell into the southeast corner of the roof. Debris from the east wall and cupola filled the crossing at Elm and Howard Streets. The congregation decided to rebuild, with Rev. E. W. McDade overseeing reconstruction. Once completed, the parish grew to more than 1,000 members before the Great Depression struck in the early 1930s. (Above, Jane Briley; below, Lynne Schlaht.)

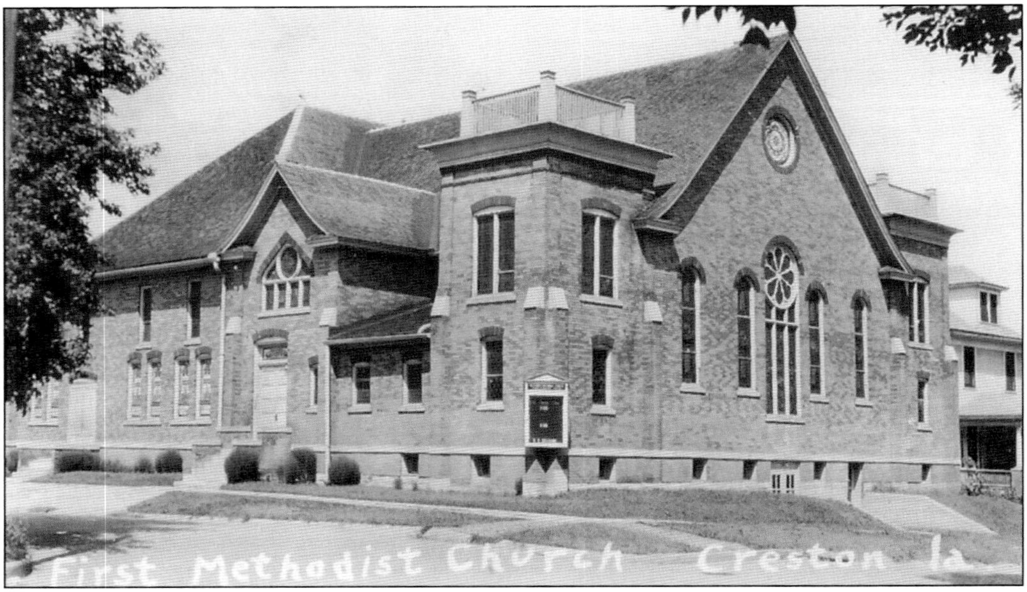

On March 21, 1905, the Immaculate Conception Parish was established. This effectively split Creston into two Catholic parishes, with Adams Street as the dividing line. A new worship center was started in August 1905 on the corner of Maple and Howard Streets. The church, which cost $28,000 to construct, was dedicated on March 20, 1907. In 1974, the two Catholic parishes merged to form one parish—Holy Spirit Parish. (Lynne Schlaht.)

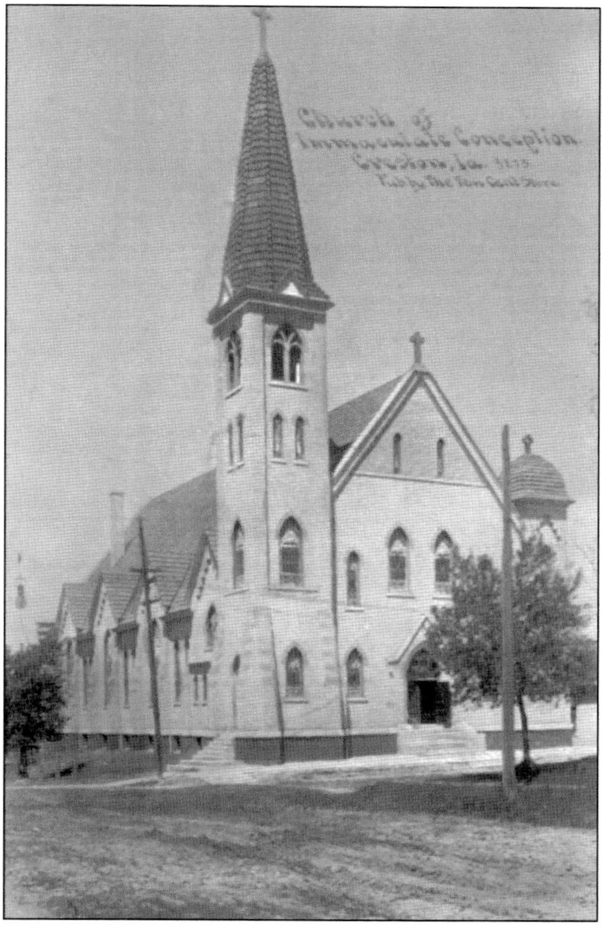

The Baptist Church was organized on October 27, 1872, with 18 charter members. The church met for 10 years in private homes and public halls before erecting the first church building in 1881 on the corner of Maple and Mills Streets. In 1906, the congregation decided to build a larger building in the same location. The new brick structure of Moorish design (shown above) was dedication on November 21, 1909. (Lynne Schlaht.)

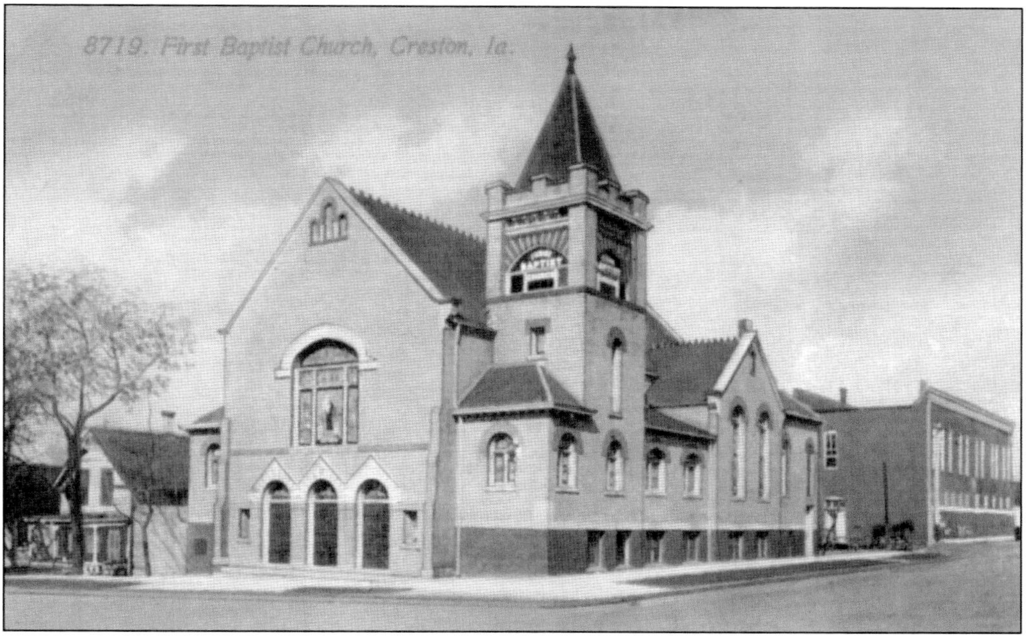

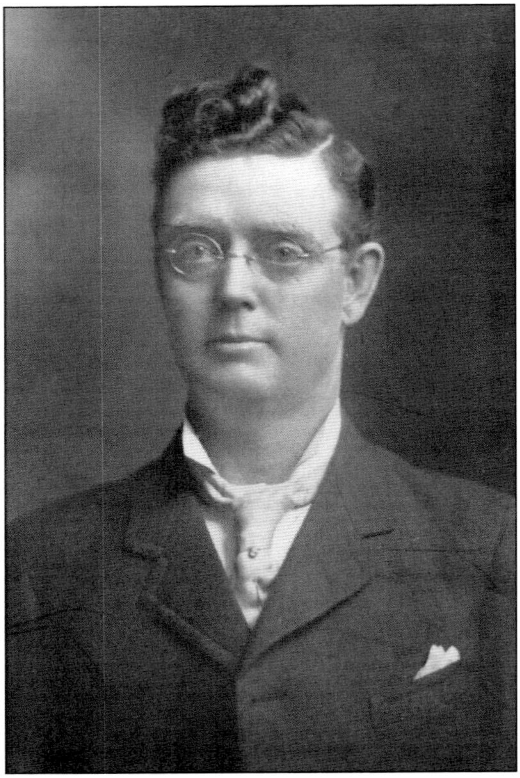

Dr. Joshua Walter Coakley came to Creston in 1906 and opened the Coakley Unity Hospital at 1200 North Sycamore Street with his sons, Dr. Cleve Coakley and Dr. Orlo Coakley. The Coakleys operated two other clinics in Creston as well. Joshua was a pioneer surgeon in Iowa, specializing in the performance of Cesarean sections. He also served as a Union County state representative in 1913, 1915, and 1917. (Union County Historical Society.)

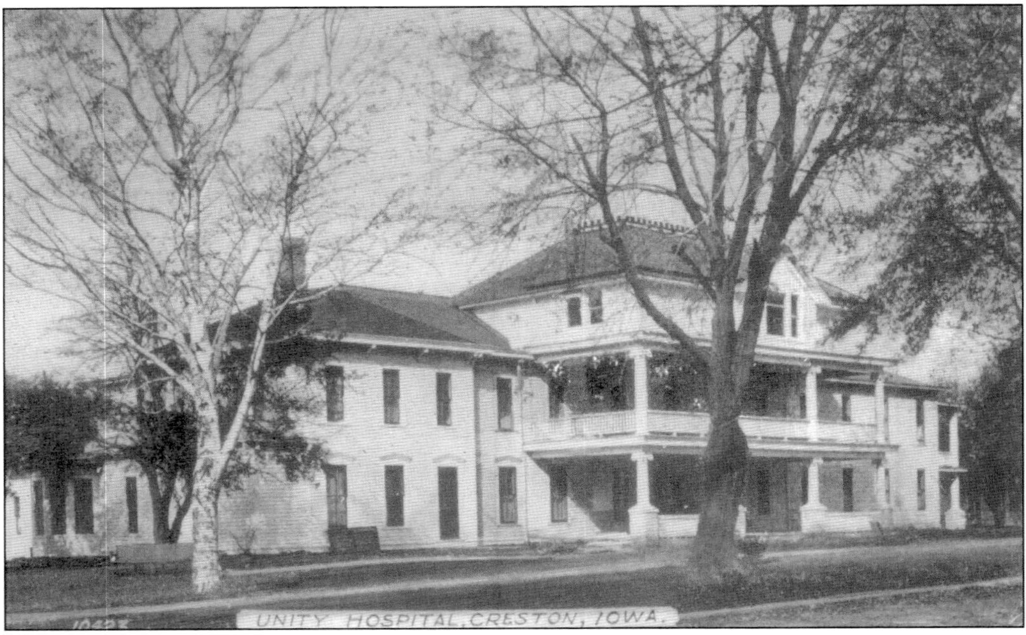

The 50-bed Coakley Unity Hospital was a state-of-the-art facility. It was described in the *Union County History of 1981* as "most beautifully situated in North Creston at the end of a fine bitulithic-paved street, one of the principal boulevards of the city where the air is purest, and far removed from the grime and smoke of the railroad yards." It is remembered for large airy rooms and big porches for convalescing patients. (Lynne Schlaht.)

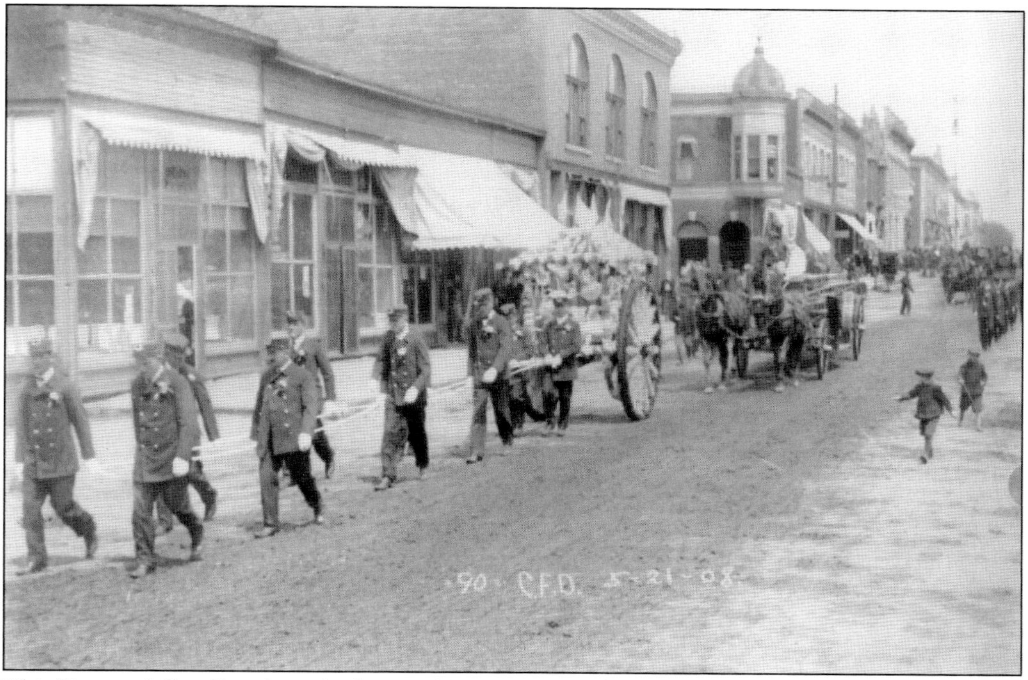

This Fireman's Day Parade took place on May 21, 1908. The firemen are leading a hose truck west on Montgomery Street. Each year the different divisions of the fire department would celebrate Fireman's Day with a parade and demonstrations of the various department apparatus. The building on the corner of Elm Street, with the arched windows on the second floor, is the only structure remaining in this block as of 2011. (Roger Nurnberg.)

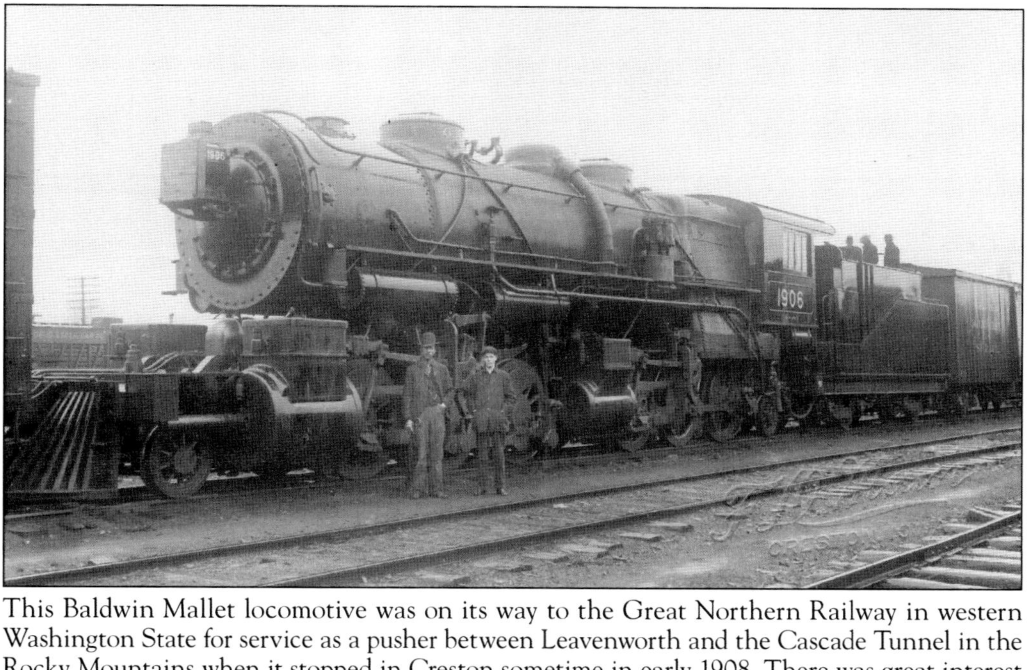

This Baldwin Mallet locomotive was on its way to the Great Northern Railway in western Washington State for service as a pusher between Leavenworth and the Cascade Tunnel in the Rocky Mountains when it stopped in Creston sometime in early 1908. There was great interest and curiosity by the CB&Q workers, as this type of locomotive was only two years old at the time. (Union County Historical Society.)

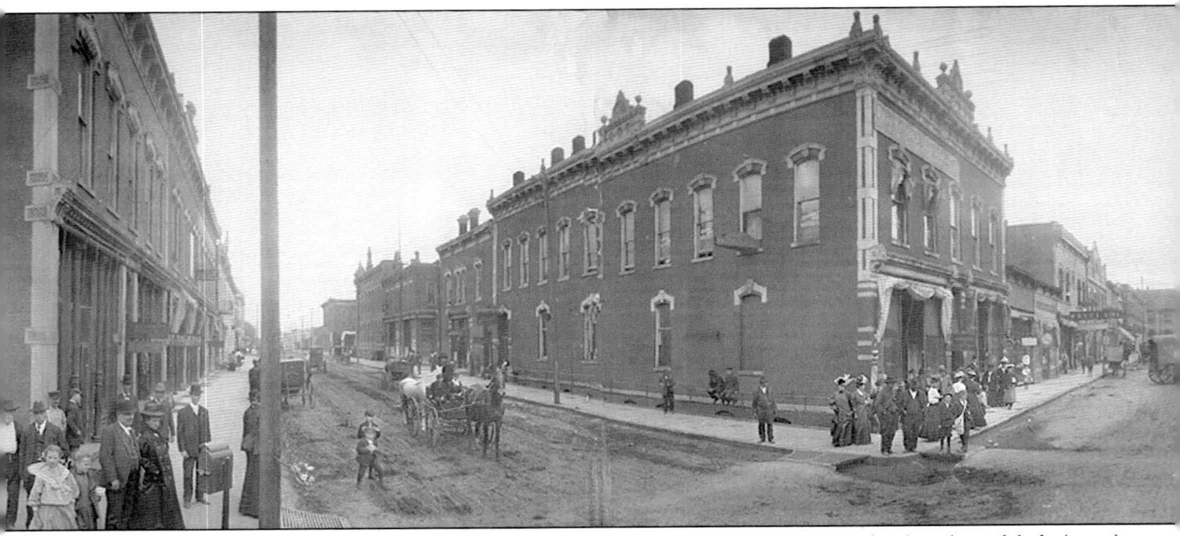

A panoramic view taken in 1908 shows Montgomery Street to the right (east) and left (west). Maple Street, looking south toward the depot, is in the center. On the far left corner, in front of the group of people, is a mail drop box. Still looking left, the Iowa State Savings Bank, the building with a pediment on the corner of Montgomery and Pine Streets on the right side, can be seen at the end of this block. The building just west of the bank was a hardware store that "wrapped around" the bank, with entrances on both Montgomery and Pine Streets. The far right building is the predecessor to the Iowana Hotel, built in the same location in 1919. Still looking

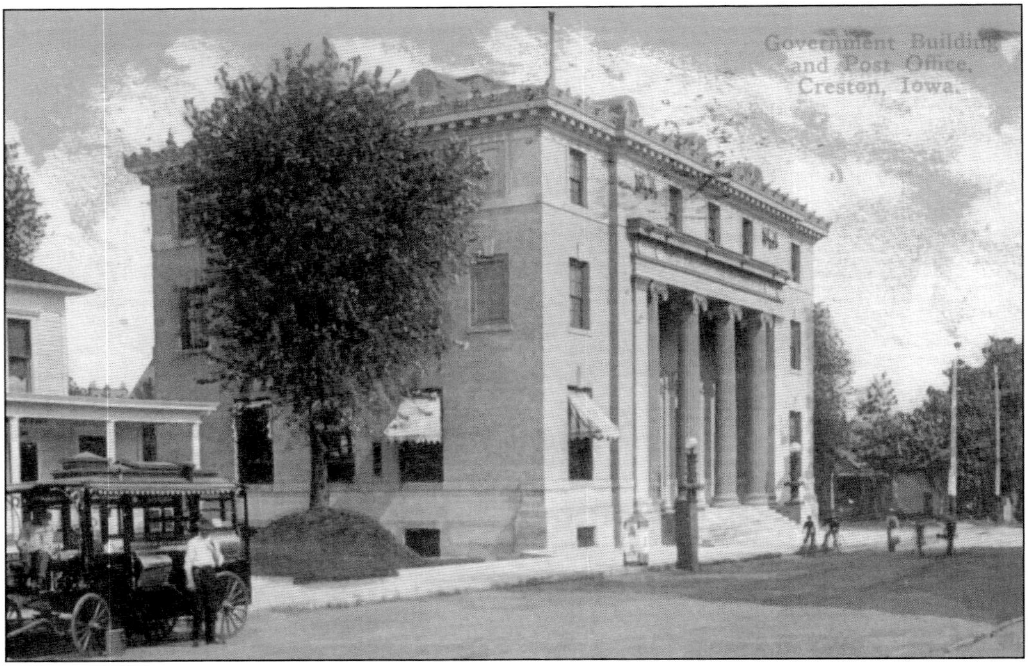

The post office, finished in 1903, is shown just after its completion (see page 46 for construction). Notice the awnings on the first-floor windows. At this time there was a house in what is now an empty lot south of the building. A horse-drawn hearse appears in the lower left corner. (Lynne Schlaht.)

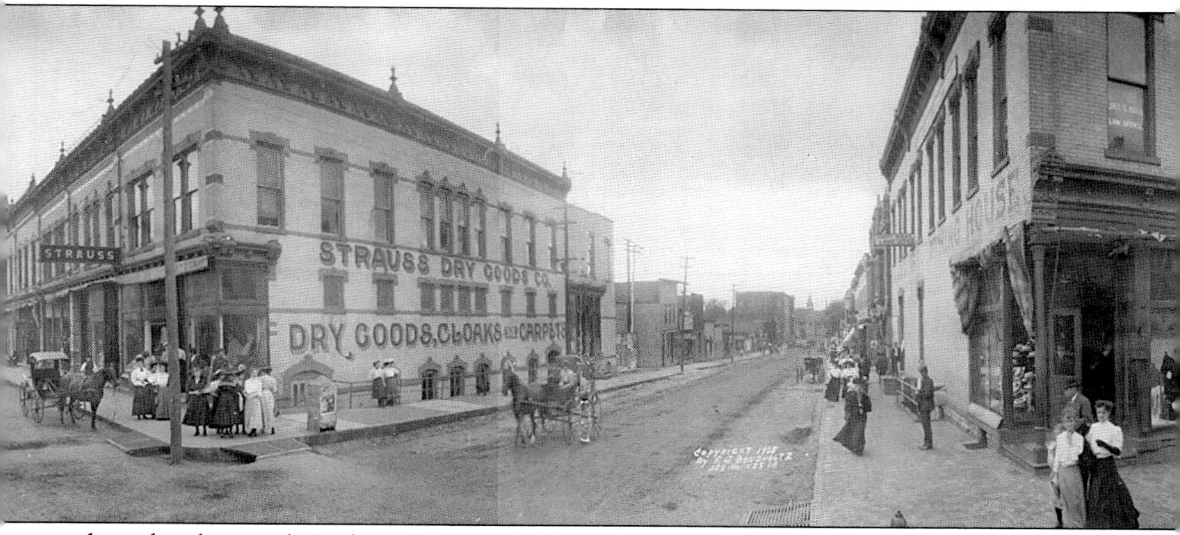

to the right, the steeple at the end of Montgomery Street is the Congregational Church, built in 1889. Just a block east of the church, on the left side of Montgomery Street, is the three-story Temple Grand Masonic Lodge and Opera House. Strauss Dry Goods Company stands on the corner to the right. There are grates or ramps that allow pedestrians access at the corners from the sidewalks to the street. Notice an ice wagon is parked in the center of Maple Street. (Library of Congress, pan 6a05006.)

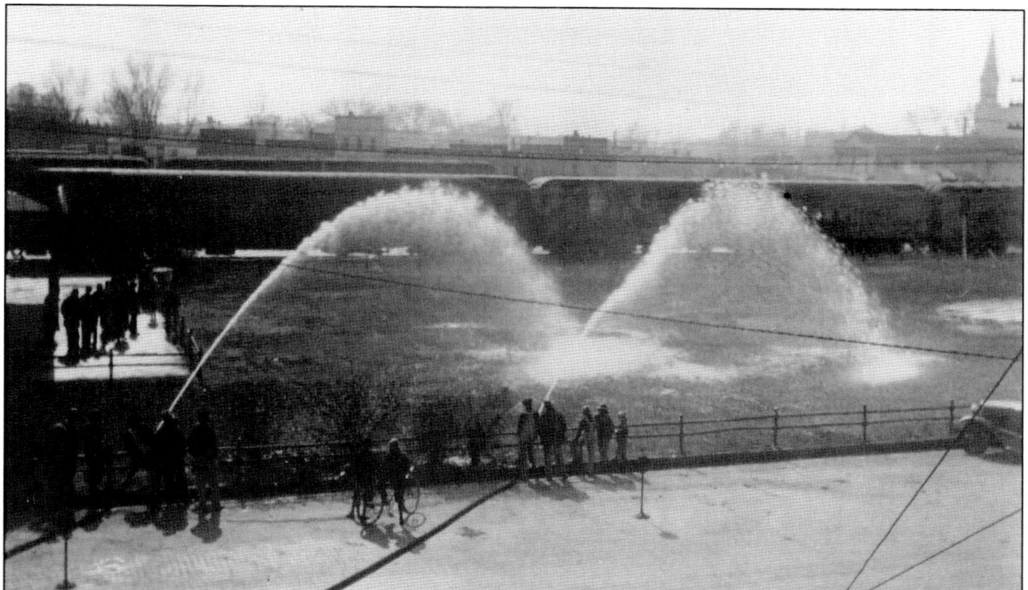

Each year, in May, the fire department would celebrate Fireman's Day with a parade and demonstrations of the various firefighting apparatus. The festivities usually had a comical, rather than a scientific, approach. Here firefighters exhibit the fire hoses on the grassy area west of the depot in 1916. Notice the railcars just beyond the exhibition area and Union Street in the background. (Roger Nurnberg.)

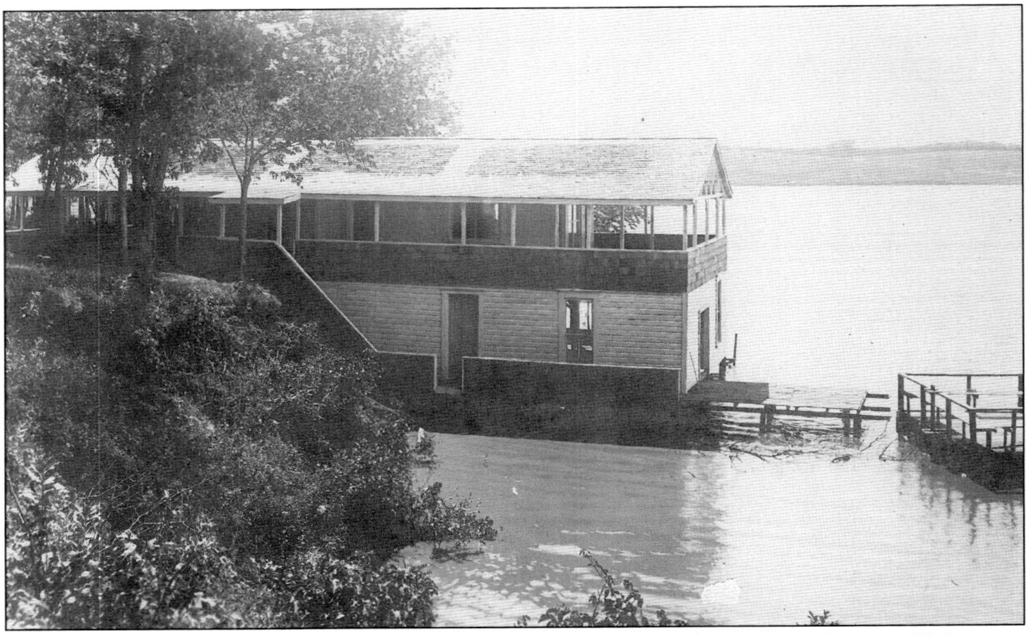

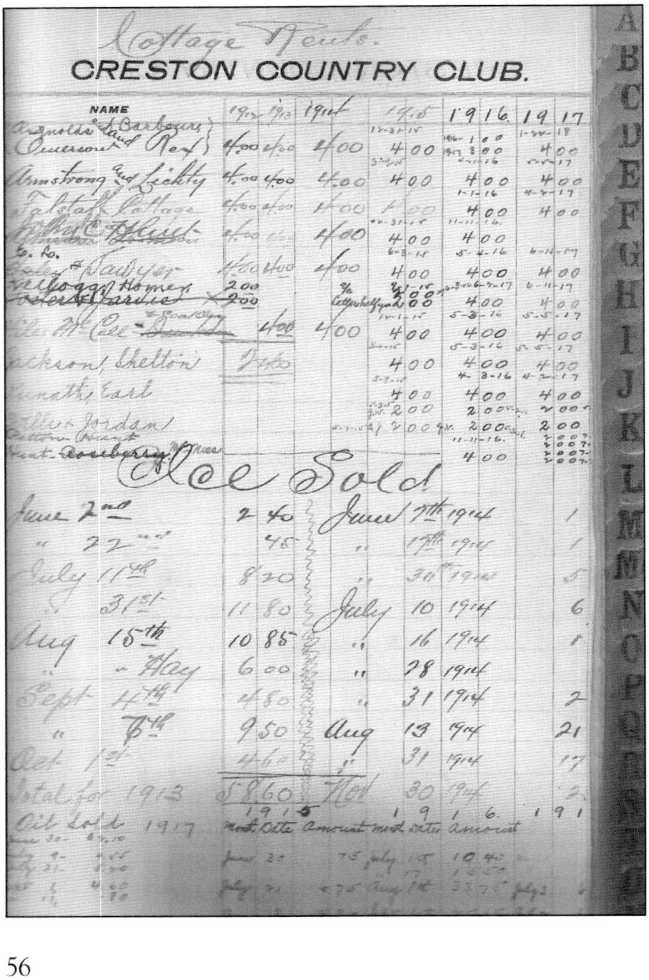

The Creston Country Club was organized in 1908 along the banks of Summit Lake, with the purpose of promoting fellowship among members; to provide a place for entertainment, fishing, shooting, boating, athletic sports, and social entertainment; and to improve and protect the fish and game on Summit Lake. This clubhouse was part of the facilities provided, along with sponsored activities, such as picnics and dances. (Lynne Schlaht.)

The Creston Country Club maintained ownership of the land on which the organization was situated, while renting lots for the construction of cottages to individual members. The group annually elected a president, vice president, secretary, treasurer, and an executive board consisting of five members. Boats could be rented either hourly or daily from the club for use on Summit Lake. (The Creston Country Club.)

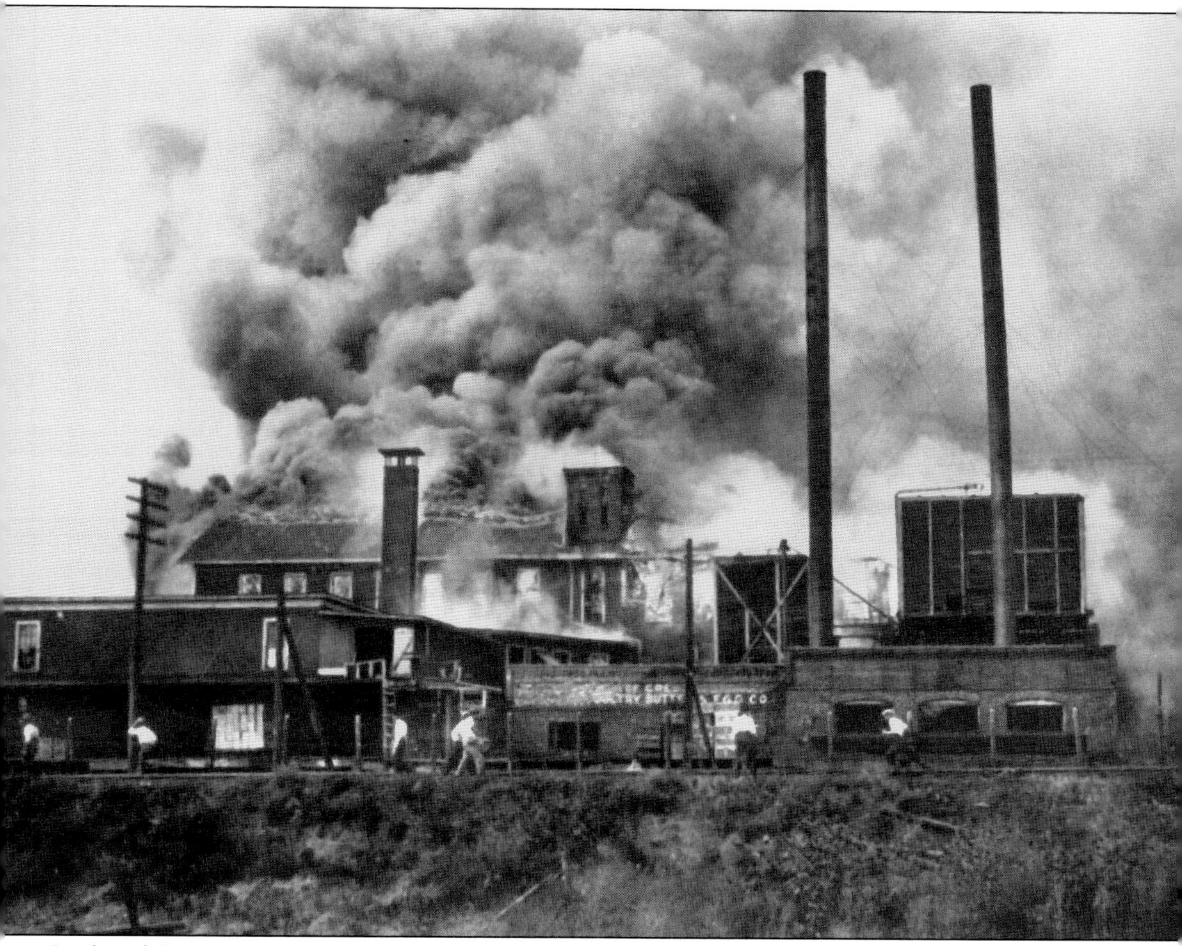

Swift and Company, a nationally known meat packer, placed a processing plant along the railroad tracks on Russell Street in the early 1900s. The Swift plant made butter, cracked and dried eggs, and processed poultry. The original Swift building was a wooden structure that burned in a spectacular fire on August 30, 1913. A four-story brick building replaced it in the same location. (Roger Nurnberg.)

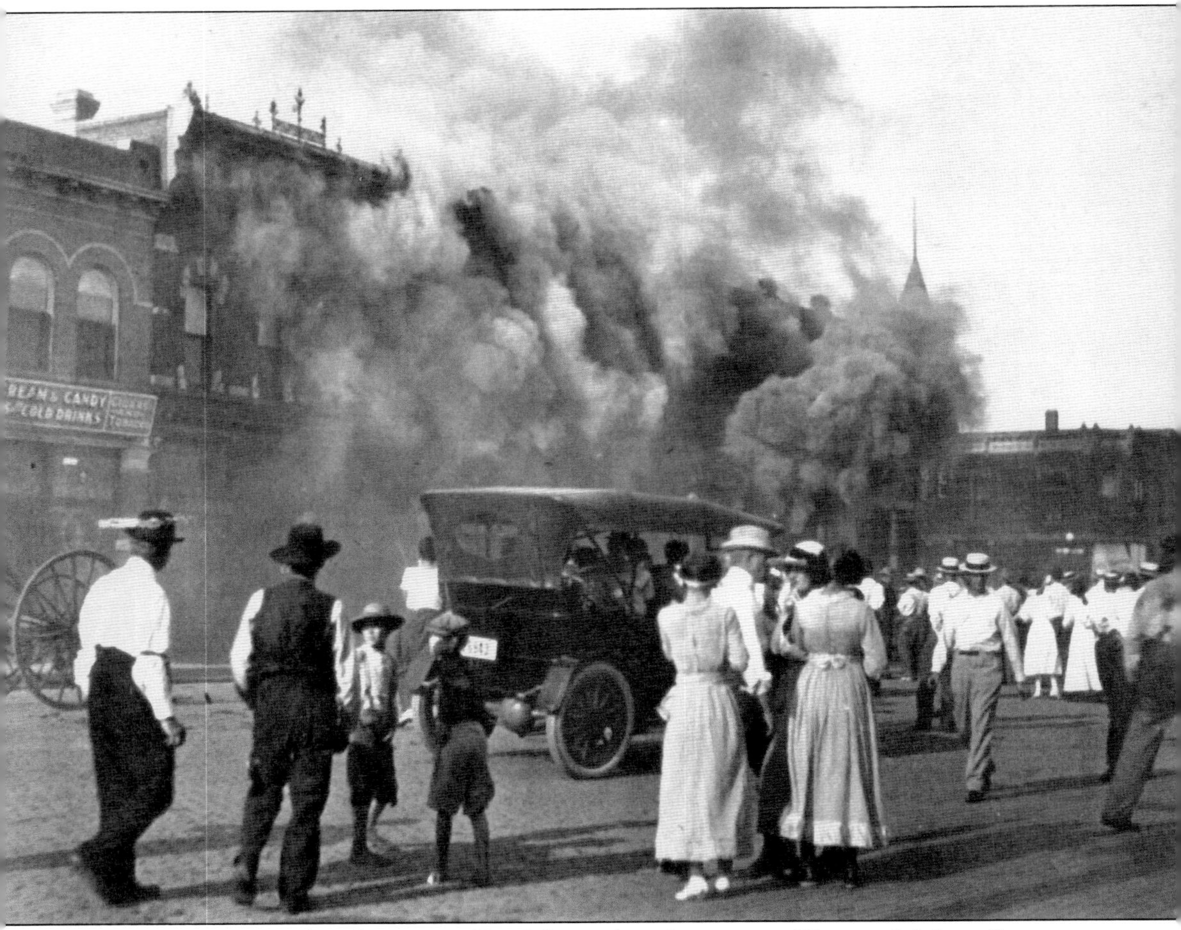

On July 16, 1913, the Blair House Hotel, located on the corner of Pine and Adams Streets across from the depot, burned to the ground in a devastating fire. The first photograph above shows a large crowd gathered on Adams Street as black smoke billowing from the blaze engulfed the structure. The tip of the turret emerged from the smoke at the corner. Many of the onlookers were passengers waiting for a train who wandered across the street to witness the blaze. The building to the far left was the Creston Opera House. The image of the 1881 Fireman's Day Parade on page 17 shows how the block looked before the fire. (Roger Nurnberg.)

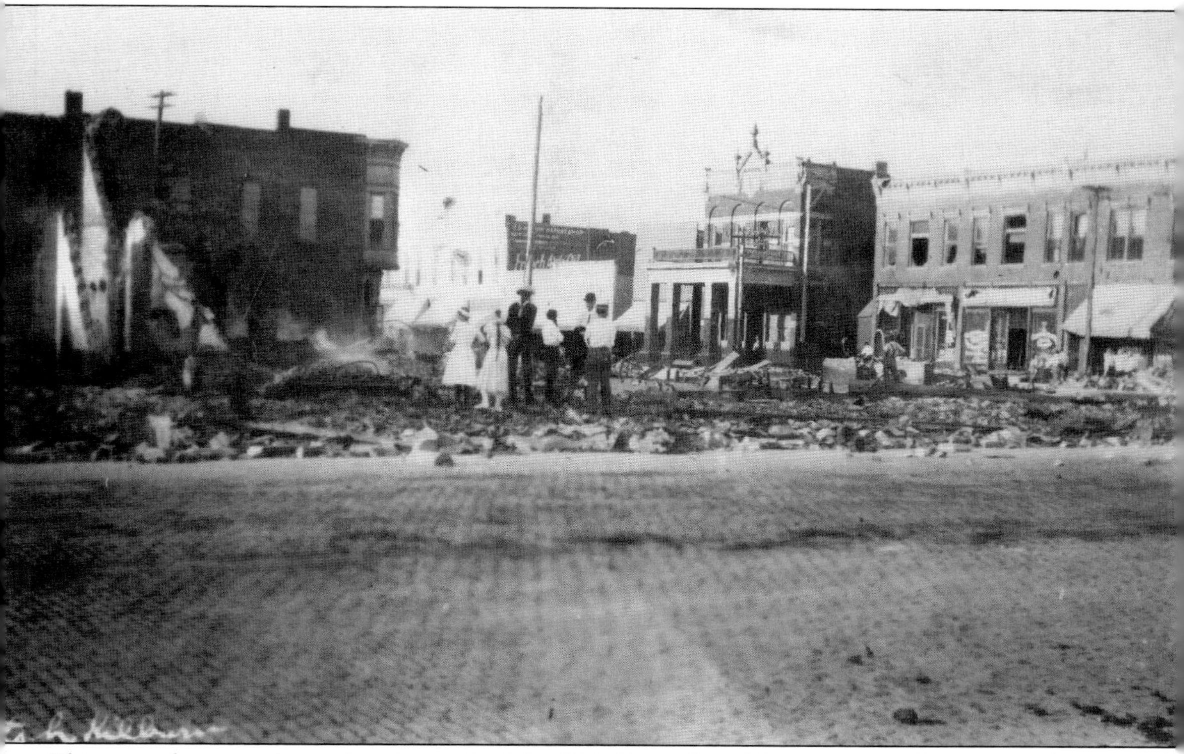

This second picture shows the aftermath of the Blair House Hotel fire. A group of young people stand among the still-smoldering rubble of the ravaged hotel. A partial double wall remains standing at left, which indicates that the building to the west of the Blair House Hotel also burned. At the time of this picture in 1913, Adams Street (in the foreground) was paved with bricks. The remaining buildings on the east side of Pine Street, shown on the right, were destroyed in later fires. (Union County Historical Society.)

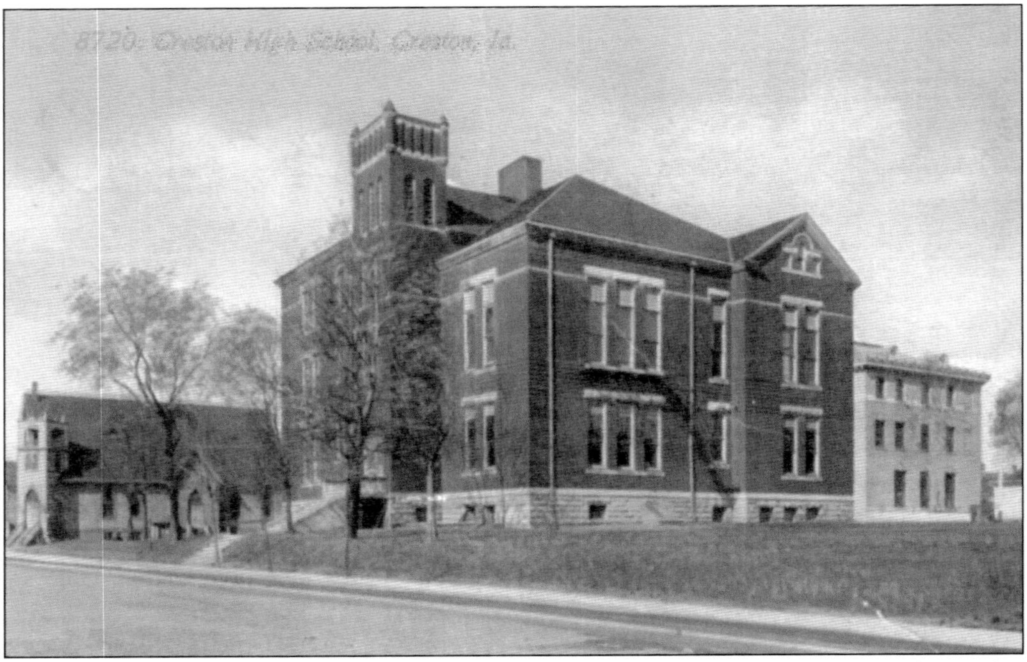

The Creston High School suffered a devastating fire on April 15, 1893 (see page 24 for pre-fire photograph). The district elected to rebuild the existing structure. The reconstructed building is shown sometime after 1903, but before it was remodeled in 1914, as evident by the 1903 post office seen behind the building. The peaked roof on the tower has been removed as well as the gable on the front, both of which were destroyed in the fire. (Lynne Schlaht.)

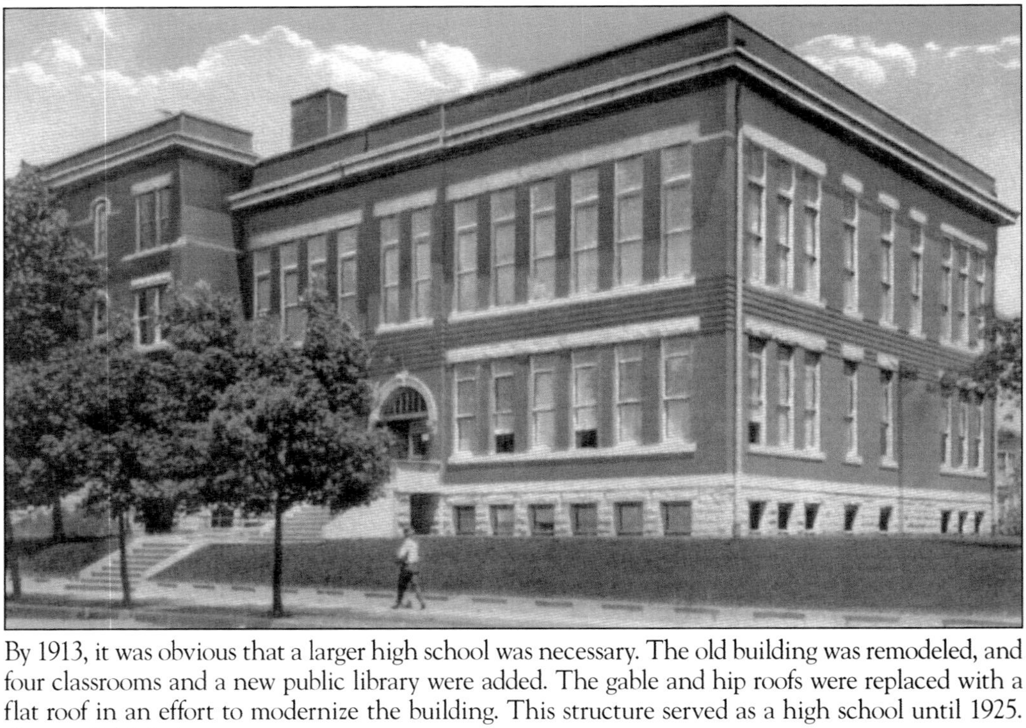

By 1913, it was obvious that a larger high school was necessary. The old building was remodeled, and four classrooms and a new public library were added. The gable and hip roofs were replaced with a flat roof in an effort to modernize the building. This structure served as a high school until 1925. (Lynne Schlaht.)

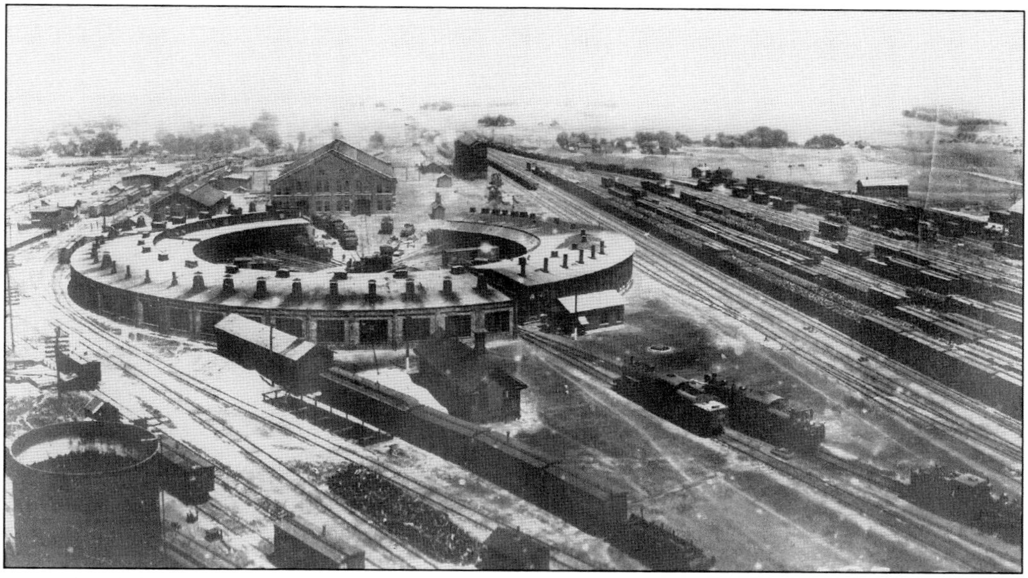

Considered the most iconic photograph of the Creston roundhouse, this image was taken from the smokestack of the city's power plant in 1913. By this time, six stalls had been removed from the roundhouse so that the Back Shop is clearly visible. Beside it to the left are the rip tracks and freight car shop that were removed in the 1930s. A corner of the icehouse is seen at the extreme right. The Creston roundhouse was the second-largest roundhouse in the nation, second only to Chicago's. This view gives a good indication of the extent of Creston's freight yard. It is easy to see how Creston earned the nickname "Little Chicago." The size of the railroad operations, along with the rough and rowdy character of the town, contributed to Creston's reputation. (Corbin-Wagner Collection.)

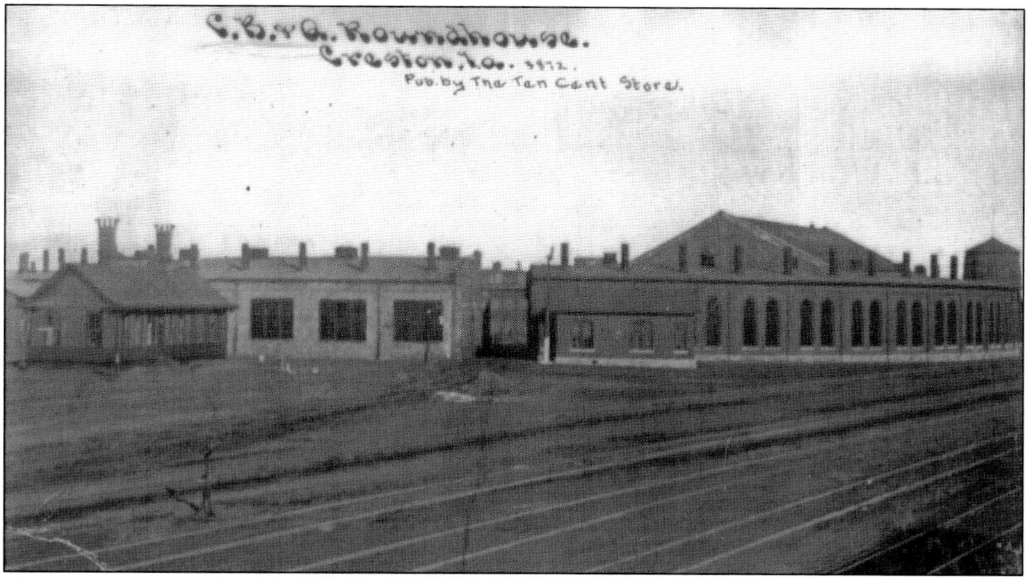

This is a street-level view of the roundhouse and shops, looking toward the northeast, taken about the same time as the image above. The roof of the Back Shop is seen in the background extending above the roundhouse with the two smaller shop buildings in the foreground. Notice that the two sections of the roundhouse have different window configurations. The section on the right, with the arched windows, contains the original 25 stalls completed in 1873 (see page 11). (Lynne Schlaht.)

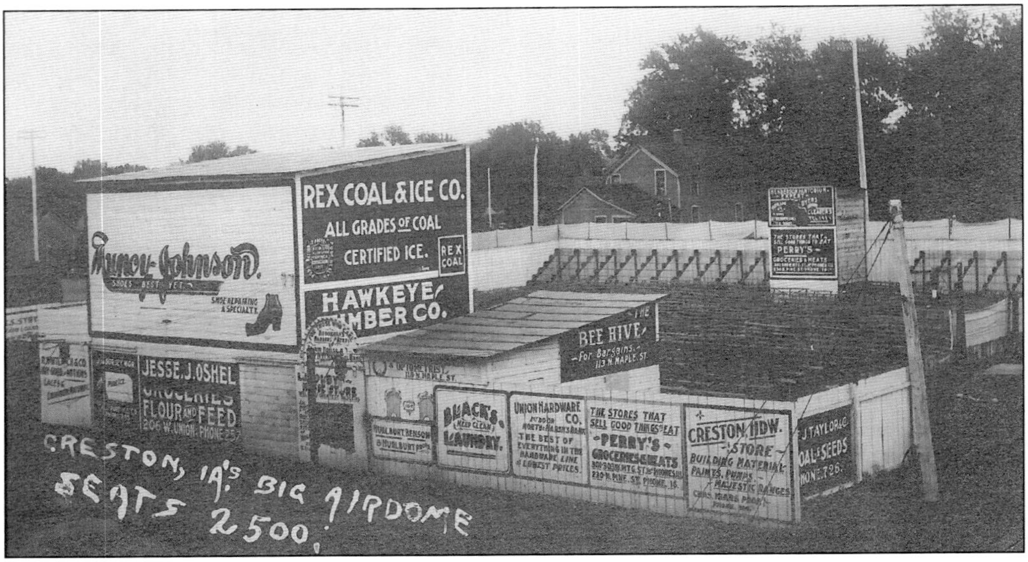

The White City Amusement Park, started by Benson and Hurlburt, was located along Walnut Street between Montgomery and Mills Streets. The big air dome (shown here) had a seating capacity of 2,500 and was used for showing outdoor movies. The entire enterprise only lasted a few years, but the swimming pool continued to be used by the city into the 1930s. (Steve Francis.)

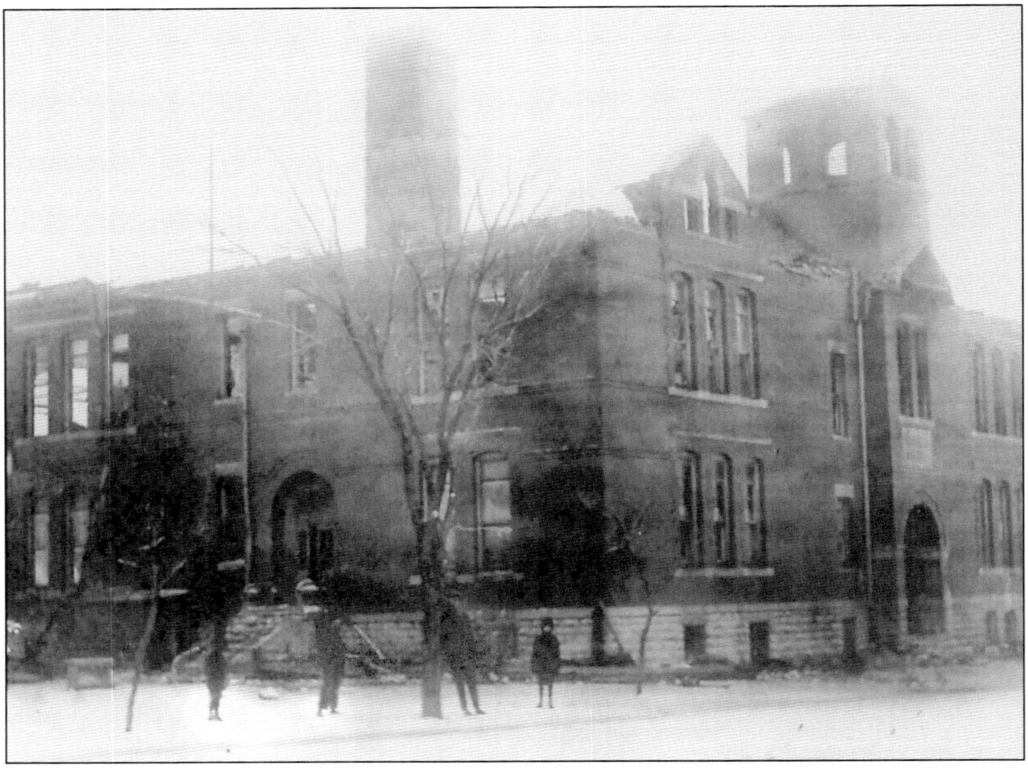

A horrific fire gutted much of the second floor of the 1893 Franklin School in 1915. The entire roof was destroyed along with most of the second-story windows. The cupola was removed in repairing the damage. The building continued to be used by the school system until 1957, when the third Franklin School was built. (Roger Nurnberg.)

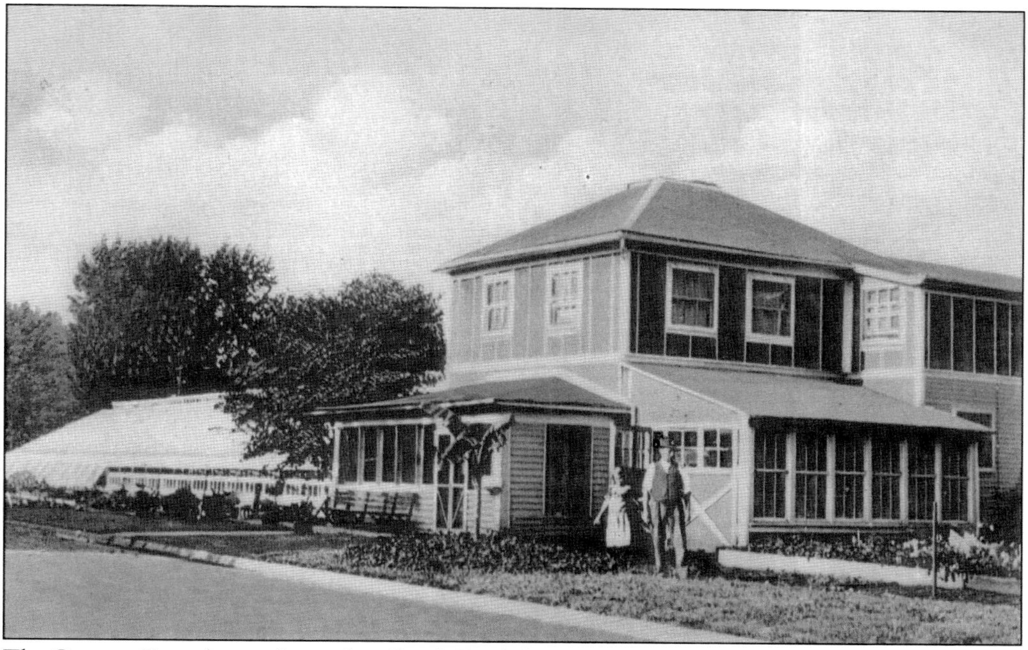

The Creston Greenhouse, located on South Birch Street across from Rainbow Park, was established in 1910 by a German family named Gahracke (pronounced *Gar-a-key*). It operated into the 1980s and was the oldest continually functioning greenhouse in Iowa at that time. Carl Gahracke came to the United States in 1909. Shortly after arriving, he obtained a job from financier and industrialist, Andrew Mellon, who became a personal friend. Gahracke was from a family of distinguished German horticulturists. He was honored by Kaiser Wilhelm of Germany for his work. During the first World War, Gahracke, who was pro-German, created quite a stir when he flew the German flag. He was fined by the city and chastised for his views. (Lynne Schlaht.)

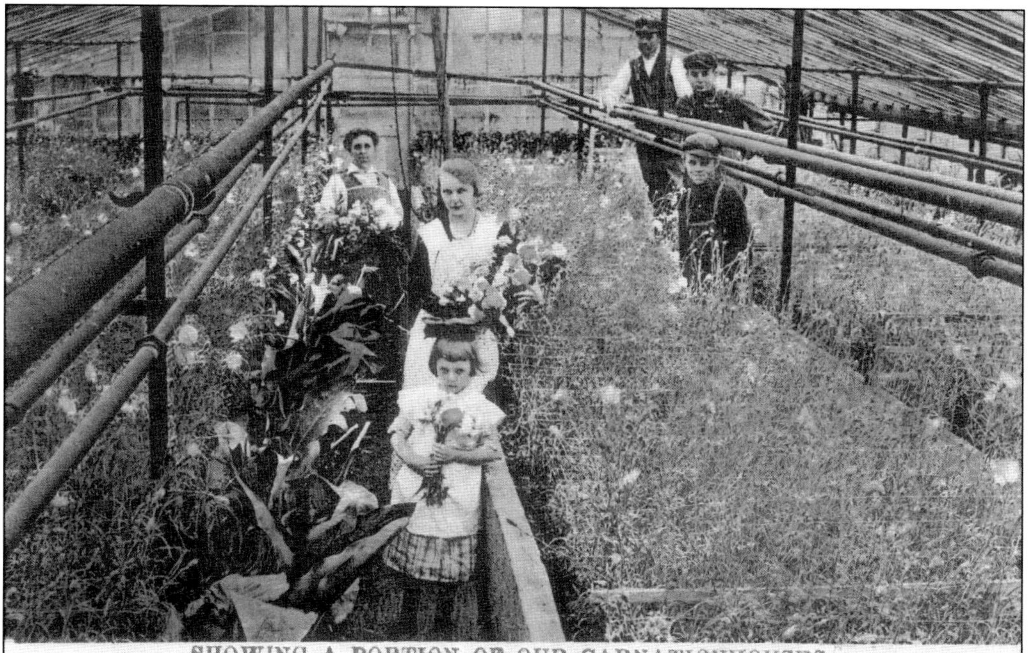

SHOWING A PORTION OF OUR CARNATIONHOUSES

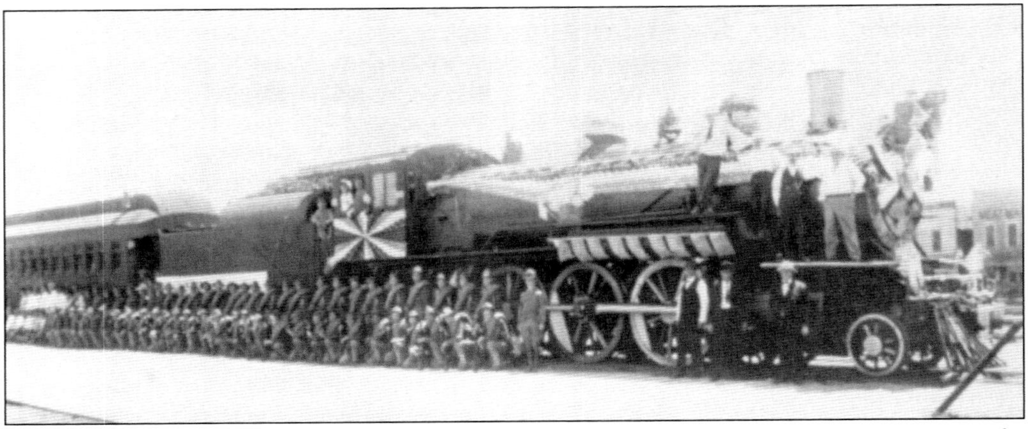

The 70 men of Company C, 3rd Infantry Battalion, Iowa National Guard pose in front of a flag- and bunting-draped locomotive on July 20, 1916. The company was mustered into federal service to fight in the Pancho Villa uprising along the Mexican border. Company C returned to Creston in February 1917, only to be recalled on July 15, 1917, for service in World War I. (Union County Historical Society.)

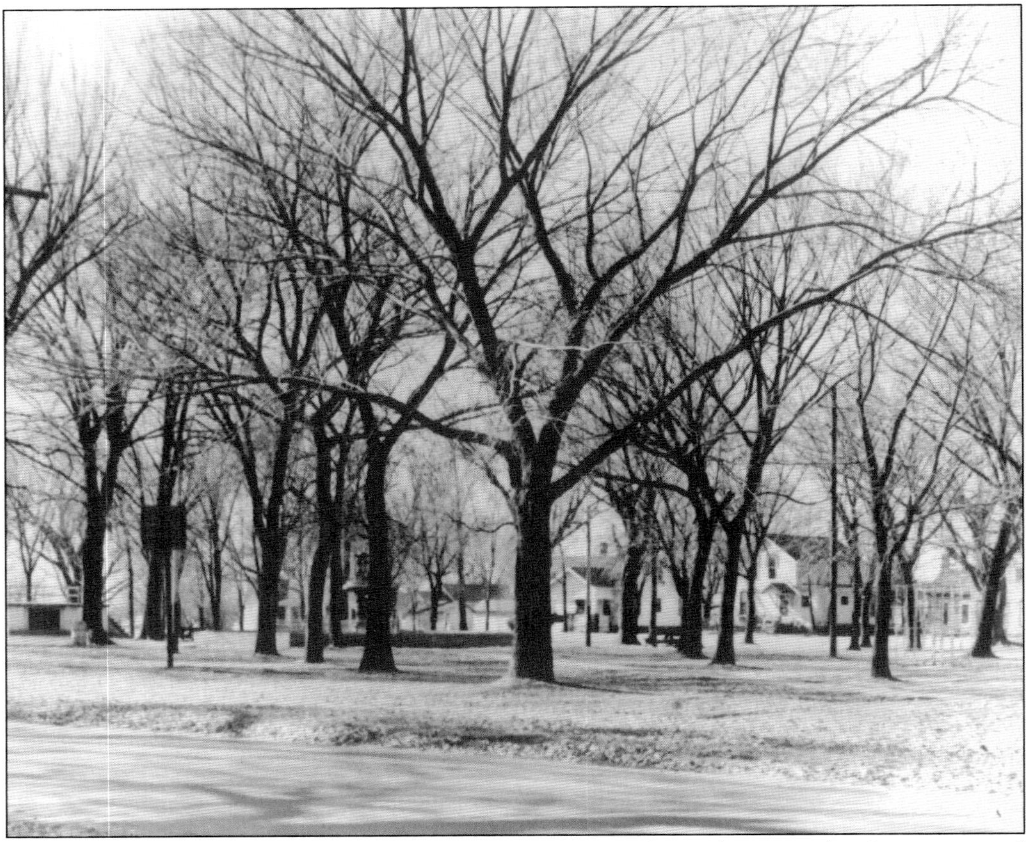

Company C of the 3rd Infantry Battalion of the Iowa National Guard, stationed in Creston, served in the Rainbow Division in France during World War I. Just after the war, the City of Creston decided to change the name of South Park, the city's first park, to Rainbow Park, in their honor. (Union County Historical Society.)

Four

The Agricultural Resilience

From the very beginning, settlers found the rich soil of Union County well suited to any kind of farming. Rarely could a more picturesque countryside that evoked the prospect of real wealth and prosperity be seen than on the fertile prairies of southwest Iowa. Abundant crops of bluegrass, fruits, grains, and native timber, along with dairy products, livestock, coal, and stone were extremely profitable.

None of this would have been of any value without a means of distributing the goods to market. The presence of exceptional rail facilities was central to Creston's development as a commercial, industrial, and farming center of Iowa. No farm within Union County was more than 7 or 8 miles from a good railroad station.

In 1919, the Farmers' Cooperative Company of Creston (also known as the Crestland Farmers' Cooperative) was established to facilitate grain shipment. The first grain elevator was built that same year. By the 1950s, it expanded to include divisions of lumber, livestock, fertilizer sales, and a feed mill.

Several industries "came to the country" to establish processing plants. Swift and Company created poultry-processing and creamery plants along the railroad. Local operators produced and processed a wide variety of products, including butter, flour, eggs, soft drinks, and milk.

The bluegrass industry evolved from the slow process of hand-harvesting to rake-like machines with beaters called strippers. Threshing facilities handled the thousands of pounds of bluegrass seeds sold throughout the United States. Creston became known as "the Blue Grass Capital of the World."

The 1930s witnessed a turning point in railroading with the introduction of diesel locomotives. Initially limited to passenger trains such as the Pioneer Zephyr, diesel units gradually began to replace steam engines in hauling freight as well. They were more efficient and experienced fewer maintenance problems.

On May 24, 1943, the Union County Soil Conservation Commission was established in part to help with the problem of soil erosion. Nearly 100 years of farming had taken its toll on the rolling hills of Union County. The organization aided farmers in implementing better farming practices. All this progress was made despite wars, drought, insect infiltration, and a national economic depression.

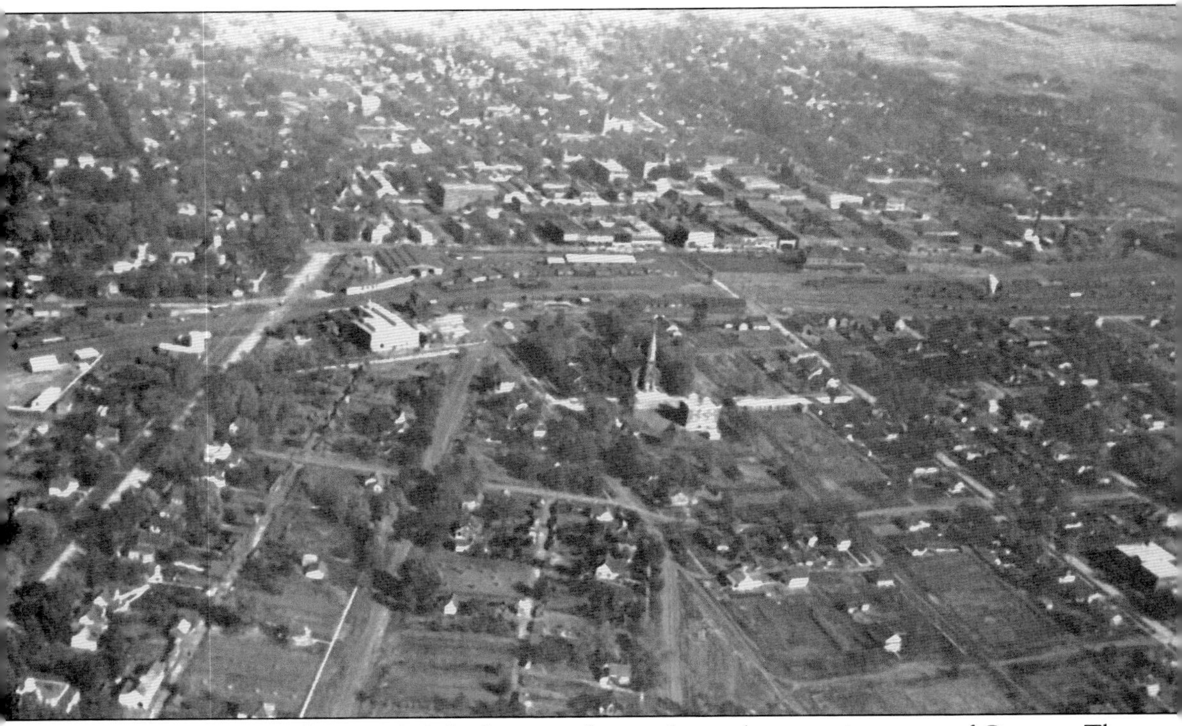

An aerial view taken in 1919, looking northeast, shows the emerging town of Creston. The roundhouse is at the far right edge with the depot due west along the railroad tracks. Just beyond the depot is the World War I Victory Arch across Maple Street. Looking north from the World War I Victory Arch to the next intersection at Montgomery and Maple Streets, the large gray building on the northwest corner is the Iowana Hotel under construction. Continuing along Maple Street, the large white building at the end of the block is the post office. The high school, with the public library, is directly behind it on Elm Street. A few blocks to the west is the Temple Grand Masonic Lodge. The prominent building in the center with the steeple is St. Malachy's Catholic Church. The brick building just across from it is the Catholic school. (*Creston News Advertiser.*)

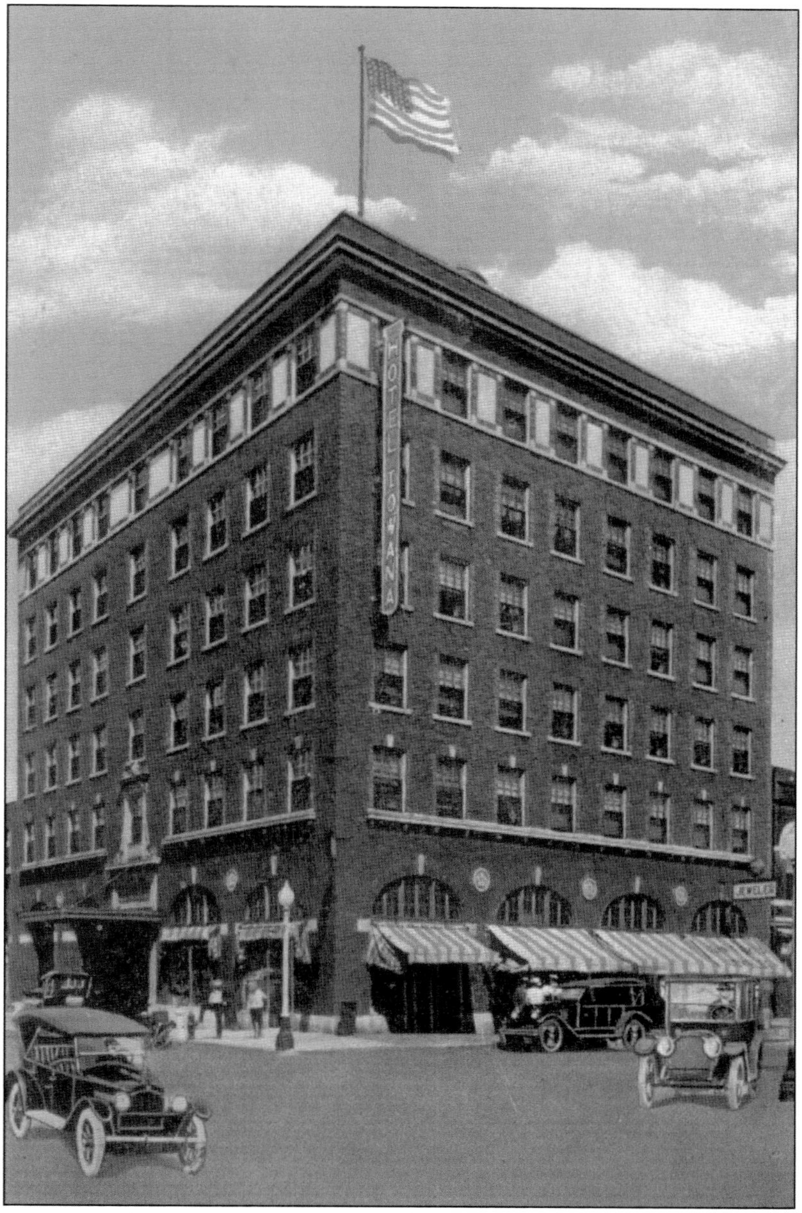

The Iowana Hotel, built in 1919 for $200,000 in the heart of uptown Creston, was considered *the* hotel in southwest Iowa. It boasted an elaborate lobby, a formal tearoom, and a beautiful dining room with a marble floor for dancing. A huge, decorated tree filled the front windows of the lobby at Christmastime. By 1921, the Iowana Hotel was bustling as other business filled the retail spaces within. A pharmacy with a soda fountain and ice cream was located just off the lobby. Shay's Jewelry store also occupied space in the Iowana Hotel. After Prohibition ended, a popular hangout for young people was a bar in the basement of the hotel called the Top Hat. It is interesting to note that a unique feature of the hotel is a second subbasement below the standard basement. As the Iowana Hotel was built at the beginning of the Prohibition era, it has been speculated that the subbasement may have been used for the manufacture and sale of illegal alcoholic beverages. There is no evidence to support or dispute this theory. A major renovation of the Iowana began in November 2010. It is expected to be completed by December 2011. (Lynne Schlaht.)

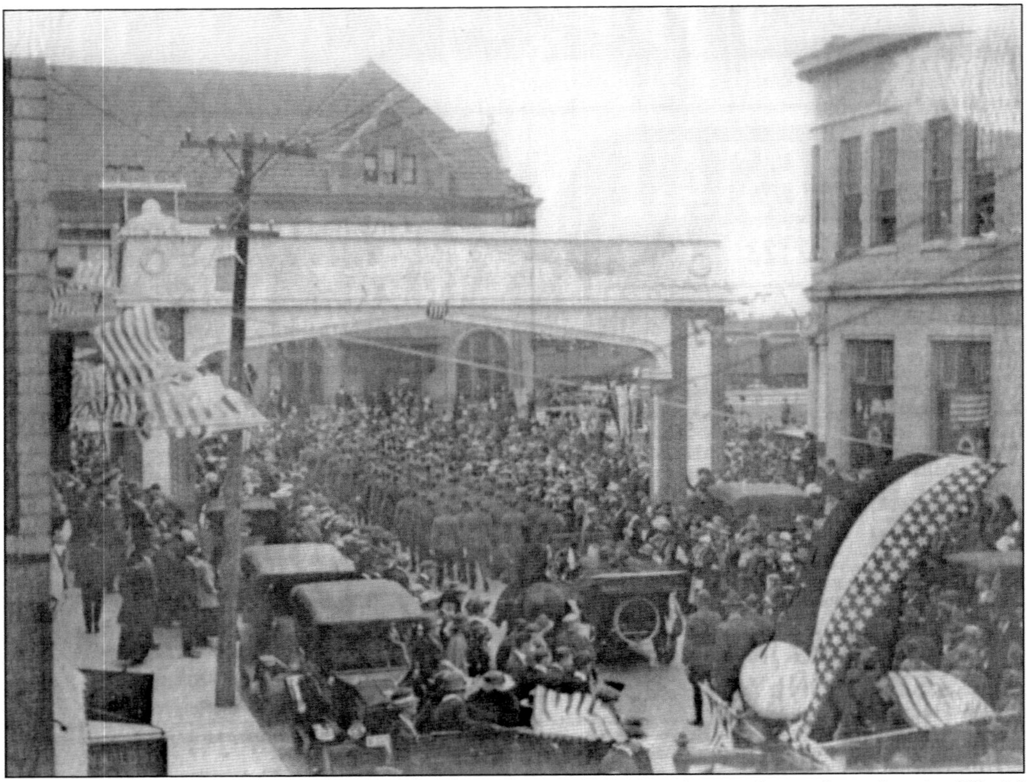

The men of Company C, 3rd Infantry Battalion, Iowa National Guard march under the World War I Victory Arch that was erected on the corner of Adams and Maple Streets to honor veterans of World War I, also called the Great War. The monument was built by Emerson Construction. It was later moved to the Lake Street entrance of McKinley Park and was eventually dismantled completely in the 1960s. (*Creston News Advertiser.*)

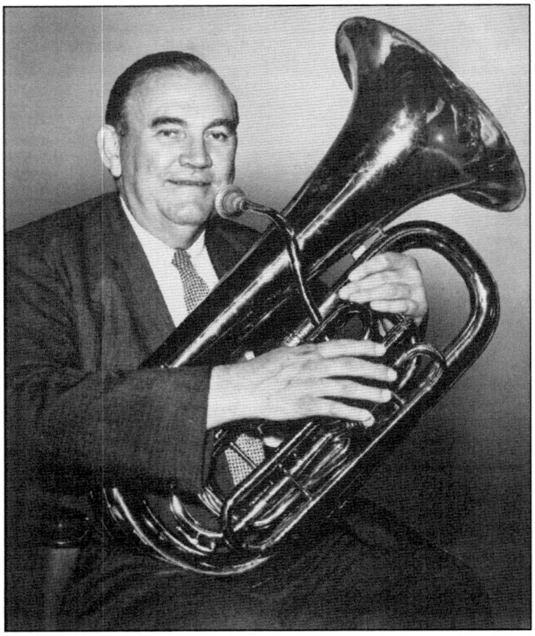

In William "Bill" Bell's hands, a tuba did much more than go oompah-pah. Recognized as the world's greatest tuba player, he made the instrument sing. Bell (1902–1971) was born in Creston on Christmas Day 1902. At 15, he received a full music scholarship to the University of North Dakota. He was the premier player and teacher of tuba in America during the first half of the 20th century. (Harvey Phillips Foundation.)

This train wreck is believed to have taken place just west of Creston, near Cromwell. Looking at the pattern on the seats, the lighting fixtures, and the general arrangement, the interior of this coach matches the 6100–6114 series of Class PB19 coaches that were built for the CB&Q railroad in 1916. There were no incident reports filed from 1919 to 1921 involving wrecks in this area. What is interesting is that this accident involved train No. 1, which is the Denver Limited, and train No. 10, of the Atlantic Coast Limited. The below picture shows what the exterior of the coach car looked like. (Right, Union County Historical Society; below, Dave Lotz.)

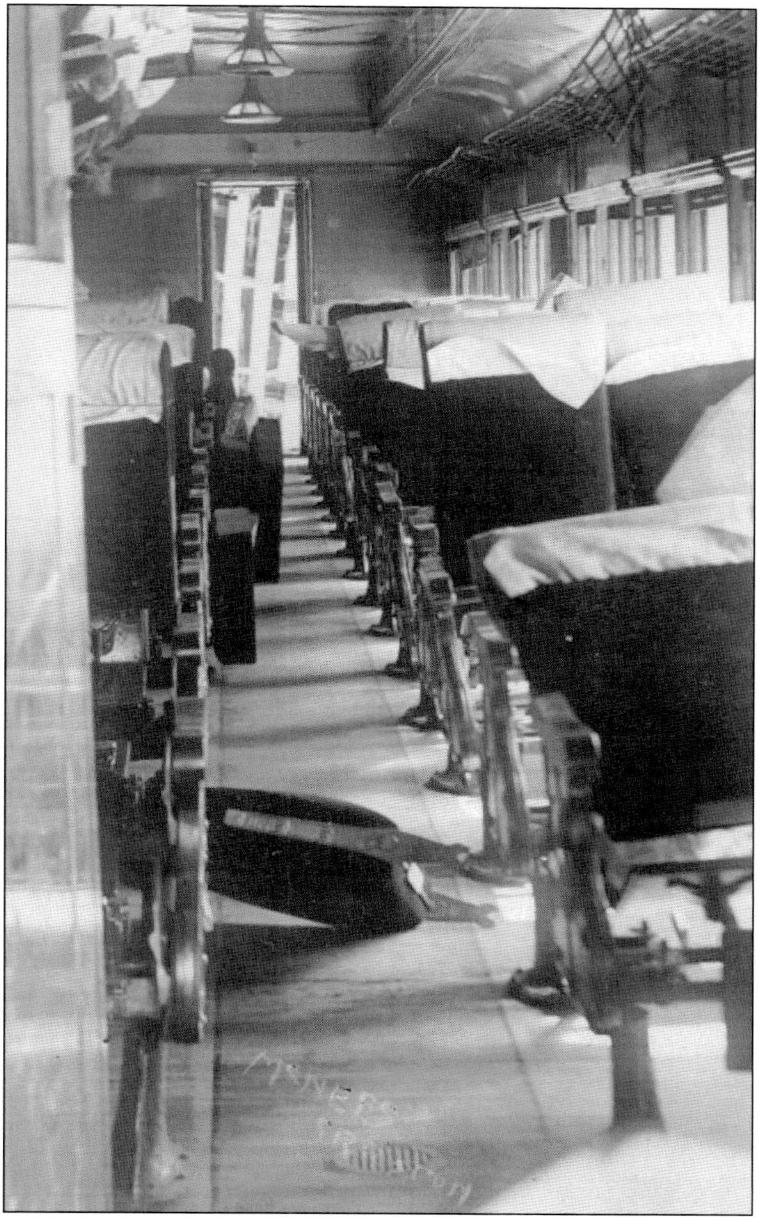

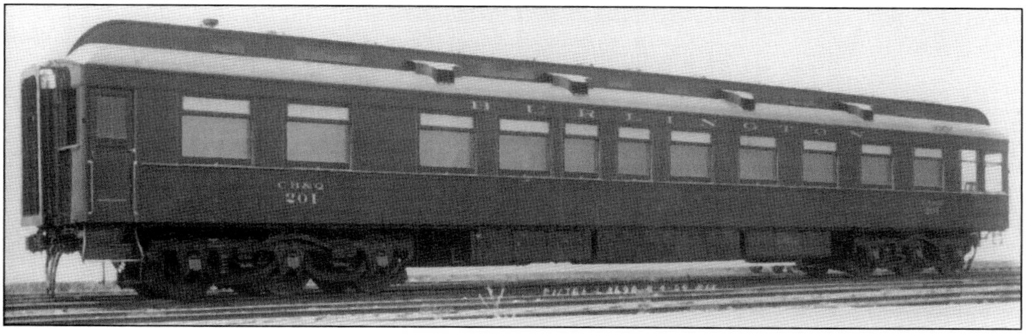

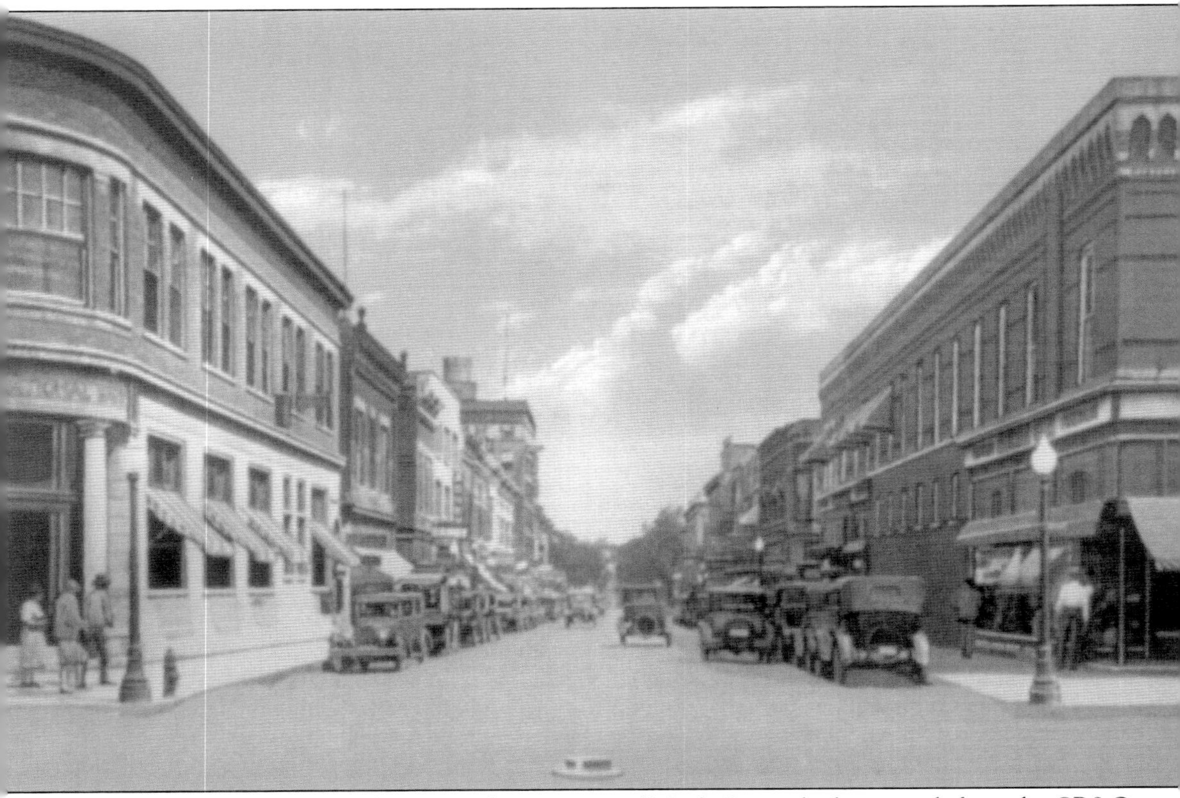

Taken sometime before the 1920s, this is a view of Maple Street, looking north from the CB&Q depot. The First National Bank is located on the corner at left. The candy sign midway down the block on the left side is for the New York Candy Kitchen. The light-colored building just beyond that point is the Agnew Building, constructed by Emerson Construction for the Agnew Clothing Store. At the beginning of the next block, on the same side, the top two floors of the Iowana Hotel can be seen. On the corner at right is a grocery store. Most of the right side of the street was destroyed by fire in October 1941. A major renovation of the First National Bank building, shown on the corner at left, began in November 2010. (Lynne Schlaht.)

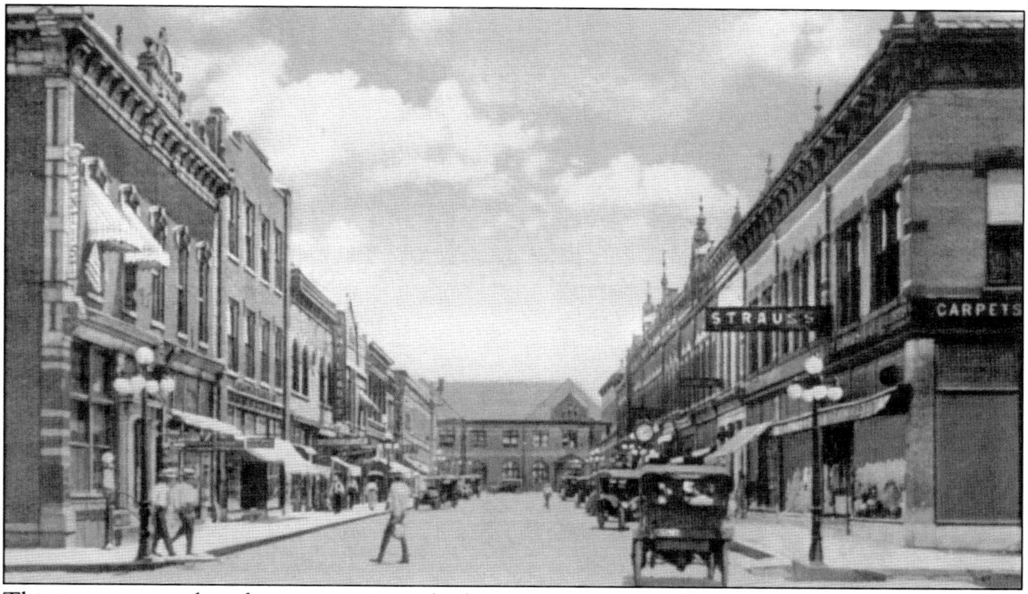

This image was taken from approximately the same position as the panoramic view in 1908 (see page 54). Strauss Dry Goods Company remained at the same location as in 1908, on the corner at right. The Agnew Building is seen in this view as well. Notice the post clock about halfway down the block on the right. The building at left has a "dentist" sign on the corner; a dentist's office remains in this building as of 2011. The basement of this building had a barbershop. The World War I Victory Arch was erected over the end of this block shortly after this picture was taken (see page 68). (Lynne Schlaht.)

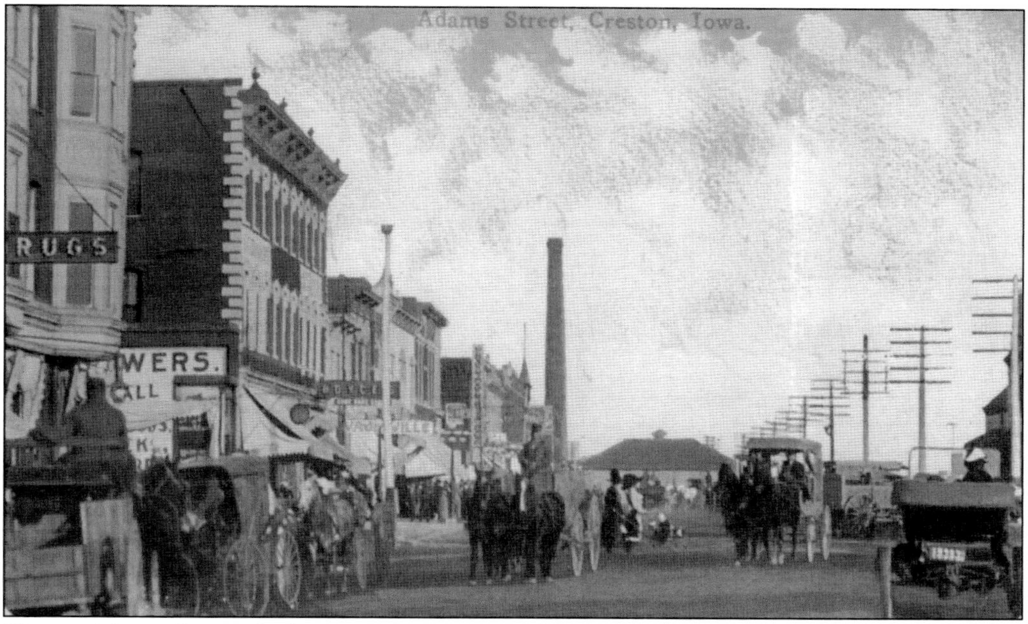

This is Adams Street, looking east, sometime after 1916. The corner of the second Summit House is visible at the left edge of the photograph (see page 32). At the end of the street is the Creston Mutual Electric Light, Heat and Power Company (see page 49). Notice there is a mix of horse-drawn carriages and automobiles at this time. The depot roof is barely visible on the right side. (Lynne Schlaht.)

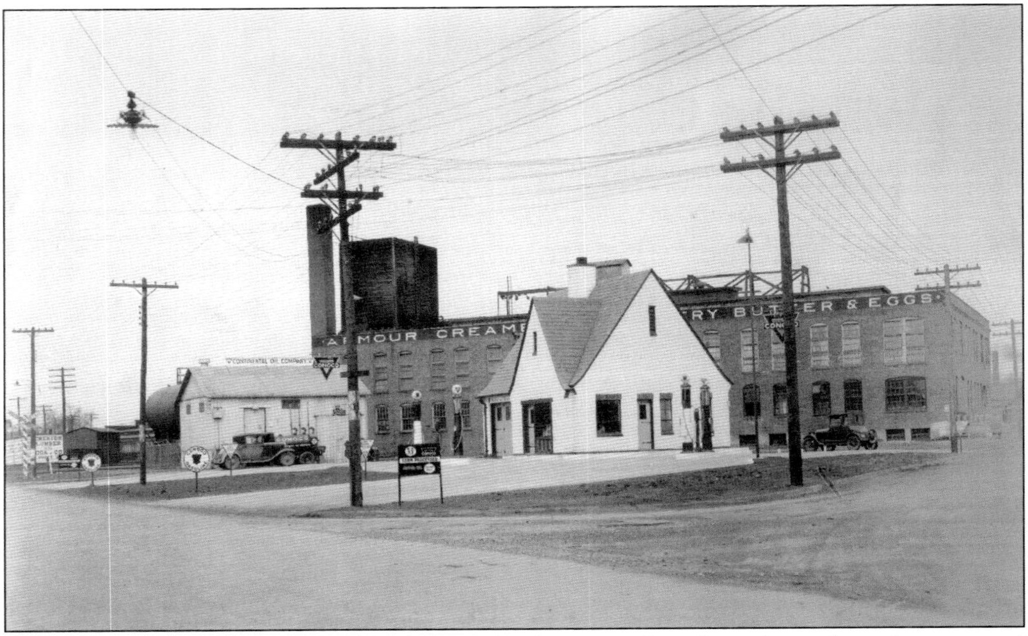

In 1923, Armour and Company bought out the Arron poultry plant, located on the corner of New York Avenue and Union Street. A major poultry- and cream-buying station was established, along with an egg-cracking and poultry-processing plant. Shown here in the 1930s, with the Continental Oil Company in the foreground, the operation closed on June 17, 1957, due to an expansion of the Farmers' Cooperative of Creston. (Dave Moffitt.)

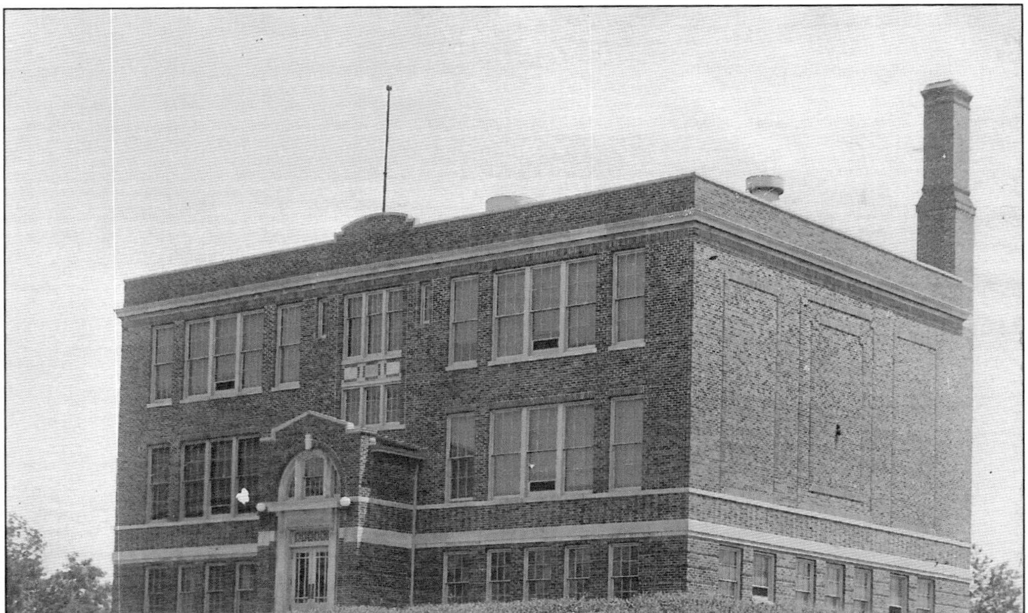

After the new high school was built on the site of the first Irving School in 1925, the second Irving School was located on Elm and Prairie Streets. Irving School was known as the "building of stairs" since it was necessary to go either up or down a flight of stairs to reach any room. (Steve Francis.)

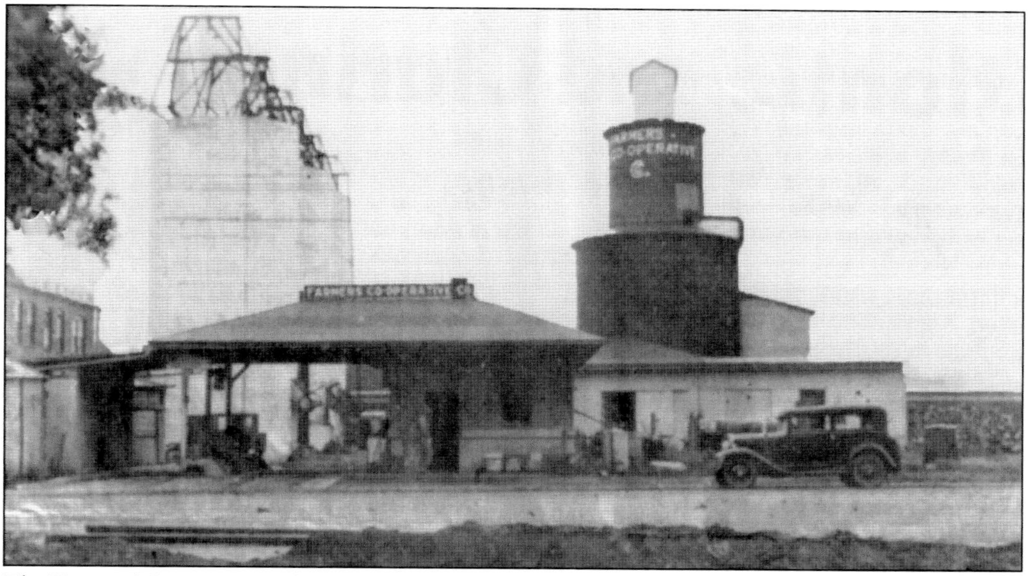

The Farmers' Cooperative of Creston, located on West Union Street near New York Avenue, lost its first grain elevator in 1919 to a fire just after the harvest, when it was full of grain. Unfortunately, due to a misunderstanding, the insurance policy had run out at noon on the day of the fire. By 1921, a new hollow, tile elevator, nicknamed "the jug," was built of fireproof material to replace the old one. It is the round, dark building on the right. (Rosalie Denton.)

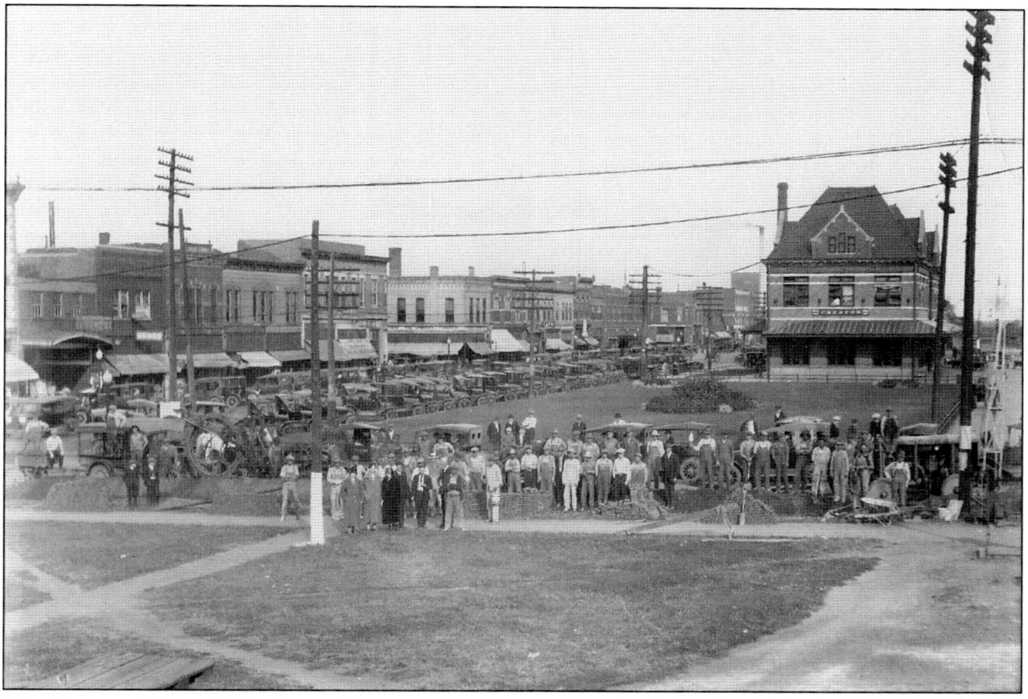

The Creston Mutual Telephone Company was incorporated on May 28, 1900. At the time, another business, Bell Company, was also providing service to Creston. Both companies continued to offer service, which meant all people in Creston needed to have two telephones. In 1924, Creston Mutual Telephone Company bought out the Bell Company. This picture shows workers running new telephone wire uptown along Elm Street in 1924. (Union County Historical Society.)

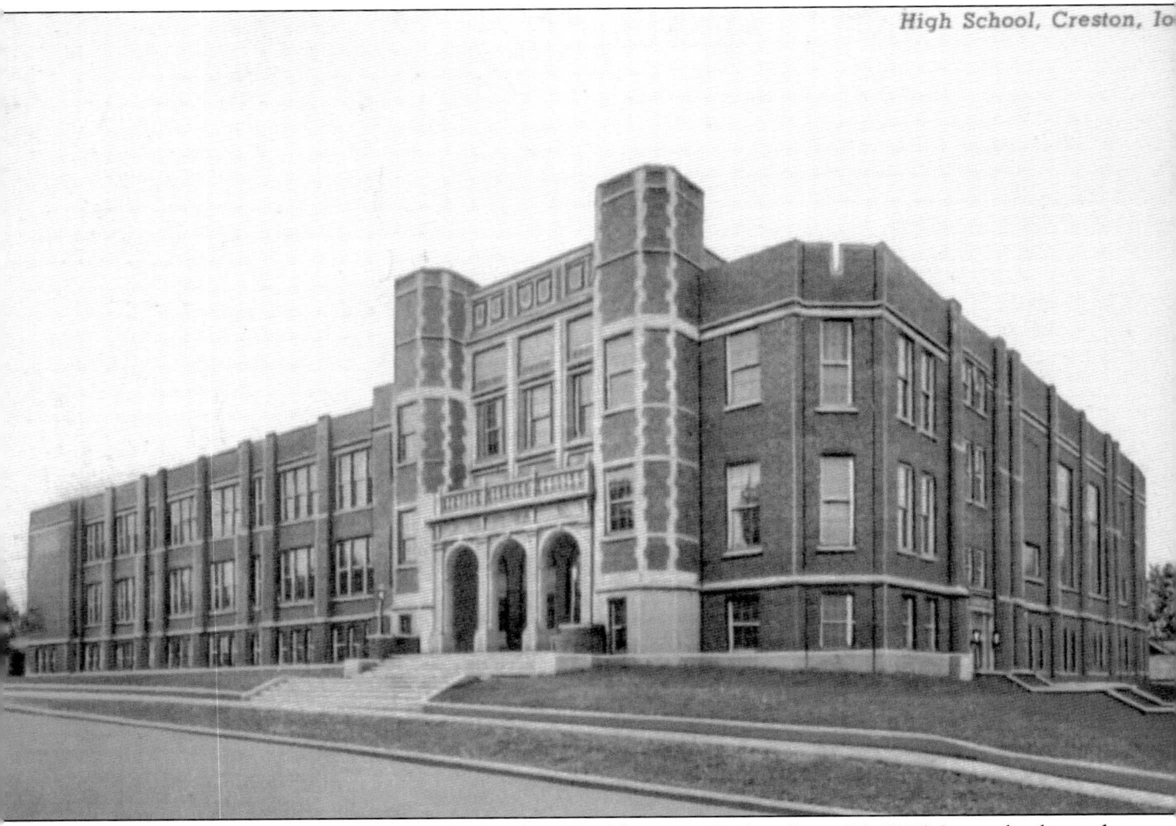

The cornerstone for a new brick high school building was laid on June 15, 1925. It was built on the old Irving School site on lots bound by Maple Street on the west and Pine Street on the east. It cost $270,000. There are 40 classrooms, a library, shop area, auditorium with seating to accommodate 1,400, a football field, and one of the "finest gyms in southwest Iowa," according to the *Union County History of 1981*. This building served the district until 1989, when a new high school was built at the former location of the Blue Grass Palace on Townline Road. (Lynne Schlaht.)

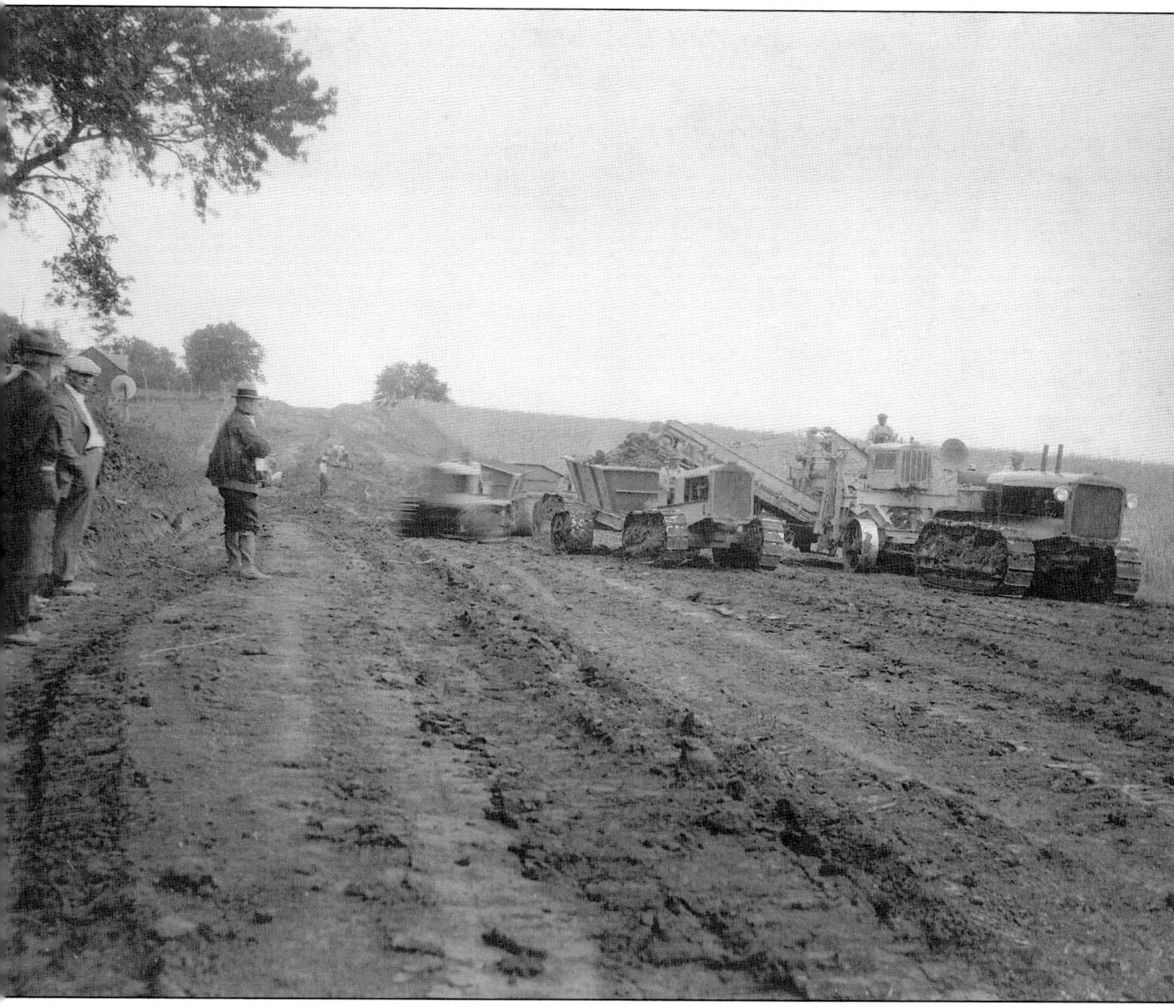

In the early days of the county, all roads or trails were dirt. The main east-west road was known as the Blue Grass Trail. It later became Highway 34 in 1930–1931, when it was paved across the state. In 1971, the roadway was straightened and widened in anticipation of four lanes in the future. It has remained a two-lane highway. (Dave Moffitt.)

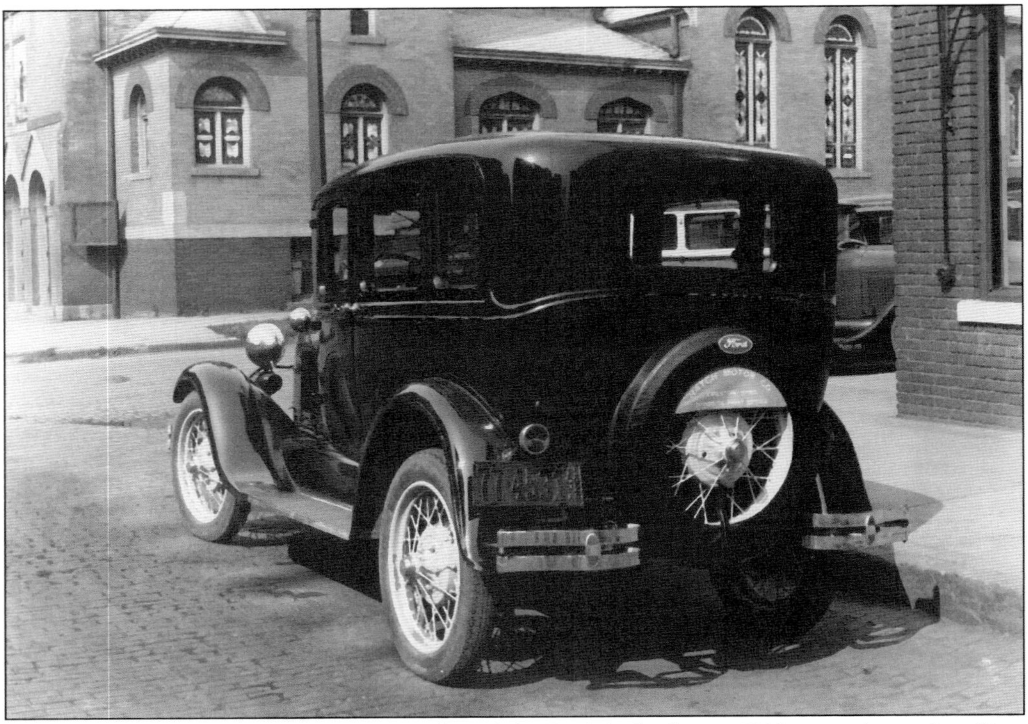

When James Brown and C. B. Elliott purchased the Ford dealership in 1913, it was located on Pine Street in a converted livery stable. By 1917, Elliot had become the sole owner of the business, and he moved it into a new brick building, shown on the right, across from the post office on Maple Street. This 1929 Ford is shown in front of the Ford garage. The First Baptist Church is seen in the background. (Union County Historical Society.)

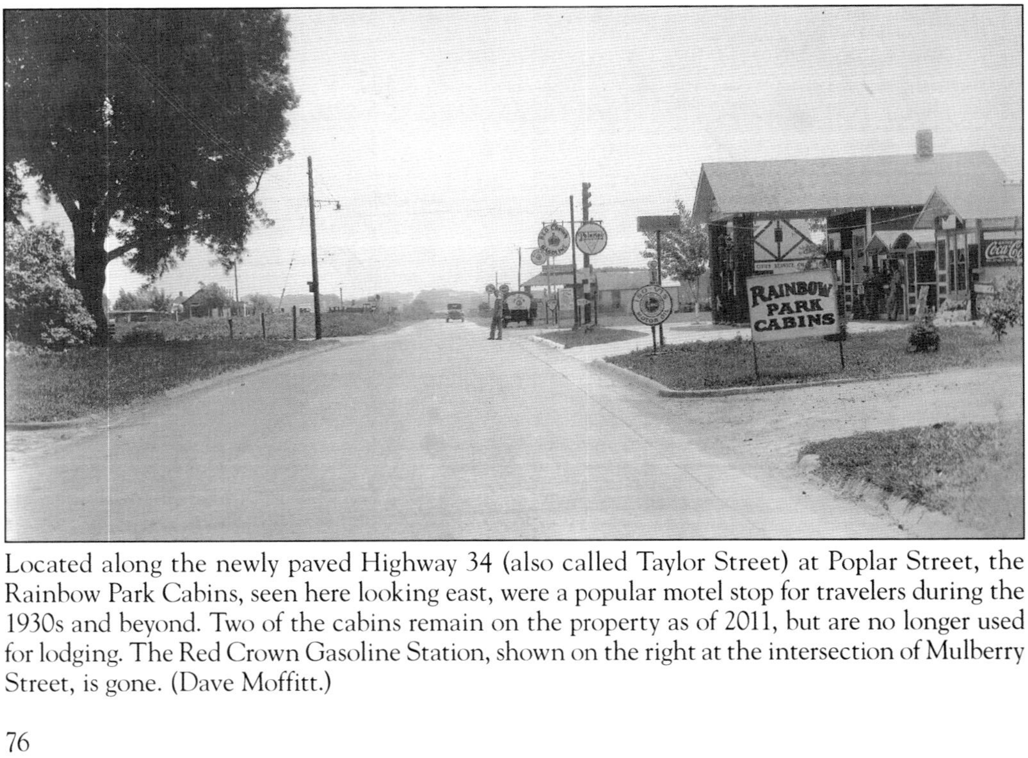

Located along the newly paved Highway 34 (also called Taylor Street) at Poplar Street, the Rainbow Park Cabins, seen here looking east, were a popular motel stop for travelers during the 1930s and beyond. Two of the cabins remain on the property as of 2011, but are no longer used for lodging. The Red Crown Gasoline Station, shown on the right at the intersection of Mulberry Street, is gone. (Dave Moffitt.)

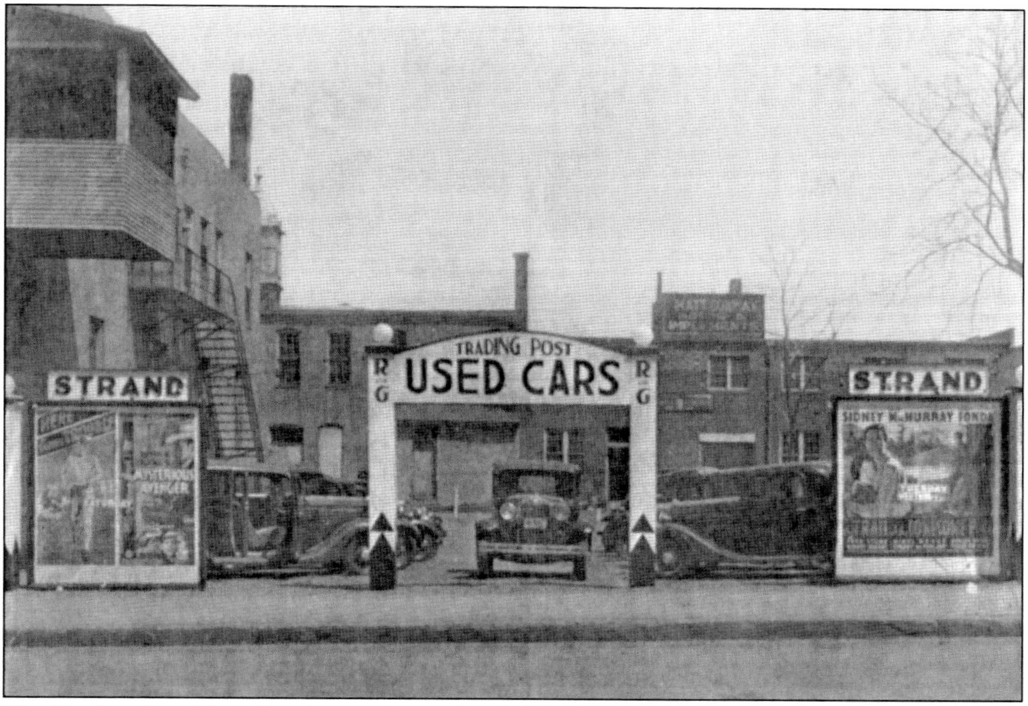

The Trading Post Used Cars lot was located at 215 1/2 North Elm Street in the 1930s. The buy of the day is front and center, under the arch. The Strand Theater Billboards show advertisements for coming attractions: *Trail of the Lonesome Pine*, *Mysterious Avenger*, and *Here Comes Trouble*. (*Creston News Advertiser*.)

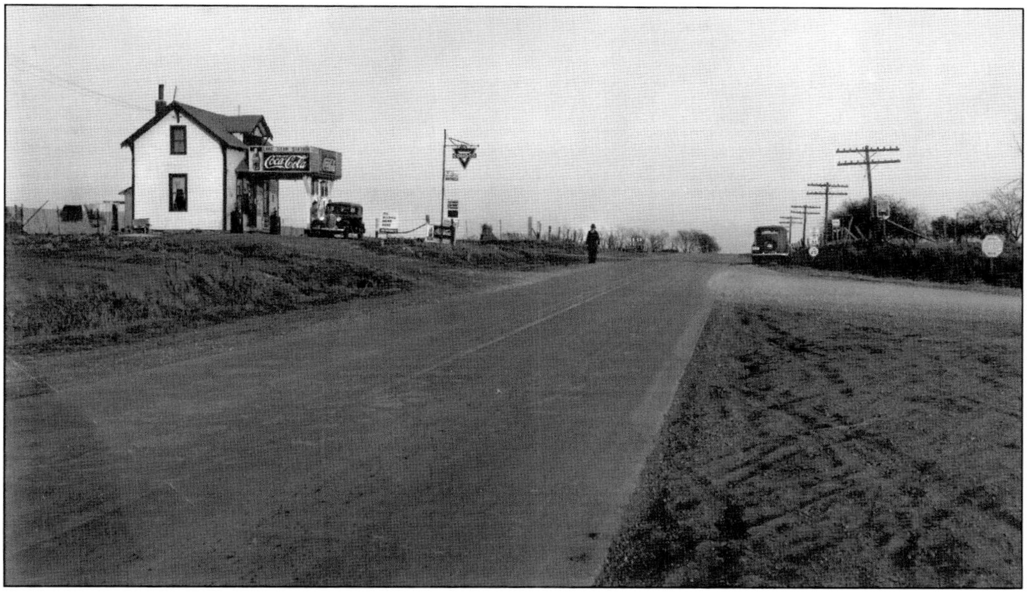

The Lone Star Station, located west of Creston at the intersection of Highways 34 and 25, was a forerunner to modern convenience stores with food and fuel available. The photographer is standing on the shoulder of Highway 34, looking east, with Highway 25 to the right. Both highways run together going east into Creston. The signs for both are posted at right of the parked car. (Dave Moffitt.)

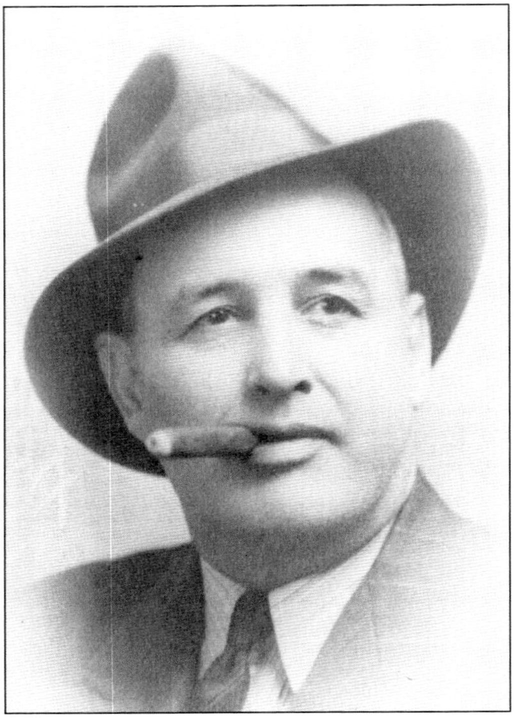

The Emerson family contributed immensely to the growth of Creston through the various construction businesses in which they were associated. It began with Lincoln Jasper Emerson, father of Stephen, called "Ray," and Lincoln, called "Don." He was a contractor and stogie joiner, which meant he framed large structures with pegs, rather than nails. He erected the large expanse of the Immaculate Conception Church. Ray and Don Emerson operated Emerson Construction, which built many of the prominent homes and businesses of the 1920s and 1930s. A partial list of their projects includes the Creston Mutual Telephone building, Gibson Memorial Library, St. Paul's Church, United Methodist Church, World War I Victory Arch, and McKinley Band Shell. Ray (left) was active politically and civically, serving as Creston's mayor from 1931 to 1938 and president of Iowa State Savings Bank. Don's son Dick took over the business around 1946. (Both, Union County Historical Society.)

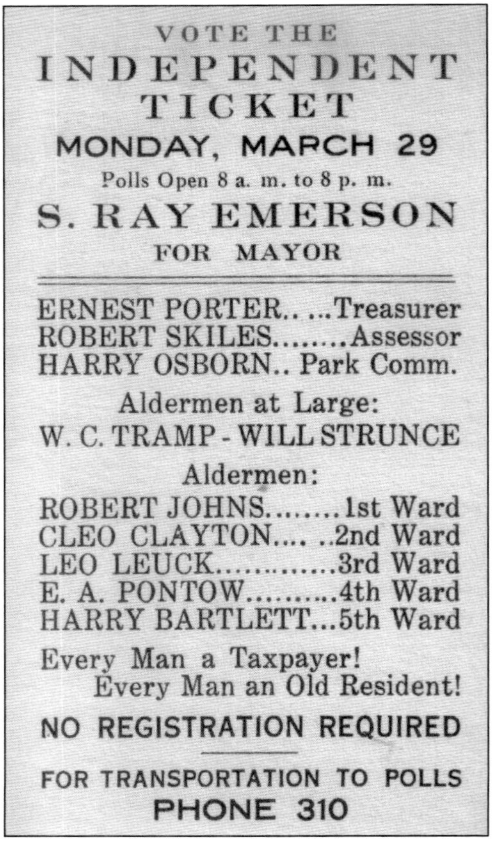

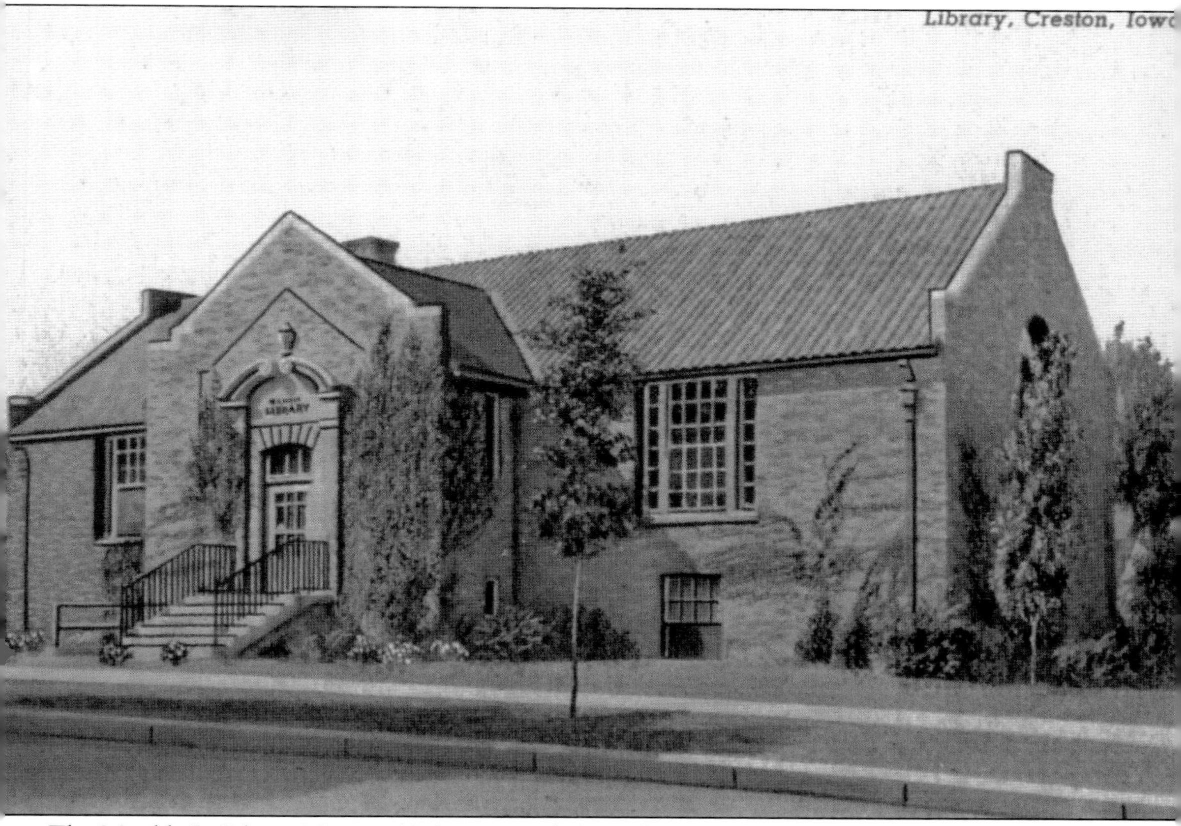

The Matilda J. Gibson Memorial Library was dedicated on April 7, 1931. Jane Gibson Phillips of Bartlesville, Oklahoma, donated $25,000 in memory of her mother, Matilda Gibson, for the purchase of the grounds and construction of a combined library and club room for the city of Creston. The library was constructed by Emerson Construction. Matilda Gibson passed away on July 14, 1902, of cholera while traveling with her husband, John, in the Philippines. John Gibson had planned to attend some business affairs in the Philippines before he and Matilda embarked on a world tour, which was to be in celebration of his retirement. The Gibson Memorial Library was placed on the National Register of Historic Places in 1983. (Lynne Schlaht.)

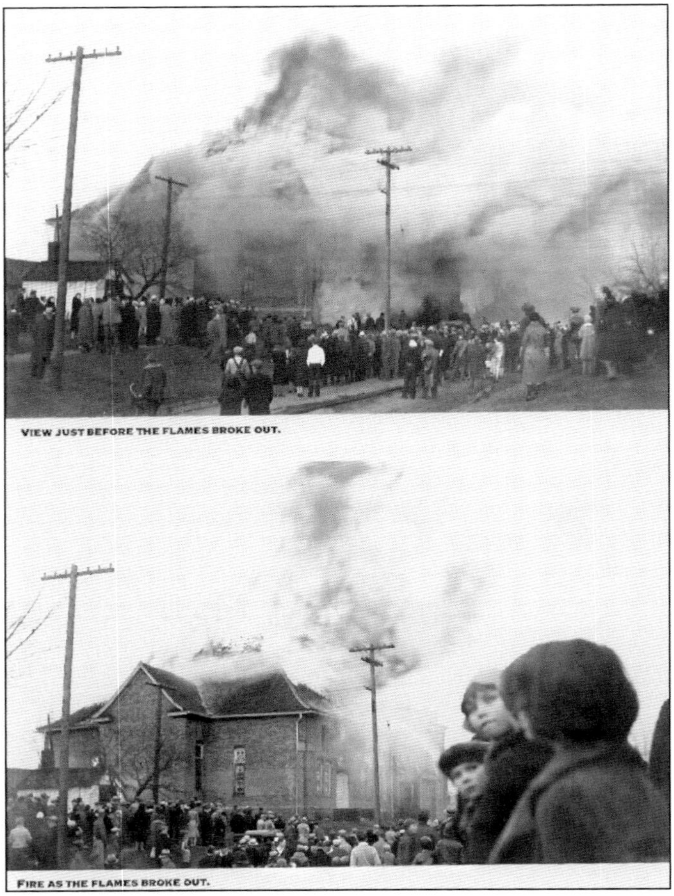

The Methodist Episcopal Church was again struck by tragedy on March 18, 1932, when the structure burned to the ground. The loss was recorded at $50,000. The congregation once more decided to rebuild, and a new church basement was completed first. It took five or six years before the present church, the First United Methodist Church, was completed. A generous donation by Frank and Jane Phillips—made in memory of Jane's mother, Matilda Gibson—made completion possible. The new edifice was finished by Emerson Construction in 1938. (Left, Jane Briley; below, Union County Historical Society.)

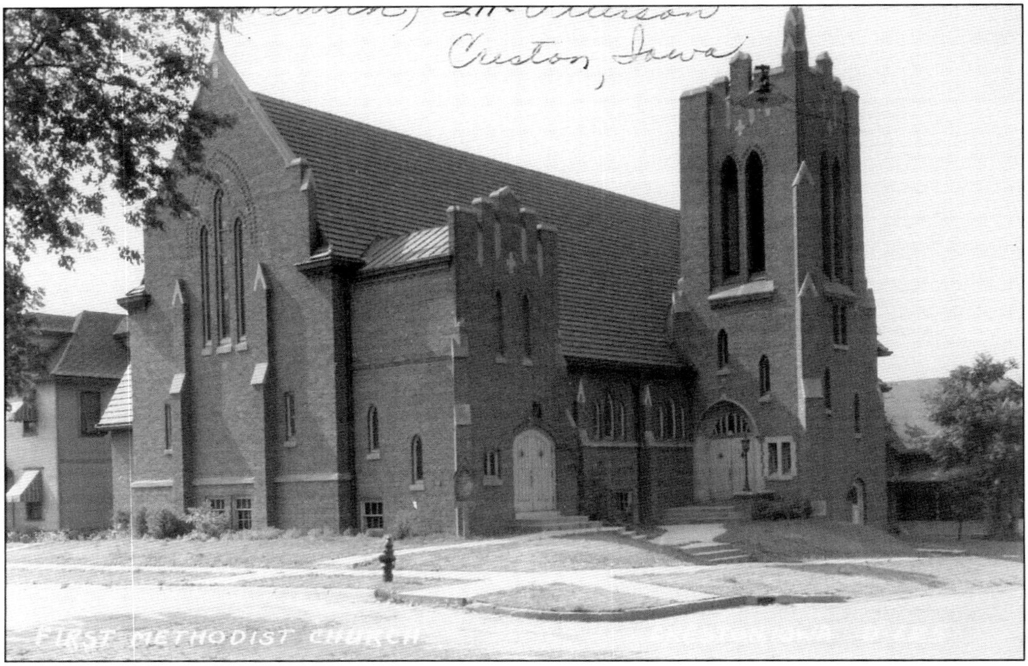

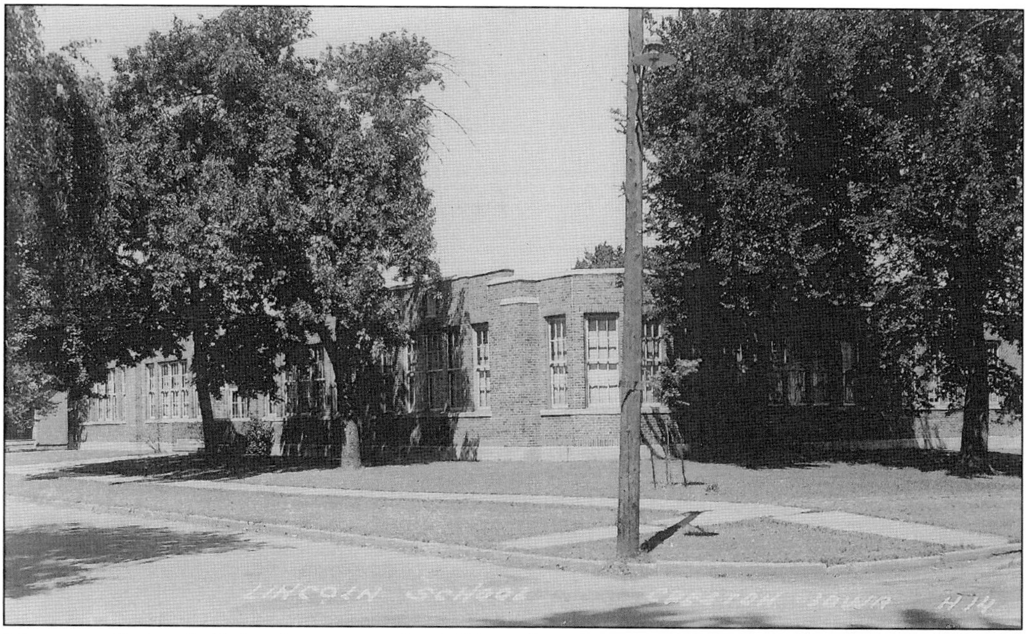

The second Lincoln School was erected in 1931 on the same site as the original Lincoln School (also known as West Brick), which was built in 1883. The new Lincoln School was a progressive building at the time. It consisted of seven classrooms, a large kindergarten room, a gymnasium, a kitchen, restrooms, a nurse's room, a shower room, large halls, and storage closets. (Steve Francis.)

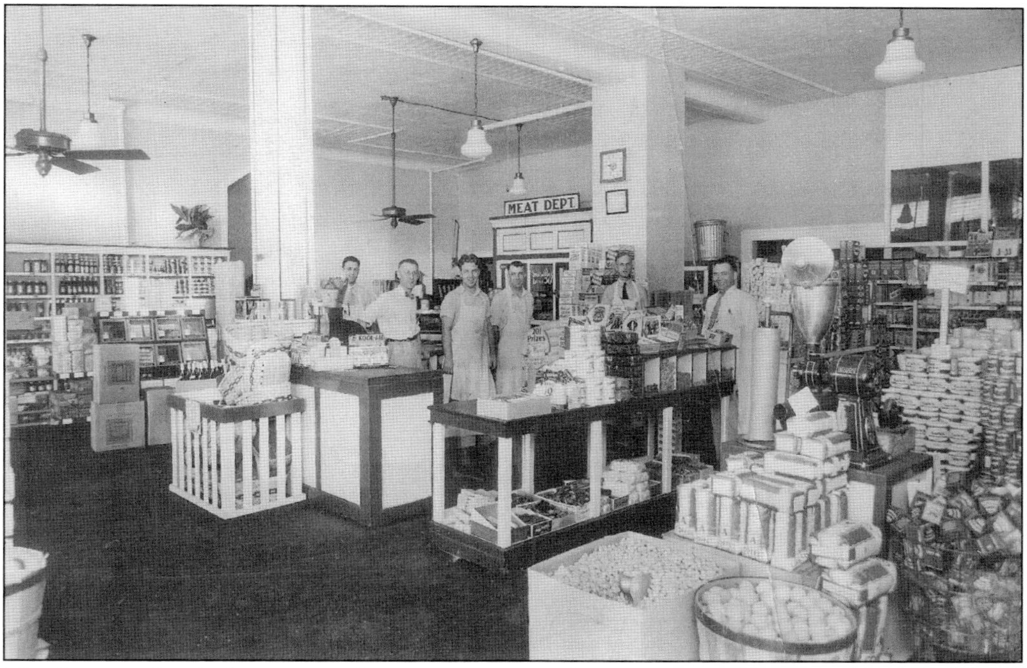

The Strunce family first operated grocery stores in Creston in 1908. In 1927, the Independent Grocers' Alliance (IGA) system was introduced into its Union Street store, which allowed for cooperative purchase of products with other stores. On July 30, 1934, the Strunce brothers consolidated the north and south side stores into the store pictured here, located just west of the corner of Elm and Montgomery Streets. (Union County Historical Society.)

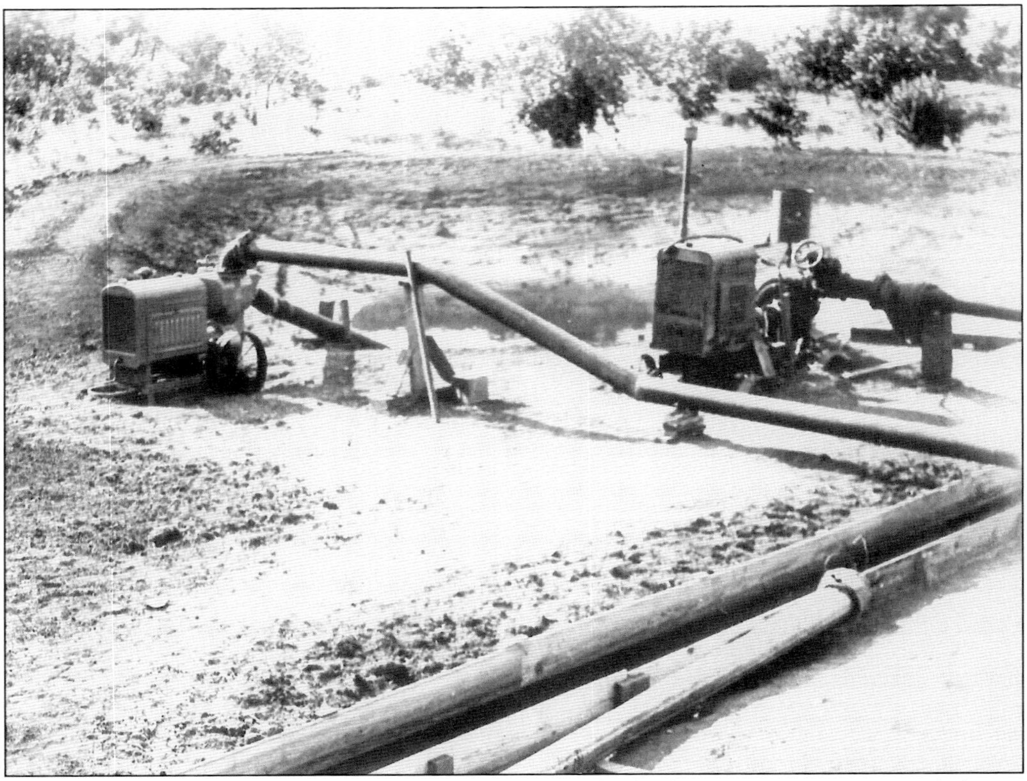

In 1934, a severe drought occurred that subsequently had a huge impact on Creston's future industry. For months, water was hauled in by trainloads because Creston ran out of water. This July 15 photograph shows water being pumped into a dry lakebed. Naturally, industrial prospects were wary of Creston. The city began work to expand its water supply. See page 96 for information about the Green Valley Lake. (Roger Nurnberg.)

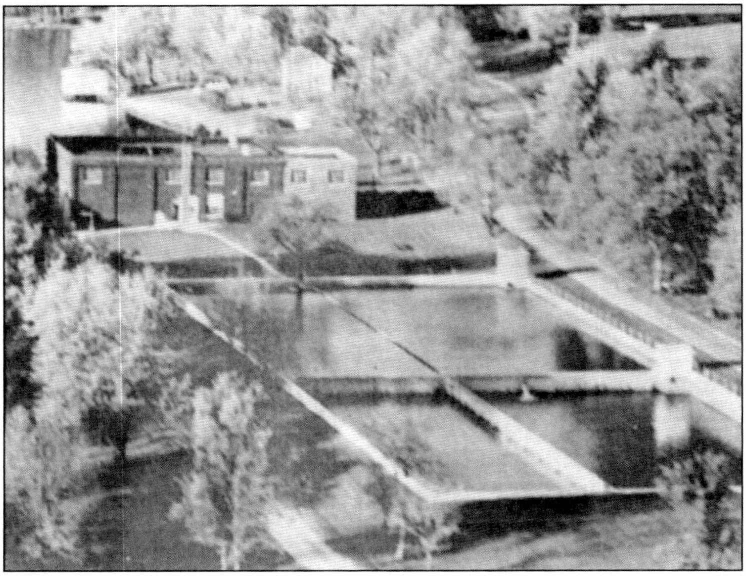

Creston had a public water supply since its earliest days, but it has only been a municipally owned system since 1935. After the drought years of the 1930s, the city purchased the waterworks in 1935. The dam at Summit Lake was raised, which doubled the capacity of the reservoir. A new pumping plant was converted from steam to electric operation in March 1946. (Union County Historical Society.)

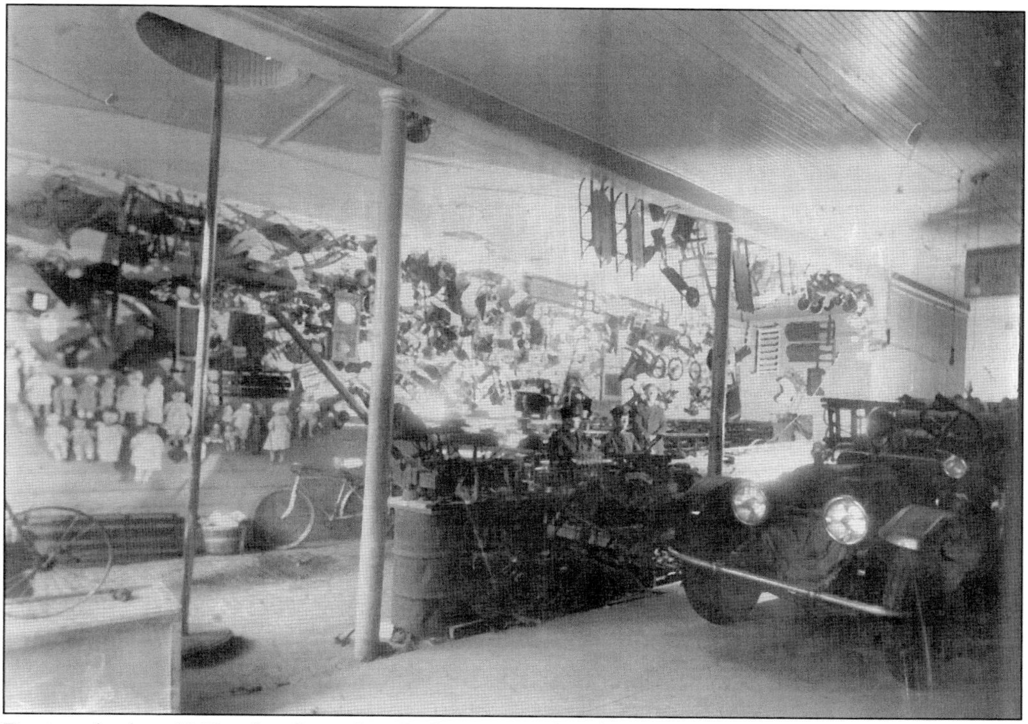

During the late 1920s, the Campfire Girls organized a Christmas toy drive for needy children in the area. The Creston Fire Department headquarters on Maple Street was the collection area. Three firemen sit in the firehouse surrounded by the toys collected by the group. Notice the fire pole leading from the second floor on the left side of the picture. (Dave Moffitt.)

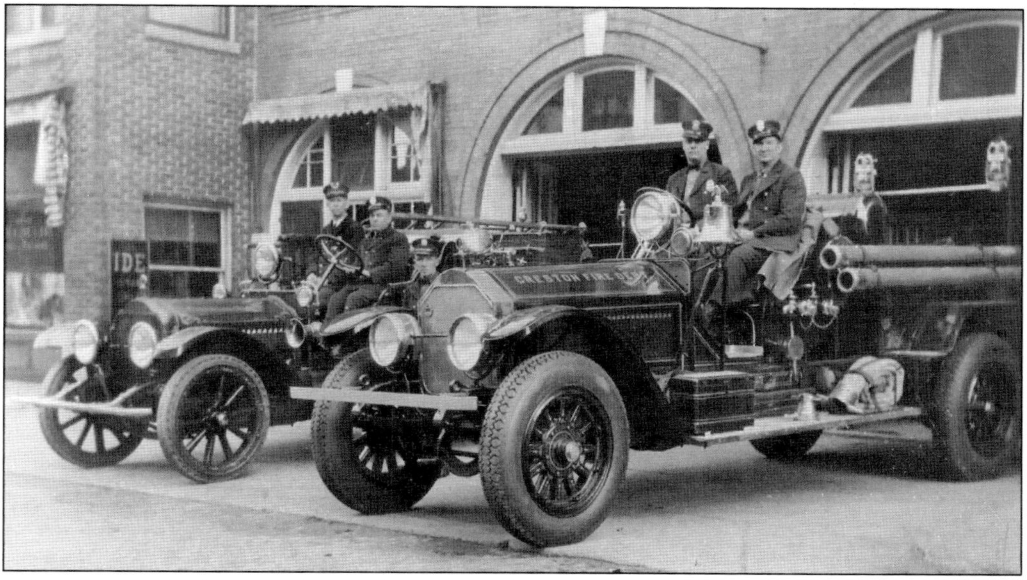

Taken in 1935 in front of the fire department headquarters on Maple Street, this photograph shows Creston's first motor-driven fire truck, a 1916 White, on the left. It was this truck that was sitting on a flatcar in the rail yards when a devastating fire burned the second Summit House. The truck on the right was the department's most recent acquisition at the time, a 1935 REO hose truck. (Roger Nurnberg.)

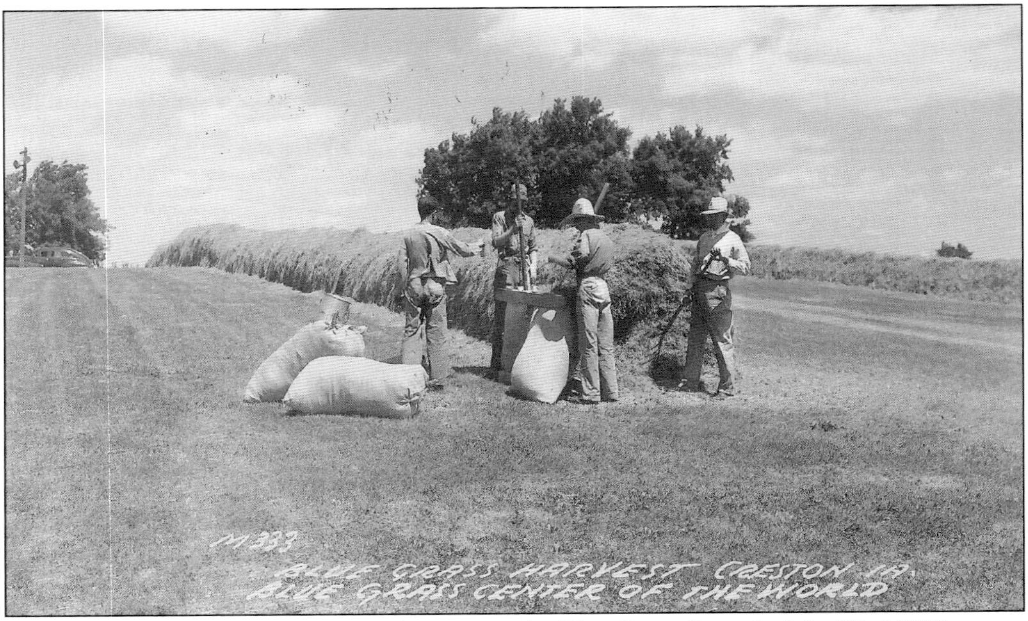

In the 1920s and 1930s, Creston was known as "the Blue Grass Capital of the World." Bluegrass harvesting was a labor-intensive process that involved hand-stripping the seed to dry on ricks, which had to be turned every few days. Once dried, it was taken to be processed, where it was threshed, cleaned, and sacked. By the mid-1930s, harvesting machines called strippers made the process much quicker and easier. (Steve Francis.)

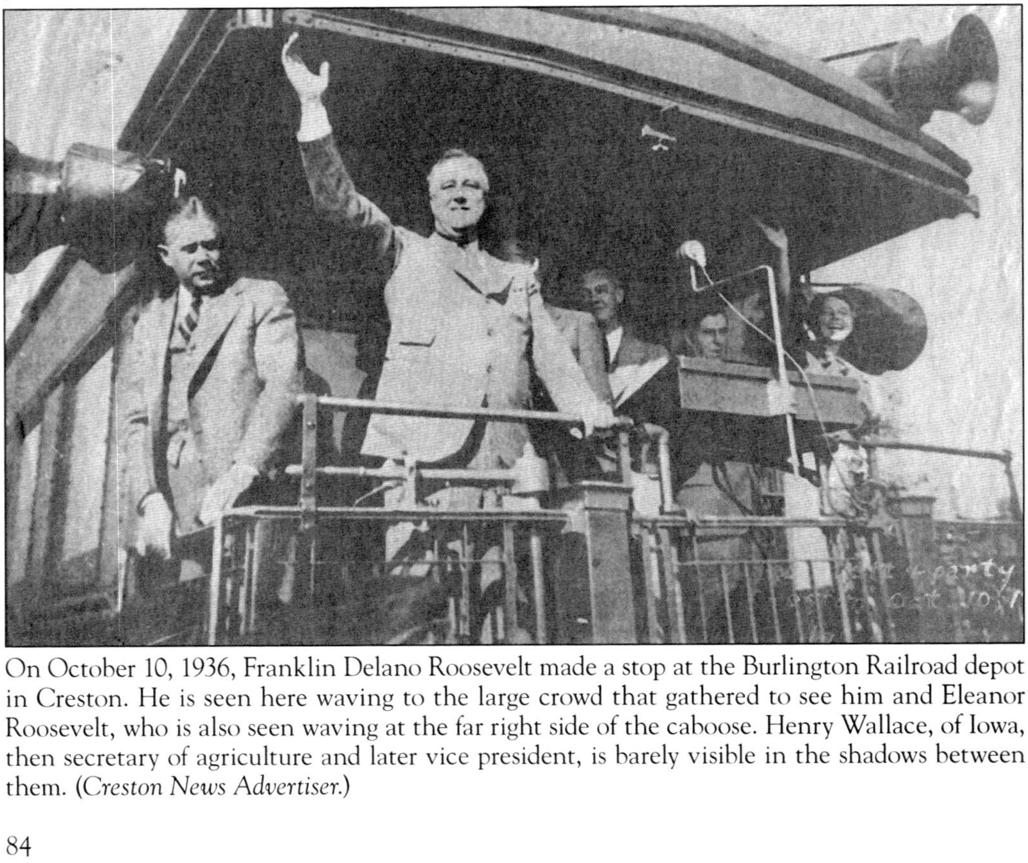

On October 10, 1936, Franklin Delano Roosevelt made a stop at the Burlington Railroad depot in Creston. He is seen here waving to the large crowd that gathered to see him and Eleanor Roosevelt, who is also seen waving at the far right side of the caboose. Henry Wallace, of Iowa, then secretary of agriculture and later vice president, is barely visible in the shadows between them. (*Creston News Advertiser.*)

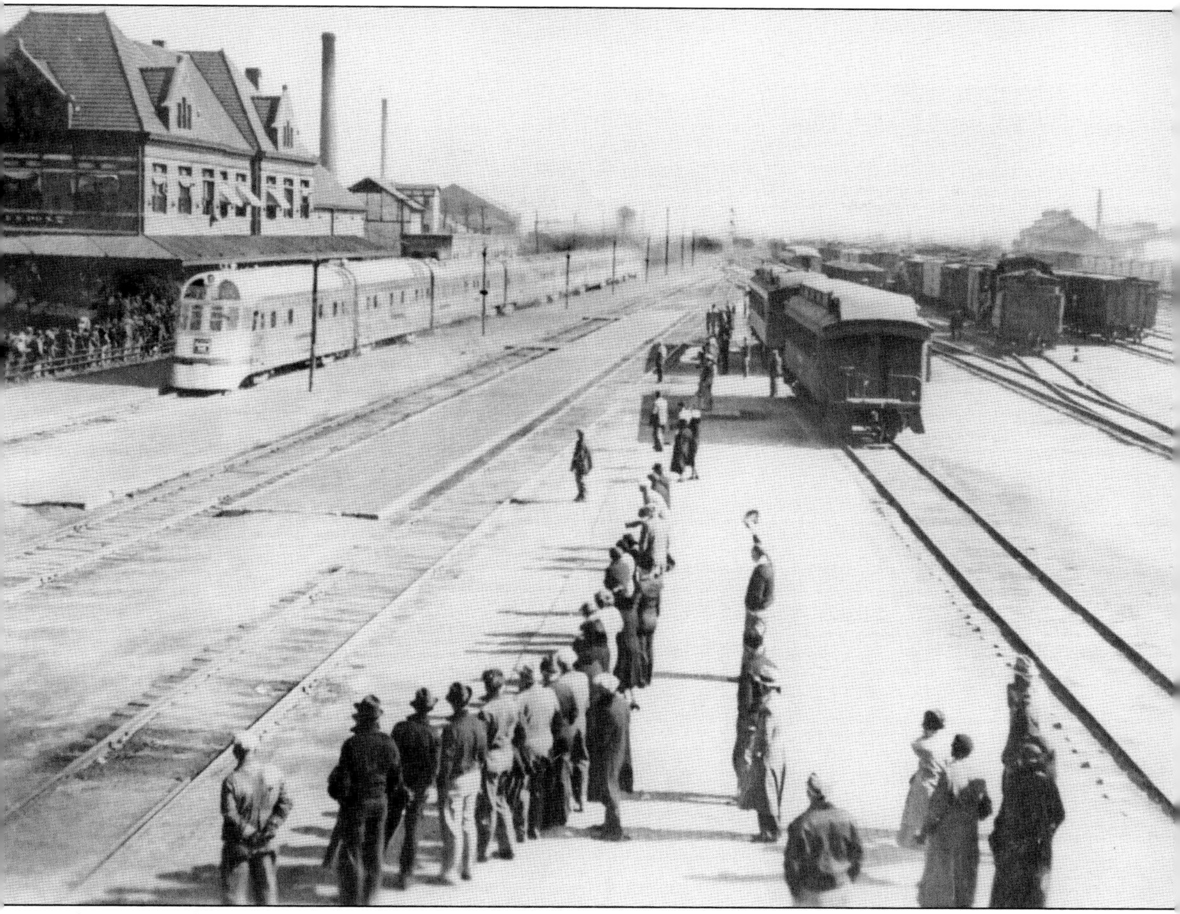

A large crowd gathers along the tracks at the Creston depot on October 23, 1936, to watch an abbreviated six-car Denver Zephyr, powered by units 9906A/B, race through town. The Zephyr was attempting to break the record for fastest time between Chicago and Denver that was previously set by the Zephyr 9900 on its maiden trip in 1934. The 9906s time was better by 52.5 minutes. (Corbin-Wagner Collection.)

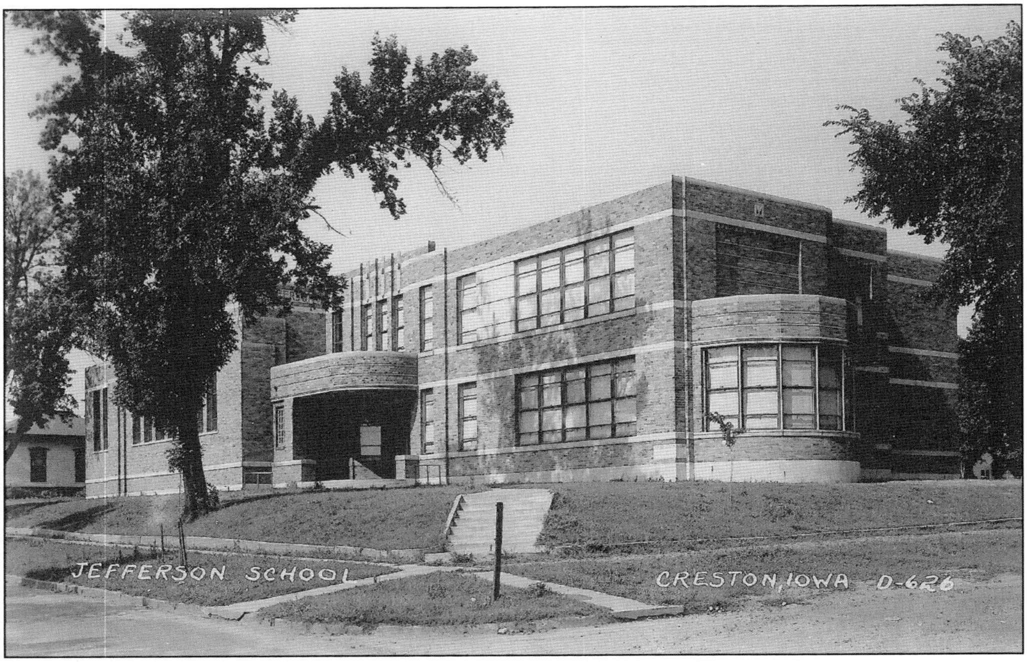

The new Jefferson School was built in 1937 on the same plot as the original Jefferson School. It was constructed as part of the Works Progress Administration (WPA) of Franklin D. Roosevelt's New Deal policy, aimed at promoting economic recovery and improving the infrastructure of the country after the economic crash of 1929 and the ensuing Depression. Jefferson School was a modern, light-brick structure consisting of two stories. As well as classrooms and a larger kindergarten room, the building contained a principal's office, a gymnasium with a stage, a kitchen, storage space, and restrooms. Jefferson School was placed on the National Register of Historic Places in 2002. (Above, Steve Francis; below, Jane Briley.)

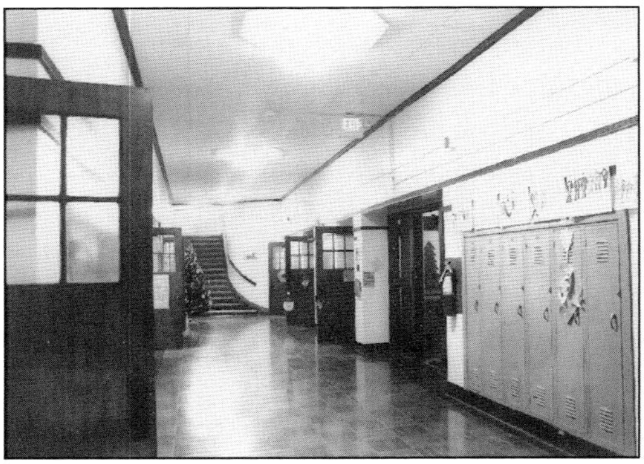

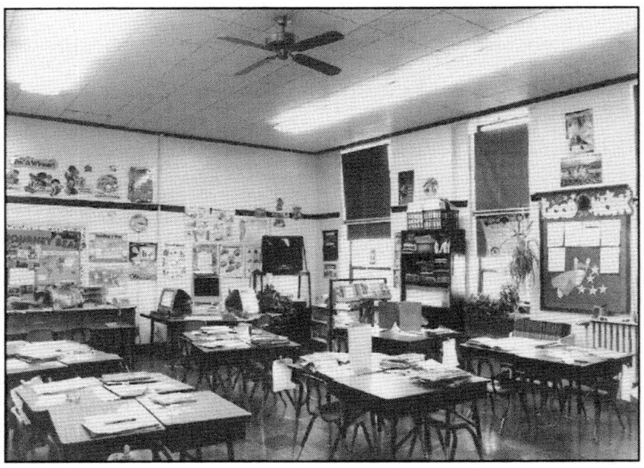

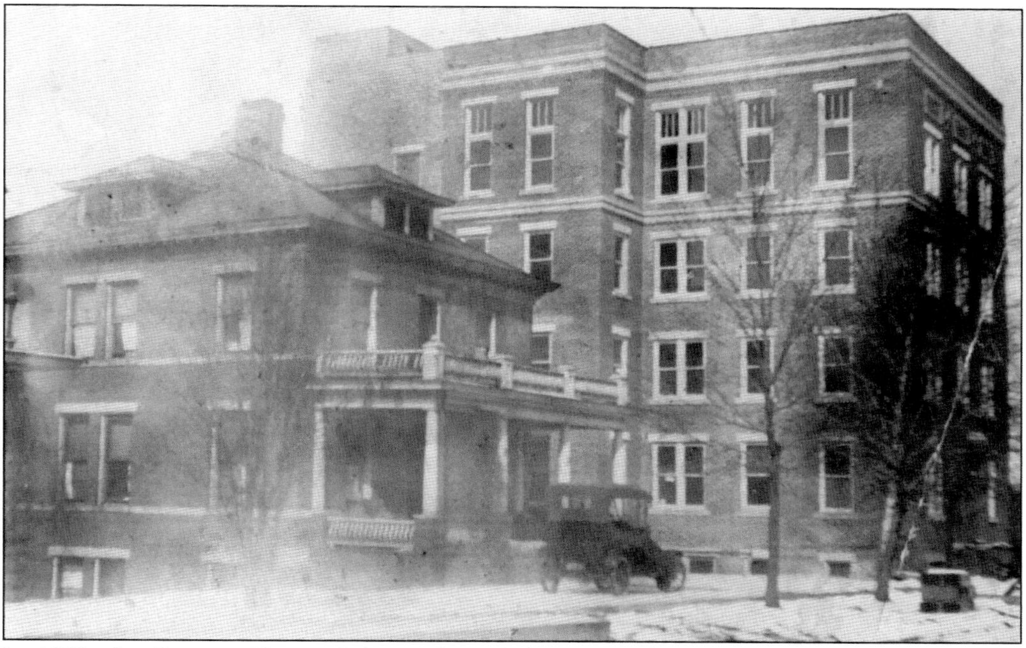

In 1938, the Cottage Hospital, located on Oak Street, along with the four-story addition completed in 1918, were given to the county debt free. The county gladly took over the facility and immediately renamed the hospital the Greater Community Hospital. J. D. Spaulding made a generous contribution, which allowed the hospital to make much-needed improvements and purchase new equipment. It was one of the earliest hospitals to have laboratory and x-ray facilities. (Union County Historical Society.)

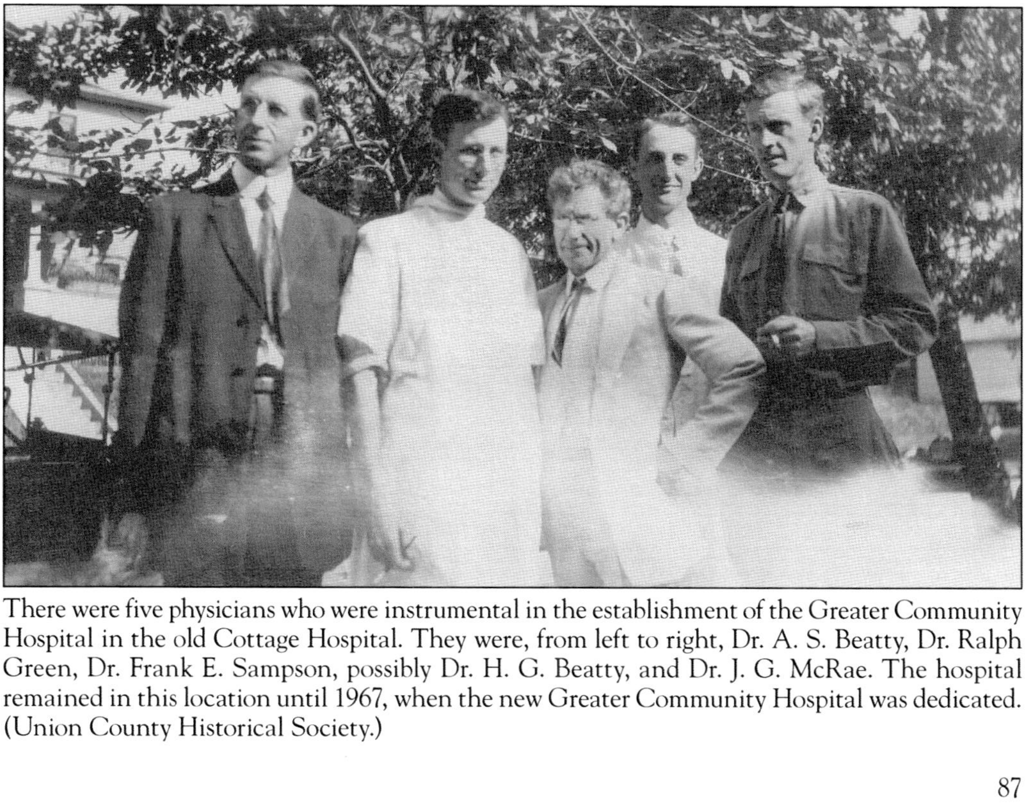

There were five physicians who were instrumental in the establishment of the Greater Community Hospital in the old Cottage Hospital. They were, from left to right, Dr. A. S. Beatty, Dr. Ralph Green, Dr. Frank E. Sampson, possibly Dr. H. G. Beatty, and Dr. J. G. McRae. The hospital remained in this location until 1967, when the new Greater Community Hospital was dedicated. (Union County Historical Society.)

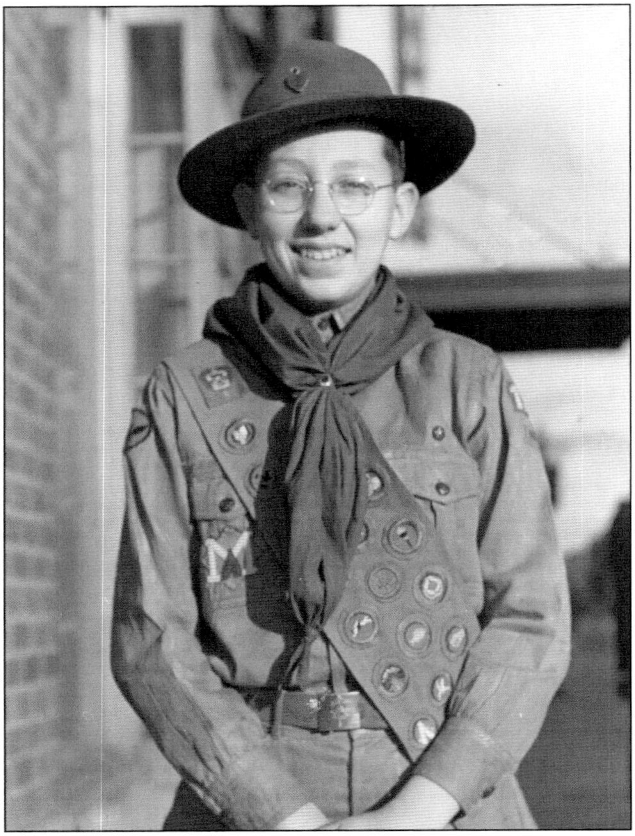

John Rivenburg was the first scout in Troop No. 135 of the Blue Grass District Tall Corn Council to earn the Eagle Award. The distinction was conferred at a public court of honor on February 11, 1938. Sadly, Rivenburg passed away on December 4, 1940, after a sudden illness. (Union County Historical Society.)

In 1939, the Creston High School boys' basketball team won their first state basketball title. The 10 teammates and the coach responsible for the championship are, from left to right, (first row) Bob Jones, Jim Gault, George Harville, Herm Harvy, and Bruce Harper; (second row) coach Harold Hopkins, Bill Strauss, Joe Healey, Kenny Hawks, Orville Double, and Harold Baughman. (*Creston News Advertiser*.)

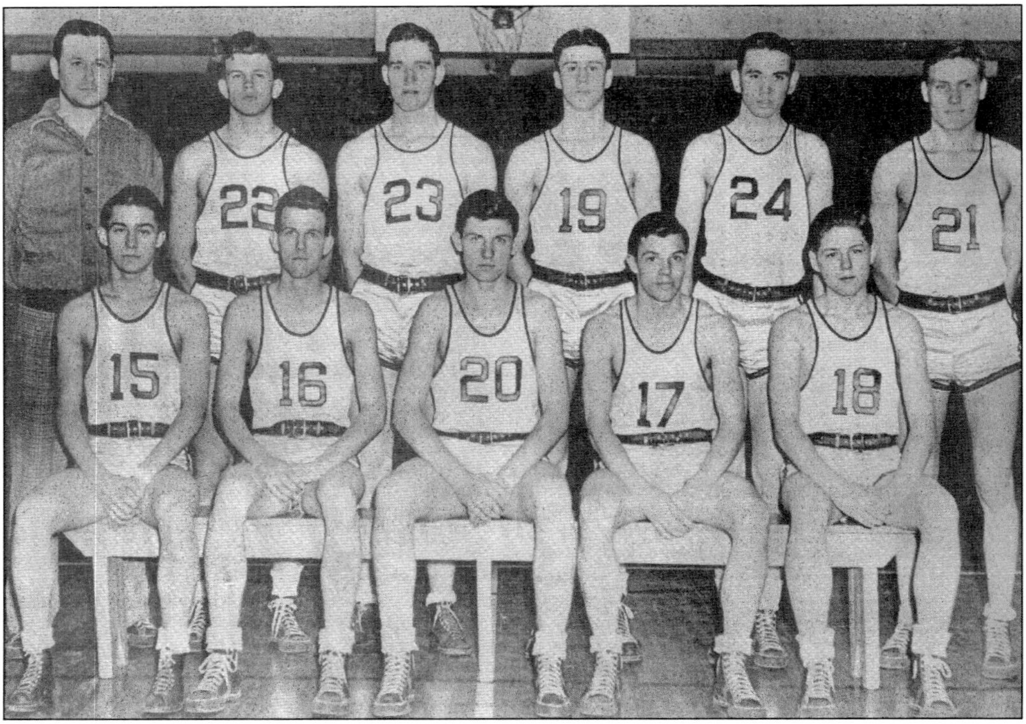

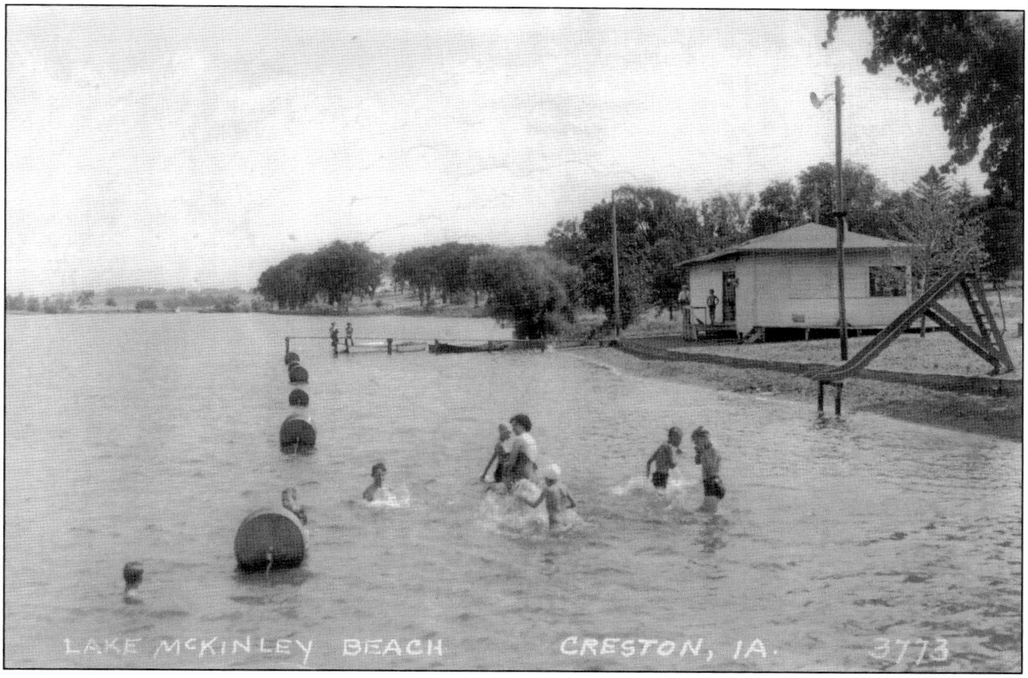

When the city purchased 30 acres of the old Lake Park in 1901, one of the first projects completed after the park commission was formed was the restoration of the lake. The new lake, like the park, was named in honor of assassinated U.S. president William McKinley. The beach, shown here in 1939, was a major source of recreation in its day. It was located on the east side of the lake, just across the road from the current city pool. The above picture was taken from the water, looking north. The bridge barely seen in the distance is Adams Street. The below image was taken from the approximate location of the parking lot built in 2010 for the city pool. Notice the diving platform located beyond the designated swimming area. (Maple Street Memories.)

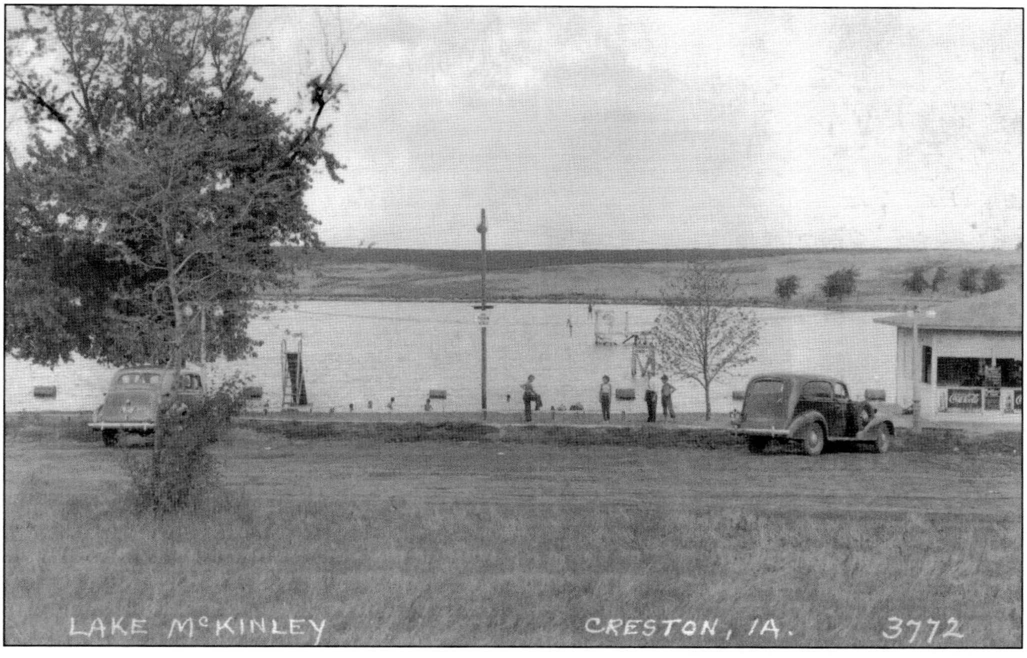

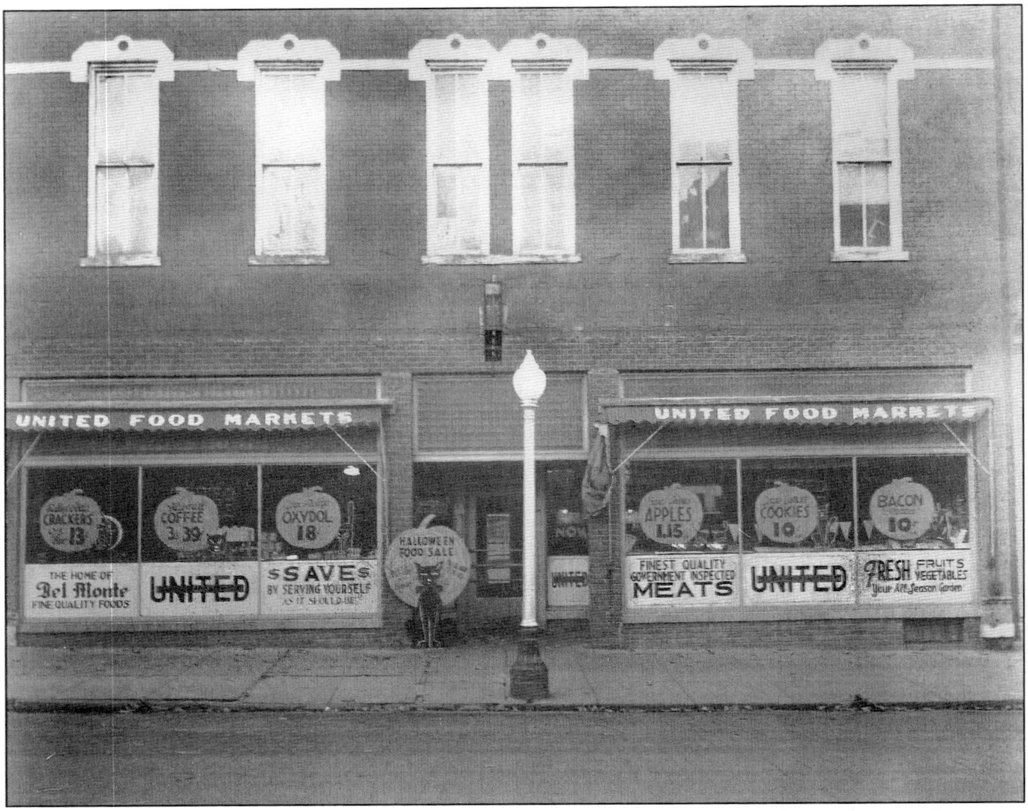

The United Food Market, located on the west side of the 200 block of North Pine Street, is shown in the 1940s. The window advertised several Halloween specials of the day. In the 1920s and 1930s, this was the location of Consumer's Grocery, which had a bakery in the upstairs area of the building. (Jane Briley.)

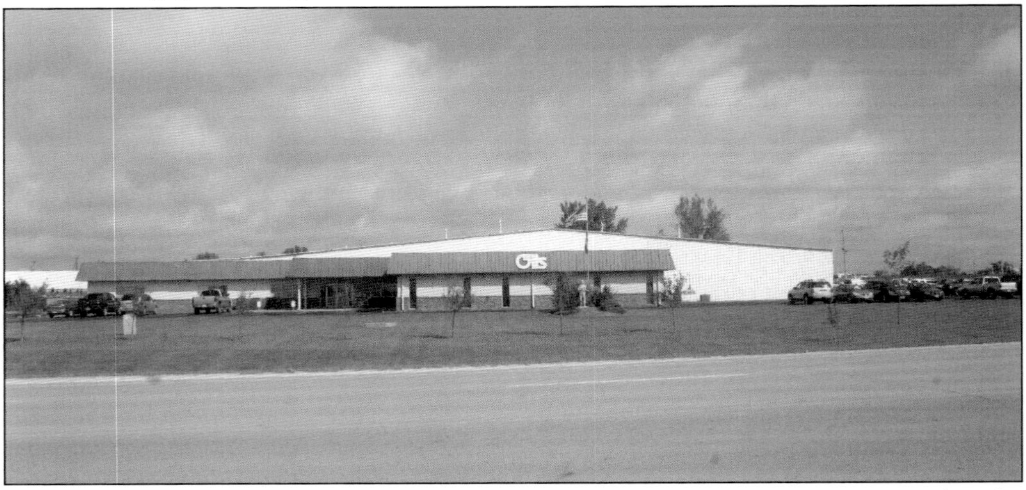

Gits Brothers Manufacturing, which moved to Creston from Chicago in 1945, started in the basement of the old junior high school. It quickly expanded and moved to the former Creston Auto Company location on Walnut Street. The company manufactures all kinds of lubrication devices, grease cups, and oilers. In 1974, the business moved to a new building in the industrial park, where it still resides today. (Photograph by Warren Woods.)

Five

An Era of Change and Growth

For Creston, the introduction of the diesel-powered engine meant the gradual decline of its steam-oriented repair shops as diesel maintenance shifted to West Burlington, Iowa. The last regularly scheduled steam-powered freight train passed through in 1956. The roundhouse and shops—once the pride of Creston—eventually fell victim to the wrecking ball and Mother Nature. With passenger service on the decline, the CB&Q decided that the 1899 depot was much larger than necessary and too expensive to maintain. Consequently, a modern brick-and-steel passenger depot was erected just east of the existing depot in 1969. The 1899 depot was sold to the city for $1.

As the community contemplated innovative ideas for attracting more industry to Creston, a new project emerged. With the decline of the railroad and the threat of another drought looming in the minds of leading citizens, the City of Creston joined with the state and the Southwest Federated Power Cooperative, established in 1946, to construct a dam at a cost of $526,000. The result was the 374-acre Green Valley Lake, which provided cooling water for the power company and a reserve water supply for the city.

In 1945, Gits Brothers Manufacturing decided to move their manufacturing plant out of the highly congested Chicago area to a smaller community. The Creston Chamber of Commerce quickly responded to the proposal, and the new industry relocated to Creston. Recognizing that something needed to be done to promote the area for more commerce, two development groups were formed in the late 1950s. A major push was underway in the 1960s to welcome new businesses to Creston, which included the purchase of 160 acres of land on the east edge of Creston for the development of an industrial park. Throughout the 1960s and beyond, several industries found a new home in Creston, and many remain to this day.

Two other significant events transpired during this period. In March 1967, the new Greater Community Hospital was dedicated with 83 beds. Just across the highway, as part of the state area college system, Southwestern Community College opened its campus in 1970.

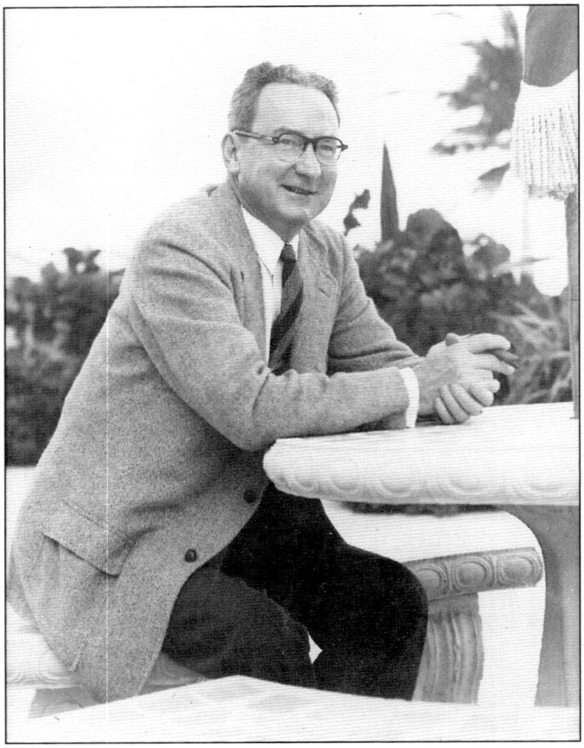

Elmo Roper (1900–1971) was a pioneer in the fields of market research and public opinion polling. He spent much of the 1920s running a jewelry store in Creston. While the store was not successful, he did learn the value of understanding customers' needs. In 1946, Roper founded the Roper Center for Public Opinion Research, the first social science data archives, at Williams College. (Roper Center for Public Opinion Research.)

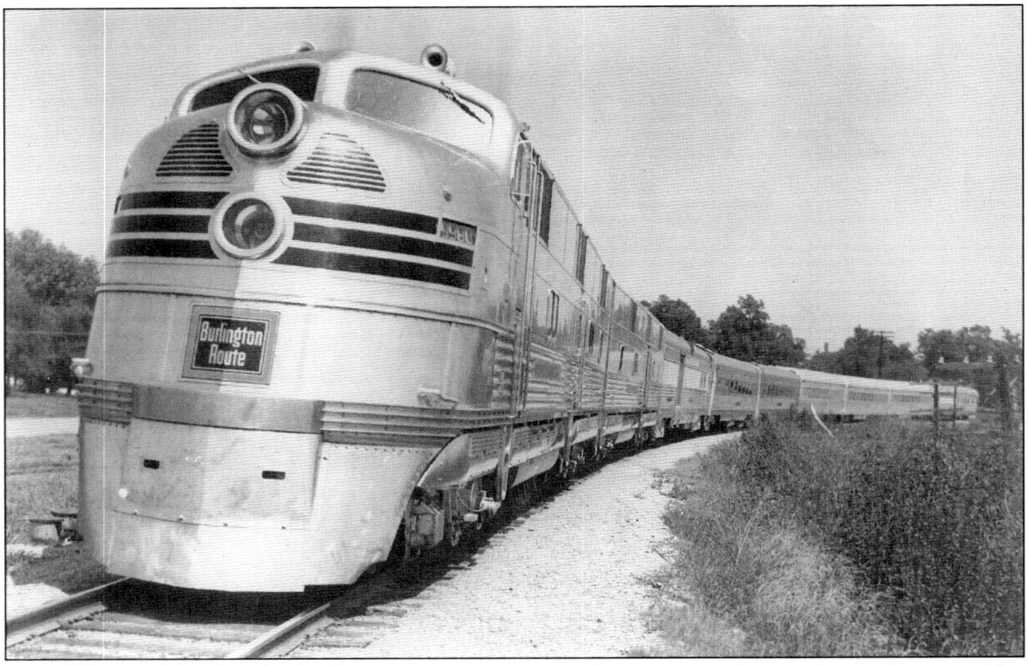

A streamliner is any vehicle that incorporates streamlining to produce a shape that provides less resistance to air. For a short time in the late 1930s, the 10 fastest trains in the world were all American streamliners. This post–World War II Burlington Streamliner, and successor high-speed train systems, have largely disappeared in the United States due to the increasing popularity of the automobile and airline travel. (Union County Historical Society.)

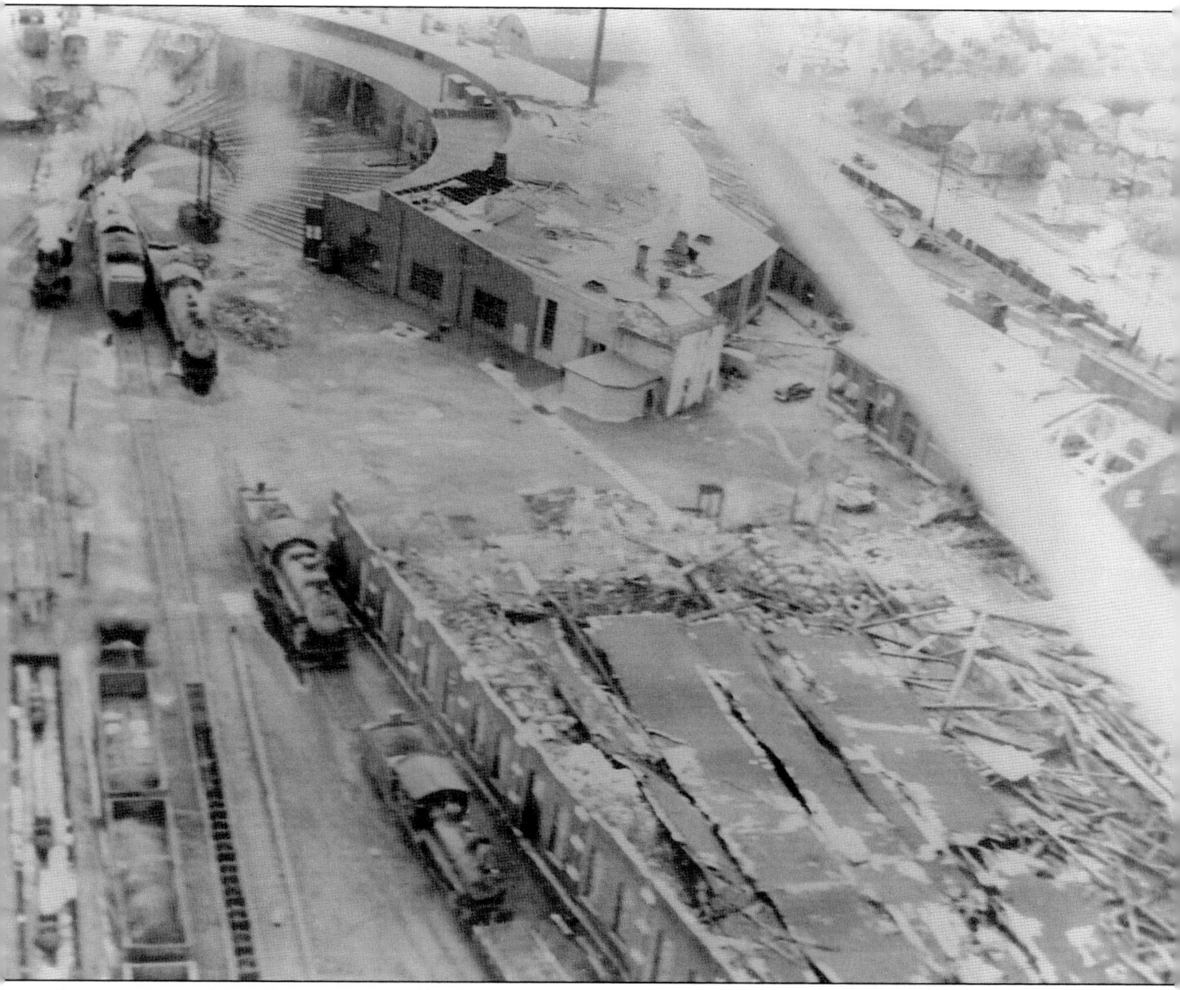

A tornado on May 30, 1946, totally destroyed the Back Shop building, leaving only its south wall standing. Two locomotives stand, protected by the remaining wall. Large portions of the roundhouse and storehouse roofs are also gone. The storehouse is partially hidden by the wing strut of the plane from which the picture was taken. The turntable for the roundhouse is in the upper left corner. The remaining section of the roundhouse was destroyed by fire in the 1980s. (Corbin-Wagner Collection.)

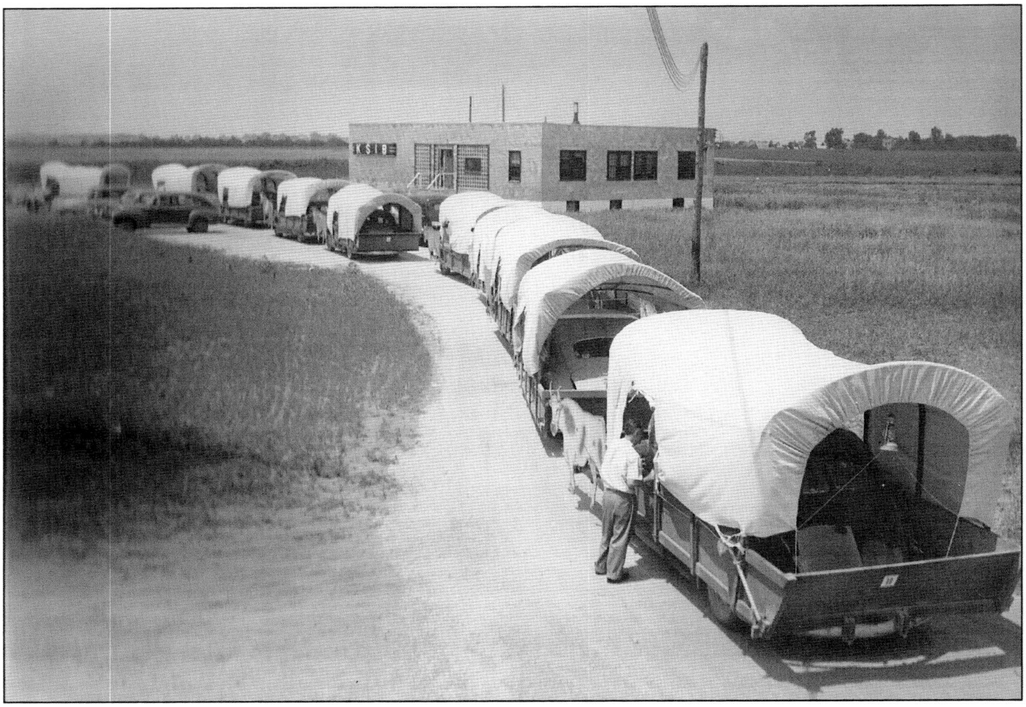

Creston Radio was started on December 7, 1946, by E. M. "Dutch" Horning and other investors around the community. The AM station was called KSIB, which stands for Keep Southwest Iowa Beautiful. The FM station, KITR, was added in 1966, and stands for Keep Informed Through Radio. On July 16, 1947, a caravan of 72 modern covered wagons sponsored by the Sons of Utah Pioneers stopped by the KSIB radio station as it trekked across Iowa. The group was following the Old Mormon Trail, which was blazed between Nauvoo, Illinois, and Salt Lake City, Utah, in 1847. These pictures were taken at KSIB when the leader of the Young Men's Mutual Improvement Association of the Latter Day Saints Church, Lorenzo Hill Hatch, stopped for an interview. (Both, KSIB Radio.)

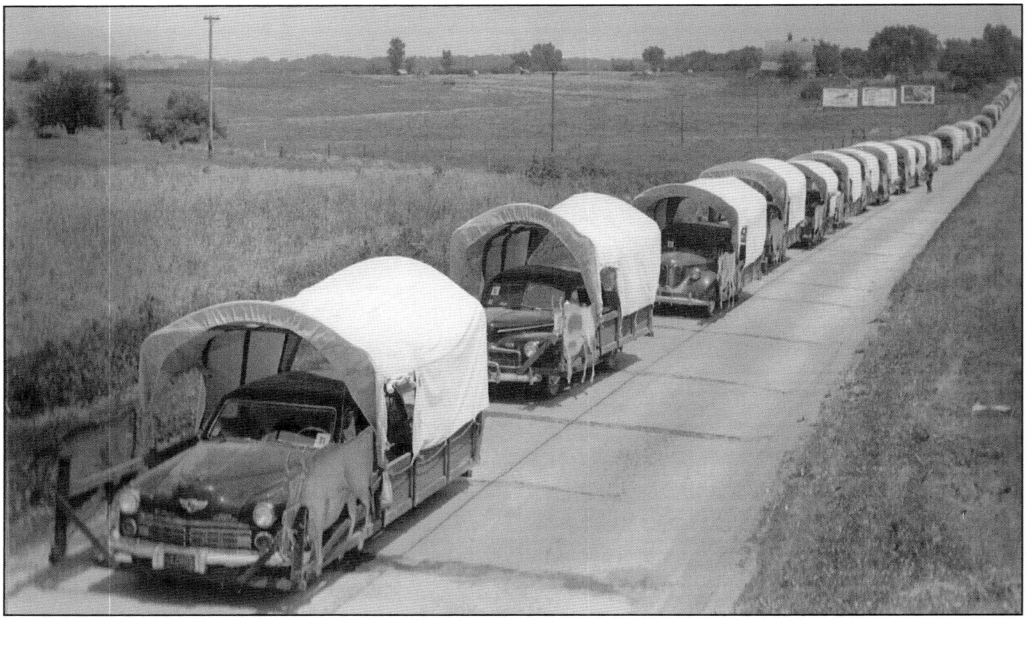

The depot gets a steam cleaning on April 27, 1949. The ornate copper awnings are still in place at this time, but they were removed two or three years later in a Korean War scrap drive. (*Creston News Advertiser.*)

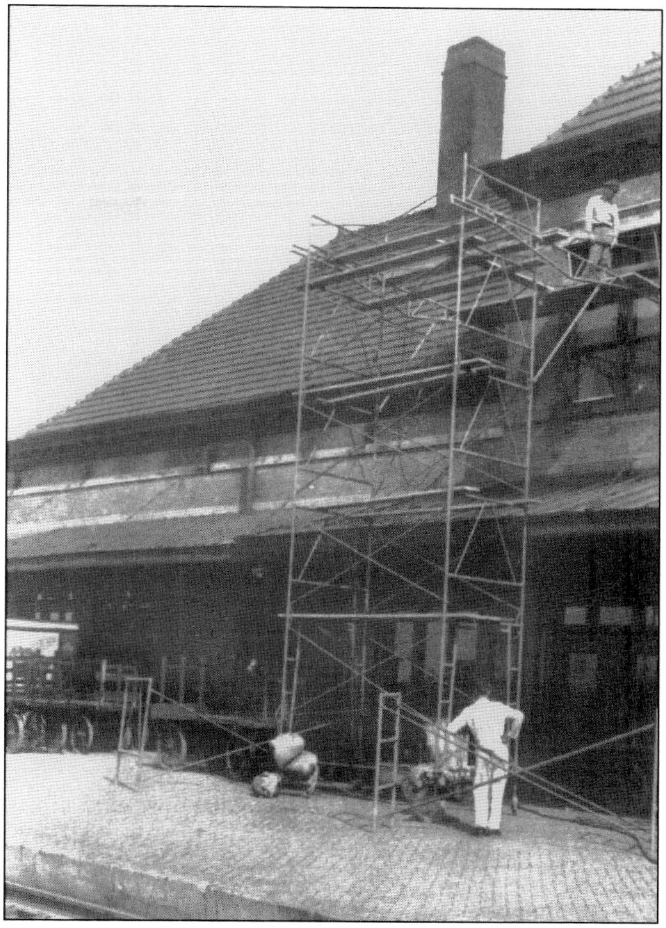

Pres. Harry S. Truman came through Creston on his birthday, May 8, 1950, during his whistle-stop campaign. He spoke briefly to the large crowd that had gathered from the back of a Burlington Railroad caboose. Truman was one of four presidents to visit Creston during the city's first 100 years. (Jane Briley.)

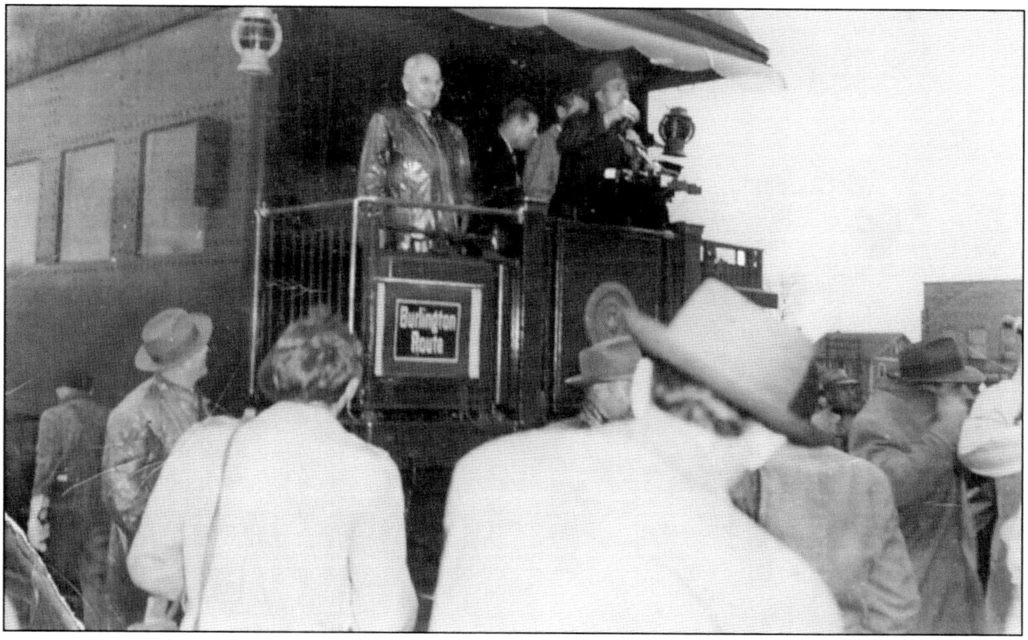

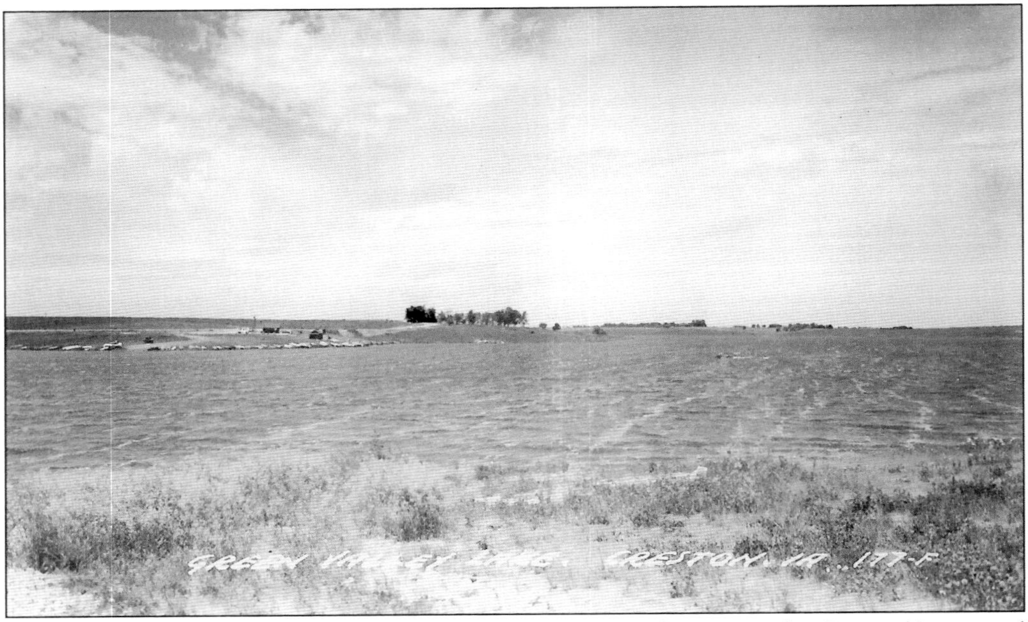

In 1951, through the remarkable joint effort by the City of Creston, the State of Iowa, and Southwestern Federated Power Cooperative, Green Valley Lake was built just northwest of Creston. The city's water supply was increased threefold. The massive reservoir of water in Green Valley Lake soon wiped out the "no water" label given to Creston, and industrial opportunities began to develop. (Steve Francis.)

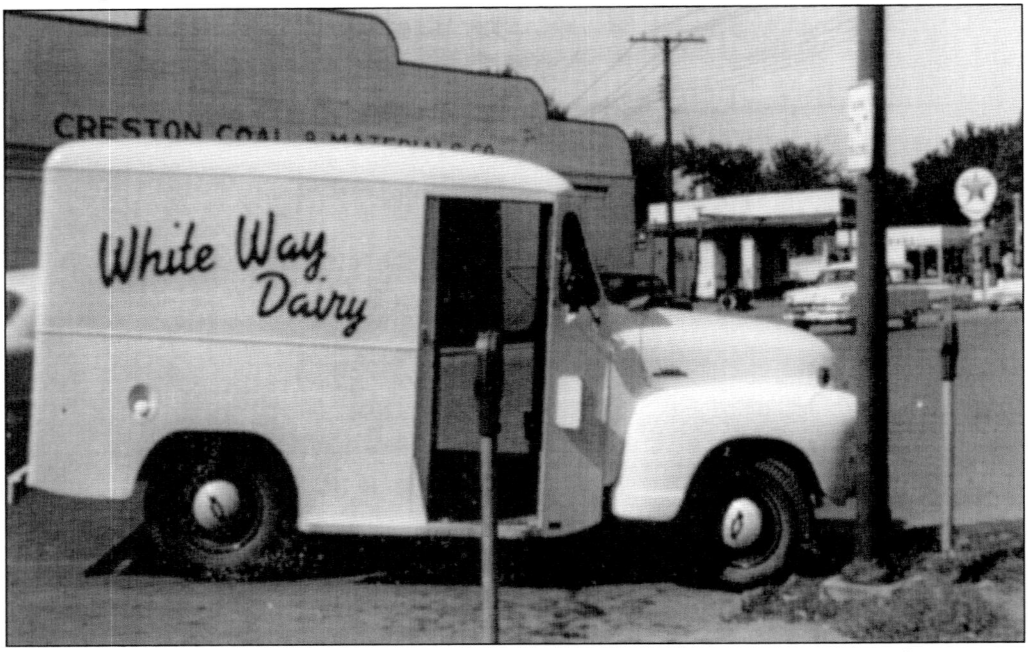

Vernon and Beatrice Boyer owned the White Way Dairy, a full-service dairy and ice cream manufacturer, on the corner of Adams and Division Streets. Milk from local farms was processed and bottled the same day for home and restaurant deliveries. Hand-packed, premium ice cream—produced in 20 flavors—was available in store or through curb-side service seven days a week, from 8:00 a.m. to 9:00 p.m. (Jane Briley.)

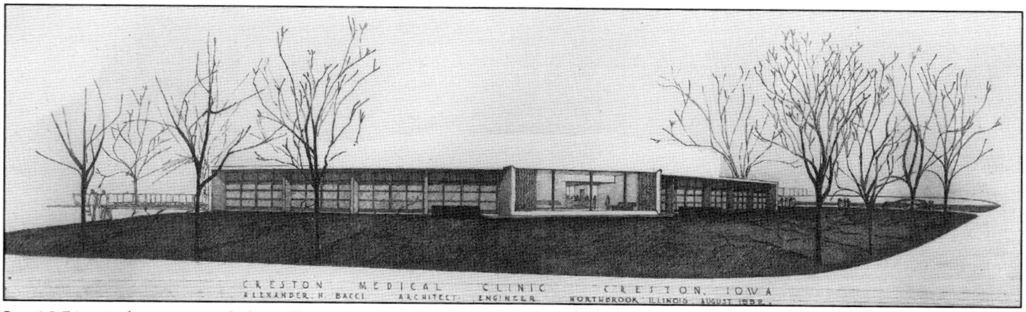

In 1951, eight general family practice doctors made plans to construct a building to establish a medical clinic for group practice. On August 3, 1953, the Creston Medical Clinic opened its doors with offices for Dr. H. G. Beatty, Dr. A. S. Beatty, Dr. J. B. Gault, Dr. J. L. Hoyt, Dr. R. H. Kuhl, Dr. J. A. Liken, Dr. M. R. Paragas, and Dr. H. J. Peggs. Later that fall, Dr. W. A. Fisher joined the group as a pediatrician. (Union County Historical Society.)

By the early 1950s, the county had outgrown the 1889 courthouse. In May 1951, the county purchased the lot intended to be the location for the new courthouse at 300 North Pine Street, diagonally across the intersection from the existing courthouse. The new building was dedicated in a ceremony held on March 10, 1953. In 1977, a new law center was constructed adjacent to the courthouse. (Union County Historical Society.)

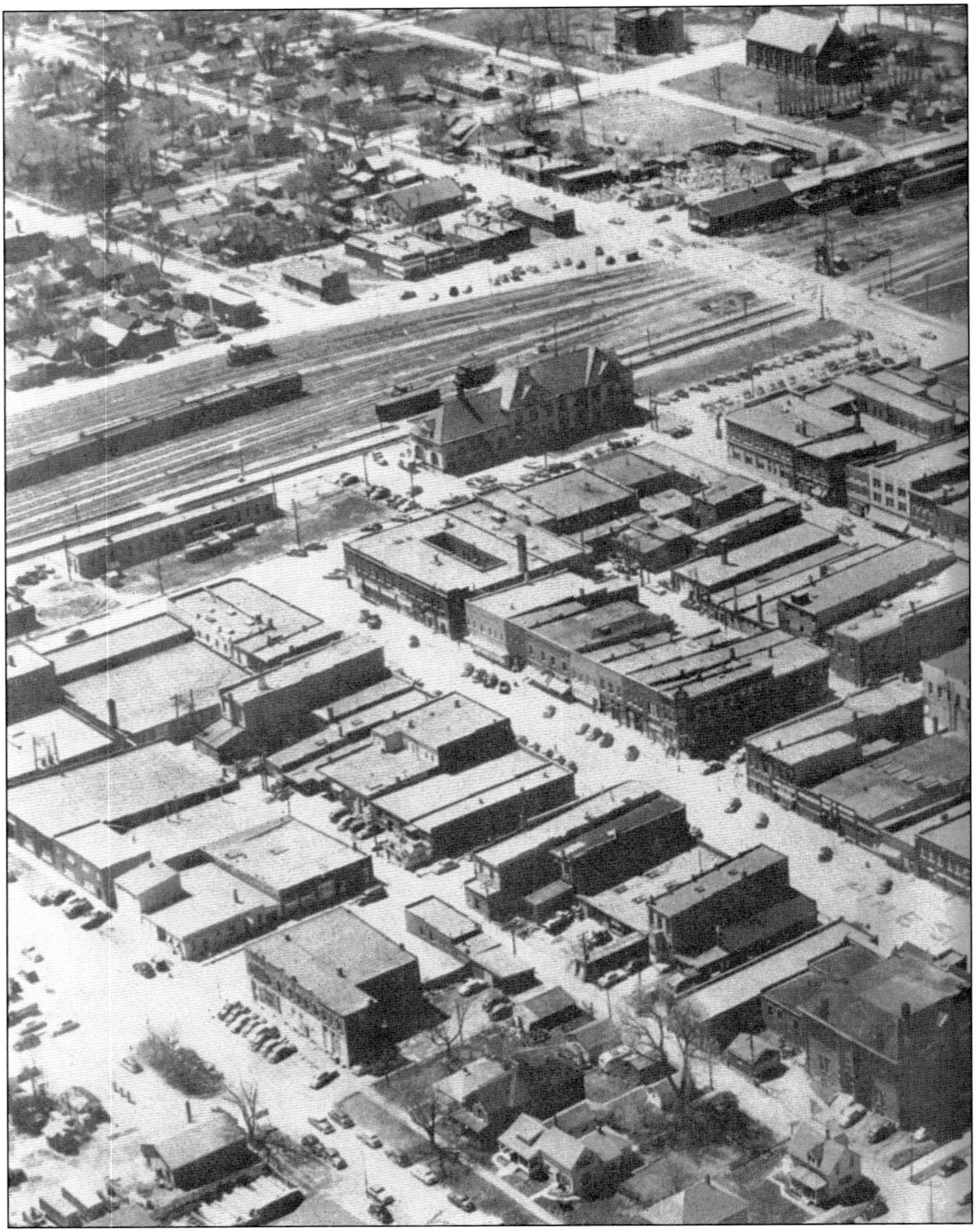

This view of uptown Creston from 1952 shows the old courthouse at the lower right, on the corner of Pine and Mills Streets. At that time, all of the buildings were still standing along Pine Street. The depot is prominent along the tracks near the top. Just in front of the depot is Maple Street, with First National Bank on the corner, just across the street and slightly to the right. St. Malachy Worship Center is the tall building along Clark Street in the upper right corner. Across the street from St. Malachy is the old Catholic school. (Rosalie Denton.)

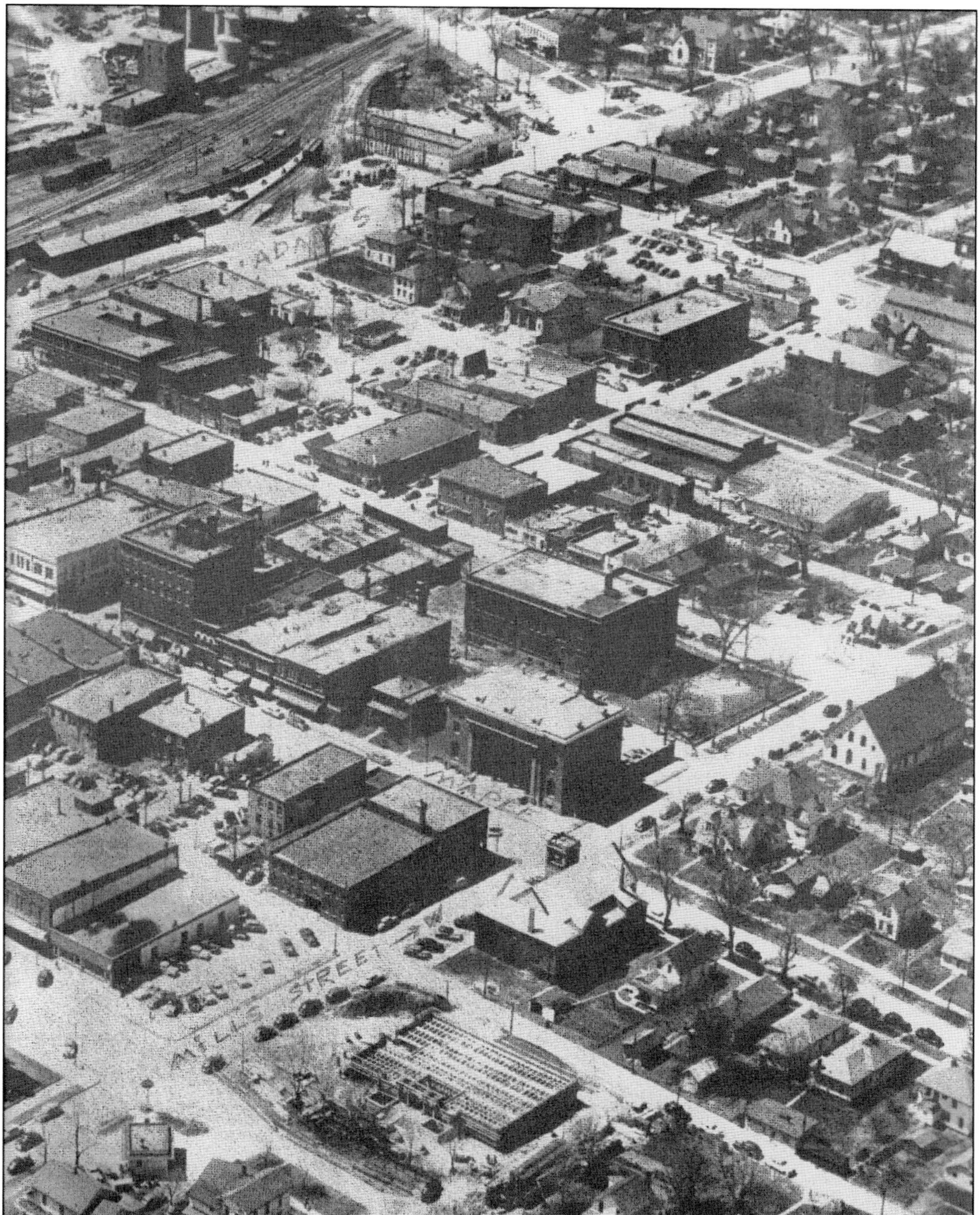

The new courthouse is under construction in the lower center of this picture. The small building on the corner to the left is Creston's first oil station. The post office is on the corner of Maple and Mills Streets. The Iowana Hotel, in the center left of the photograph, is up the street from the post office. The junior high school, originally the high school, is seen behind the post office. One block farther west and one block south is the second Masonic Lodge. Across Montgomery Street to the north (right) is the Elks Lodge. (Rosalie Denton.)

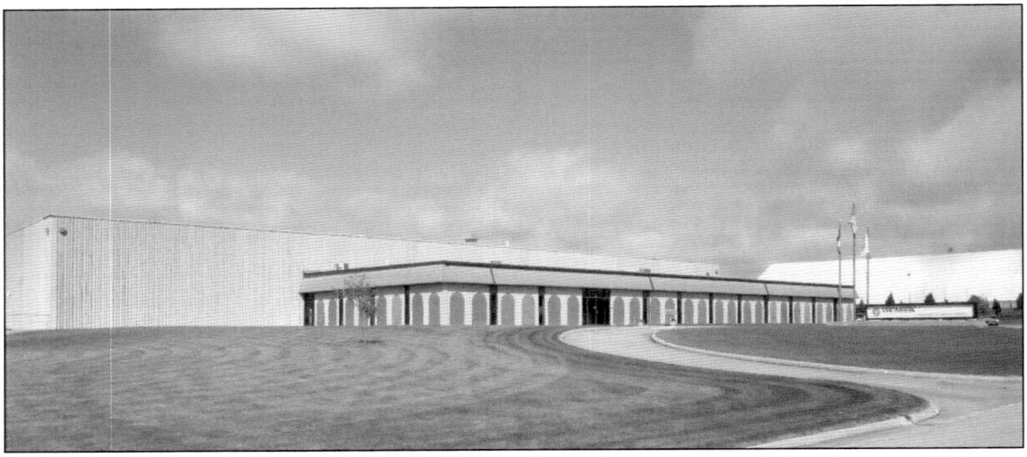

A local engineer, Harry Banks, designed a machine that was intended to be a small, home potato and vegetable peeler. Subsequent efforts by other engineers resulted in a commercial volume machine for potato chip manufacturers. Veg-A-Peel, started in 1954, developed into an international business with sales nationwide and abroad. The company began operating under the name Vanmark Equipment, LLC, in 2006. (Photograph by Warren Woods.)

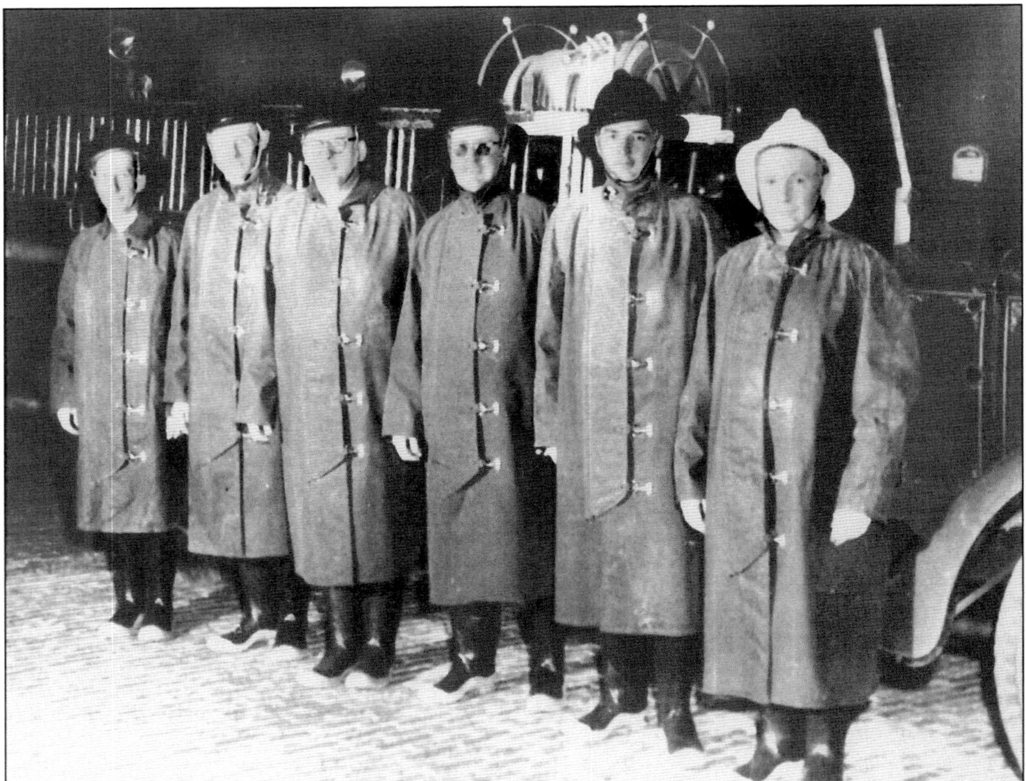

These 1956 volunteers are shown in turnouts, also referred to as bunker gear—the common protective clothing worn by a firefighter when fighting structural fires or performing rescues. Turnouts are so named because, when not in use, they are kept ready to wear by "turning out" the pants over the boots. This way, the firefighter simply steps into the boots and pulls up the pants. (Roger Nurnberg.)

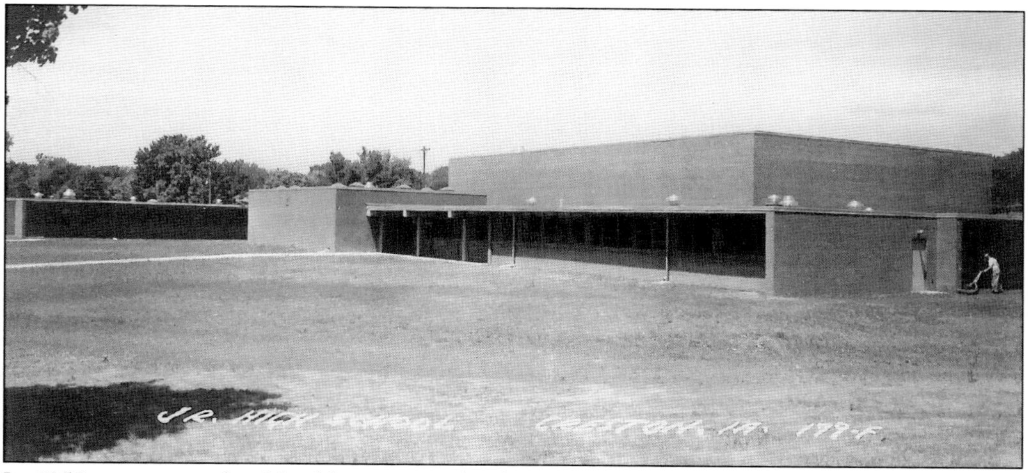

In 1958, two new school buildings opened. The new junior high school (above), later named Burton R. Jones Middle School in honor of the district superintendent who passed away in 1957, was erected on property already owned by the district on the old football field at Elm and Swan Streets. The third Franklin School was erected on an unoccupied site between Oak and Division Streets, which was south and west of the second Franklin School building. The new school had nine classrooms, a kitchen, a gymnasium, a music and art room, storage, and offices all on one floor. The total cost of both buildings was $664,000. A unique feature of Franklin School was the Miracle Learner Swimming Pool (below), which was a two-lane pool built in the gymnasium. Students from all the neighborhood primary schools were bussed to Franklin School for swim lessons. (Above, Steve Francis; below, Gary Wimmer.)

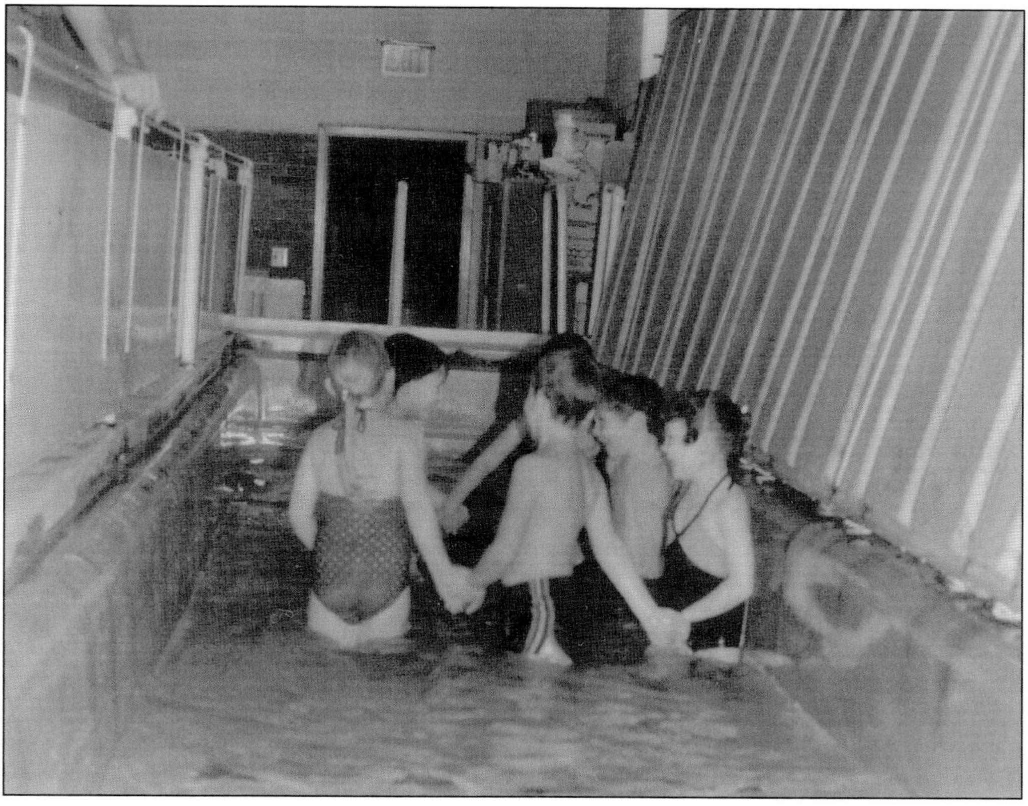

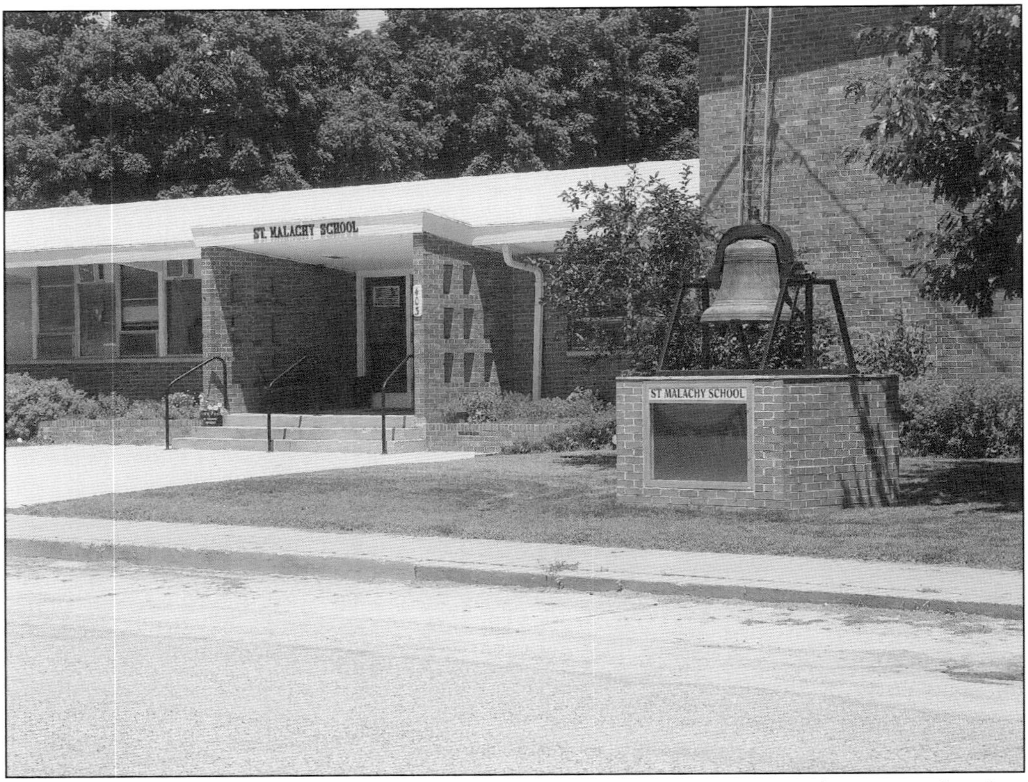

Construction of the new St. Malachy's School started in August 1956 and was completed in 1957. The cost of the new building was $160,000. The original two-story, brick Catholic school was torn down in 1958. A new convent was built in its place to provide living quarters for the Benedictine Sisters, who taught at the school. (St. Malachy School.)

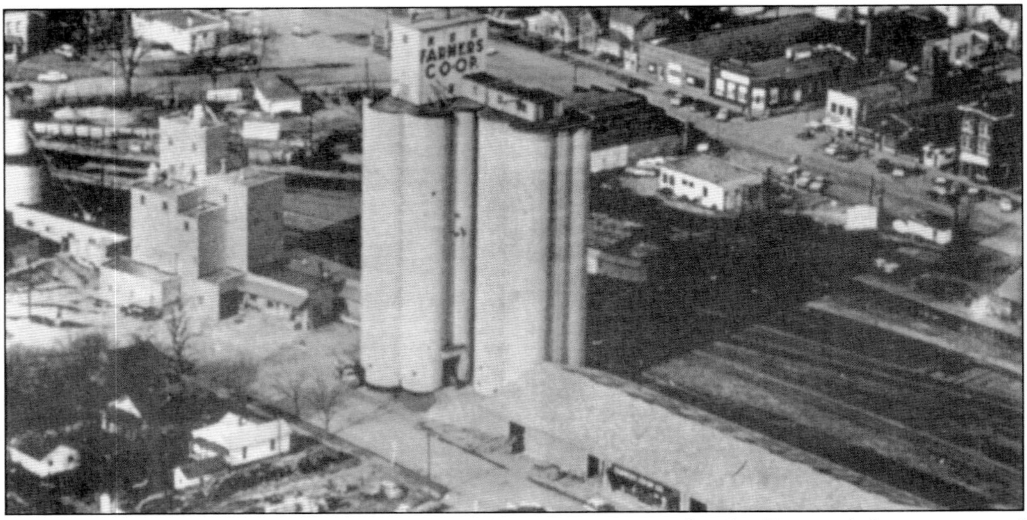

The period from 1947 to 1963 heralded the largest expansion for the Farmers' Cooperative of Creston. By 1959, when this photograph was taken, the organization had grown to include a mill added in 1948, concrete grain elevators added in 1954 and 1959, and a lumberyard added in 1952. The biggest year in the company's history to that point was 1962, with a total volume of business just short of $3 million. (Rosalie Denton.)

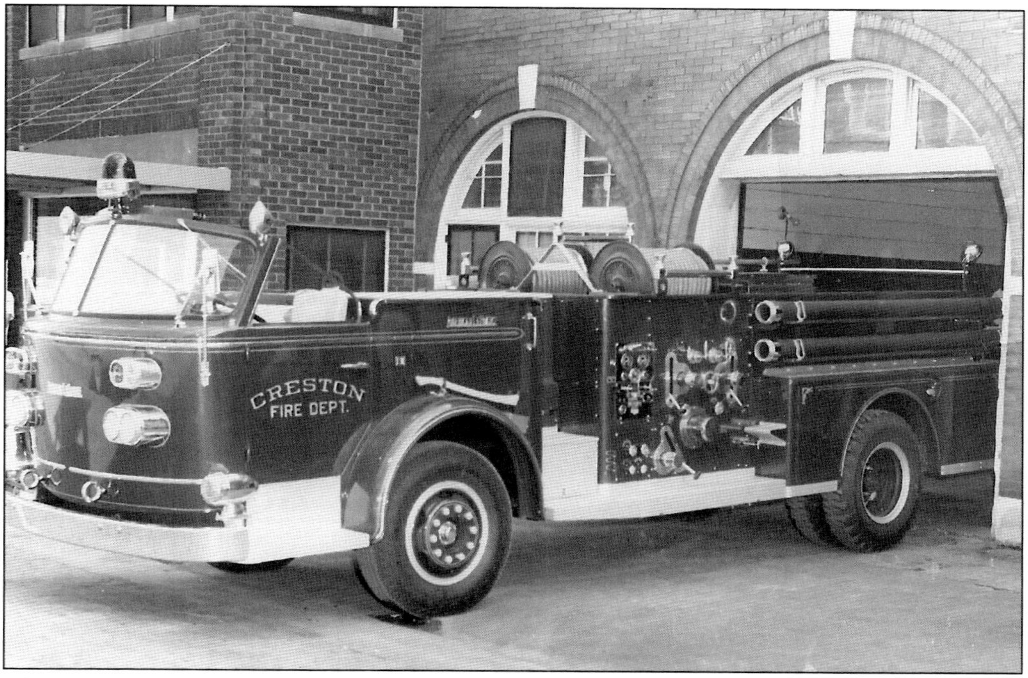

This 1959 American LaFrance hose truck replaced the truck purchased in 1935 (see page 83). The new truck had a centrifugal pump capable of pumping 750 gallons per minute. By 1959, the fire station was remodeled so that the haymow served as the fire chief's office, a courtroom, city offices, and city council chambers. The north arch and stall served as a ladies restroom for city shoppers. (Roger Nurnberg.)

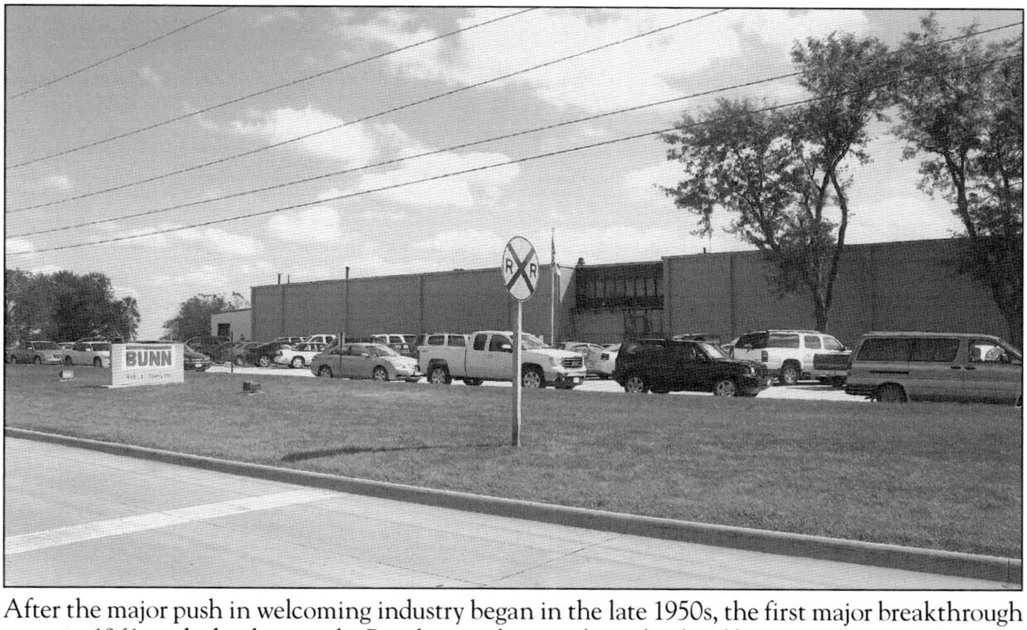

After the major push in welcoming industry began in the late 1950s, the first major breakthrough came in 1961, with the decision by Purolator to locate a branch of its filter manufacturing business in Creston. A factory was built in northeast Creston on Townline Road. Purolator was later taken over by Bunn-O-Matic, a coffeemaker assembly company. Bunn-O-Matic currently operates two locations in Creston. (Photograph by Warren Woods.)

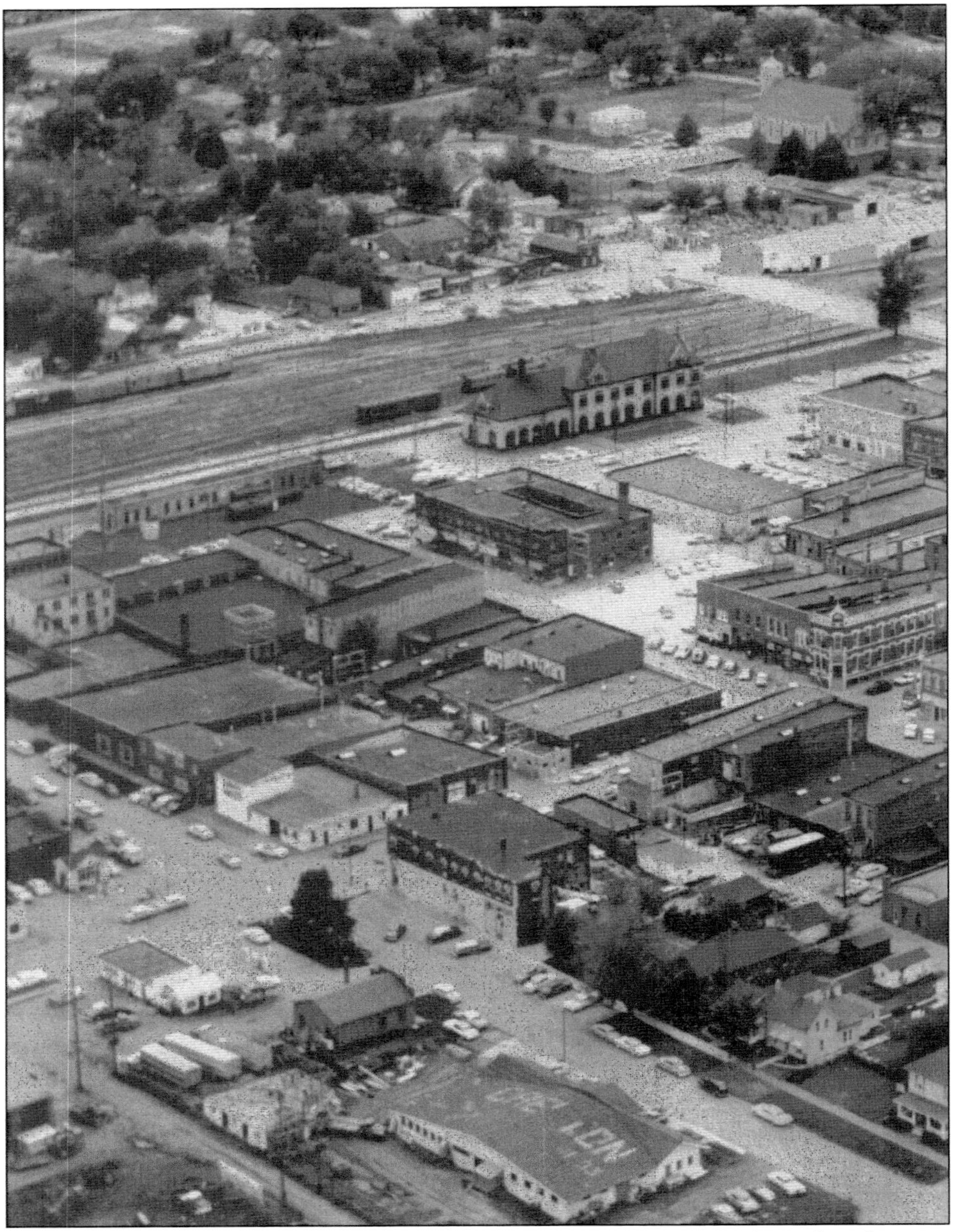

Taken in 1963, this aerial view shows the changes in the uptown area since the earlier photographs shown on pages 98 and 99. The depot stands prominently along the tracks. From this angle it is easy to see that the canopies have been removed. This was done for a Korean War scrap drive. Directly across the street to the north, the buildings at the corner on the east side of Maple Street have been replaced by a parking lot and a one-story structure, which was a Fareway Grocery Store in 1963. A large section of buildings have been removed along Pine Street. At the end of Pine Street, along the tracks, is the service building (shown on page 107) that was torn down to make way for the third passenger depot, built in 1969. The long white building in the upper right corner, just south of the railroad tracks, is the new Farmers' Cooperative of Creston lumberyard. Just beyond that, to the southwest, is St. Malachy Church. The old Catholic School that was across the street in 1952 is gone. (Rosalie Denton.)

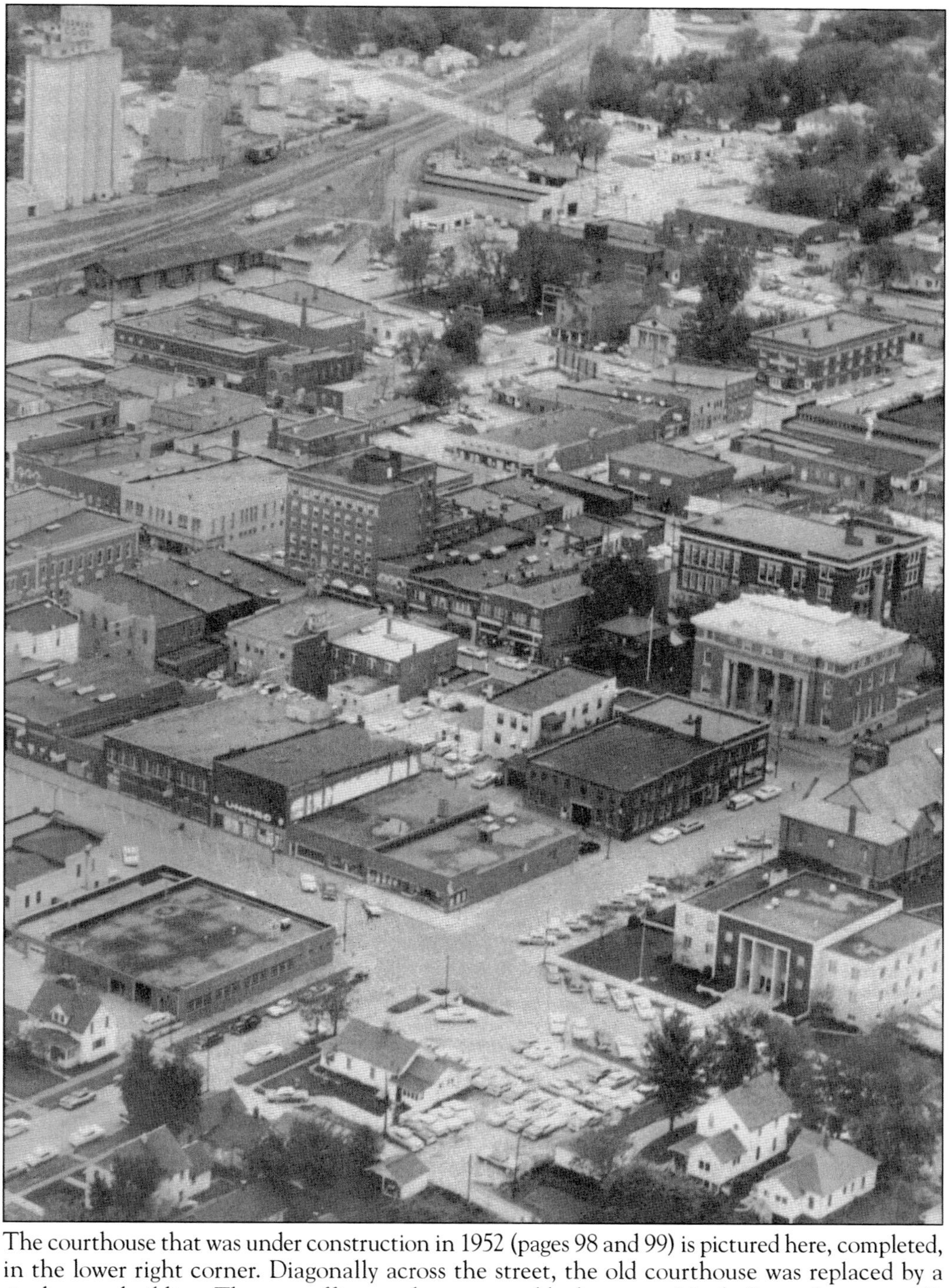

The courthouse that was under construction in 1952 (pages 98 and 99) is pictured here, completed, in the lower right corner. Diagonally across the street, the old courthouse was replaced by a single-story building. The post office can be seen one block west on Maple Street (see page 46). The original brick high school is directly behind the post office on Elm Street (see page 60). In 1963, the building was used by the community college. The Iowana Hotel is the tall building in the center of the picture (see page 67). The Farmers' Cooperative of Creston grew to dominate the south side of the tracks with its concrete grain elevators and new lumberyard, shown on the previous page. (Rosalie Denton.)

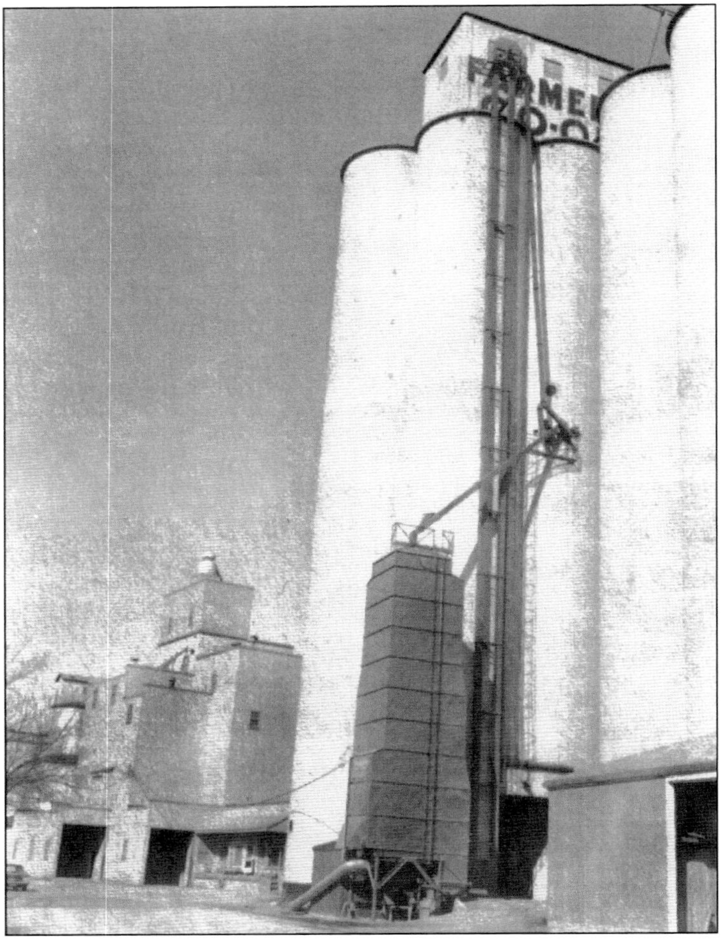

In April 1963, the Farmers' Cooperative of Creston installed a new $32,500 drier in its elevators on West Union Street. The cooperative's original tile elevator, "the jug," was still in use and can be seen in the background behind the feed mill. (Rosalie Denton.)

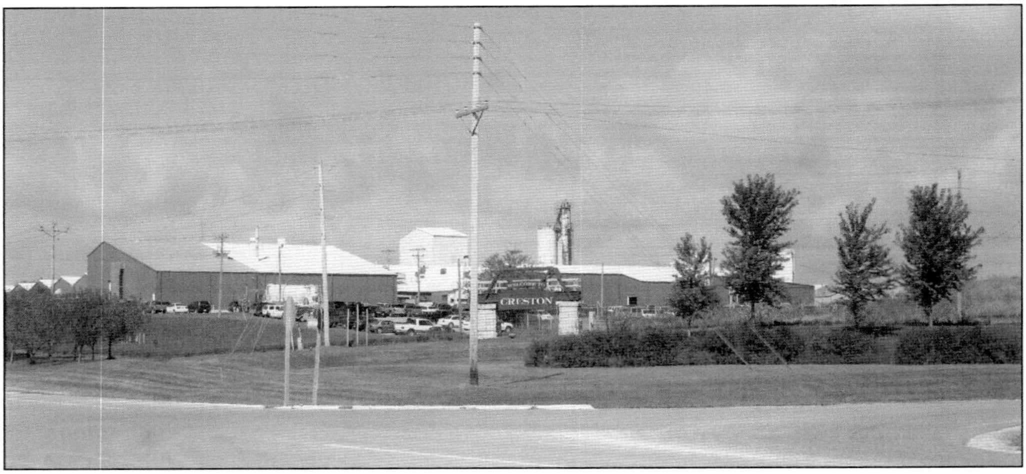

In 1964, the well-known Hills-McCanna Company of Carpentersville, Illinois, chose to locate a magnesium foundry in Creston. The new plant was built at the east edge of the industrial park. Later, an aluminum foundry was added. In 1971, Wellman Dynamics of Michigan took over the company. Many parts for airplane and space vehicles are still made here as of 2011. (Photograph by Warren Woods.)

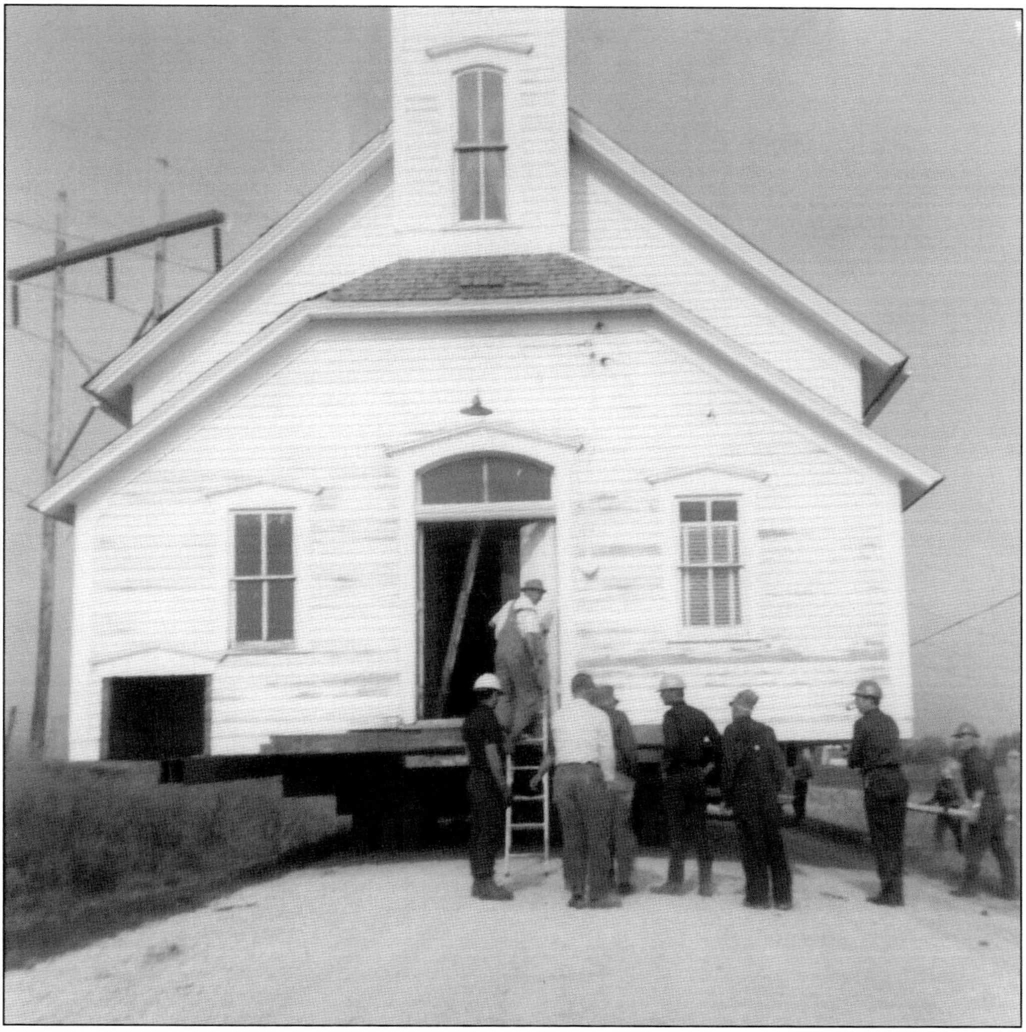

Preserving the history of Creston was a concern as early as 1894, when C. S. Rex and J. B. Harsh formed a group to recognize the 25th anniversary of Creston's founding. A similar concern prompted the reorganization of the Union County Historical Society in 1966 to prepare for a centennial celebration. The group is shown transporting Lincoln Township School No. 5 to the new historical complex. See page 111 for more information. (Union County Historical Society.)

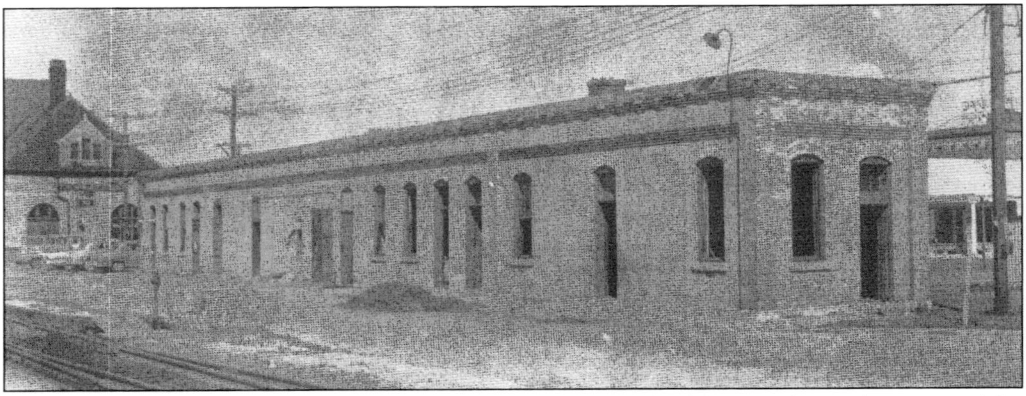

Popular along the Burlington Route, this long, narrow service building was located just east of the depot. It was constructed in the same yellow, pressed brick and used primarily to store supplies, such as coal, oil, and ice, and to provide space for the crews of passenger trains. It is shown here in September 1968, shortly before it was razed to make room for a new passenger depot. (*Creston News Advertiser.*)

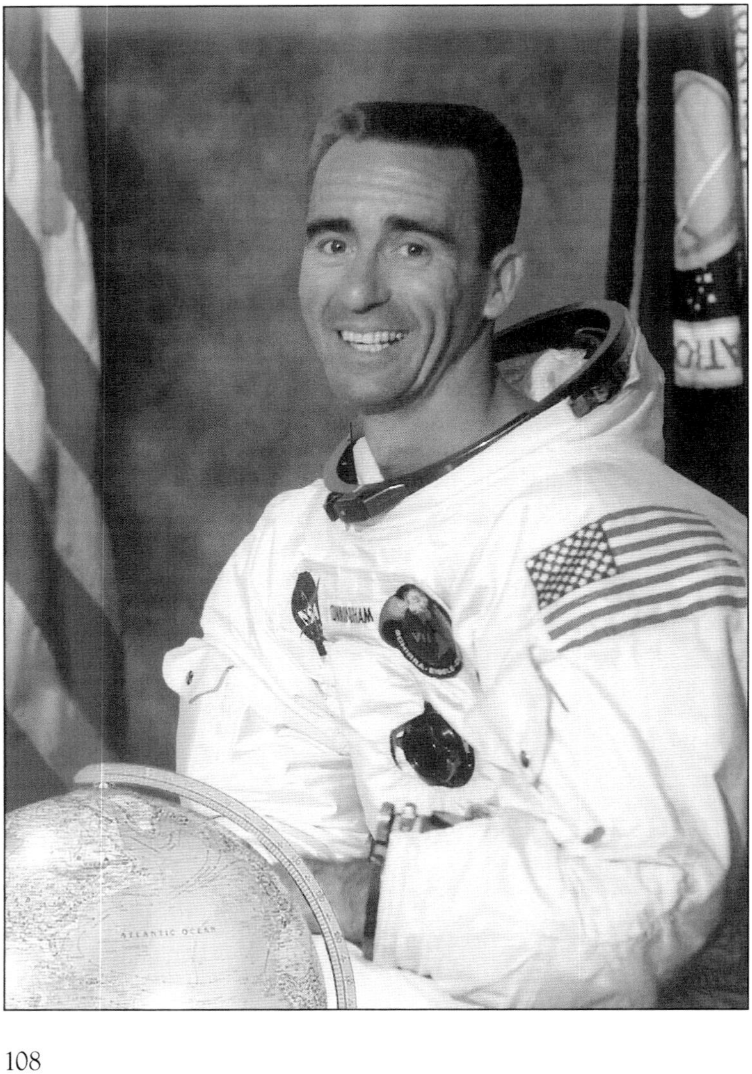

Ronnie Walter Cunningham, born in Creston on March 16, 1932, was a member of the third group selected for the NASA astronaut program in October 1963. On October 11, 1968, he occupied the lunar modular pilot seat for the Apollo 7—the first manned launch of an Apollo mission. He retired from NASA in 1971 and later went on to publish a book, *The All-American Boys*, reminiscing his astronaut days. (Walter Cunningham.)

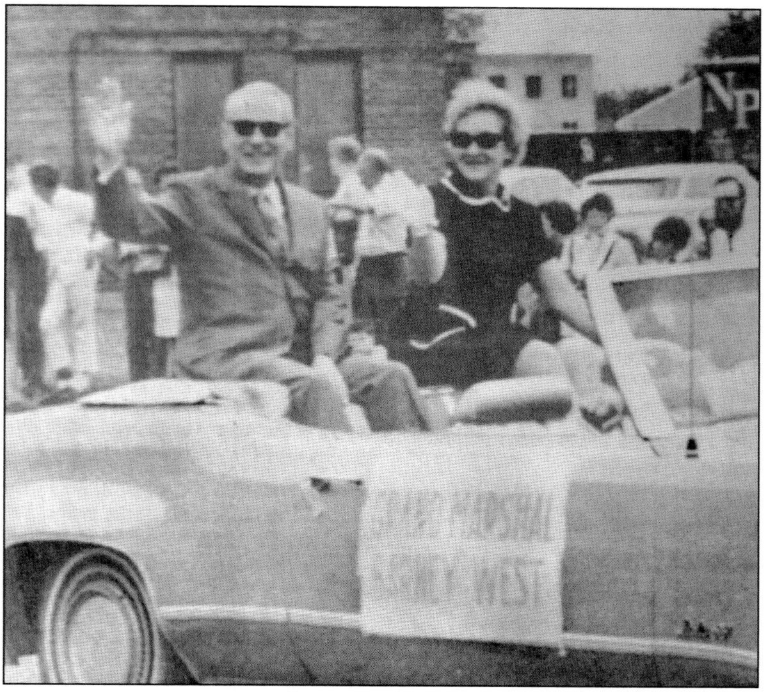

J. Bernard West, a 1930 graduate of Creston High School, was chief usher at the White House and served under six presidents. He later documented his experiences in the executive mansion starting in 1941, with the book *Upstairs at the White House (My Life with the First Ladies)*. West, shown with his wife, Zella, rode in the "Crestennial" Parade as grand marshal for Creston's centennial celebration in 1969. (*Creston News Advertiser.*)

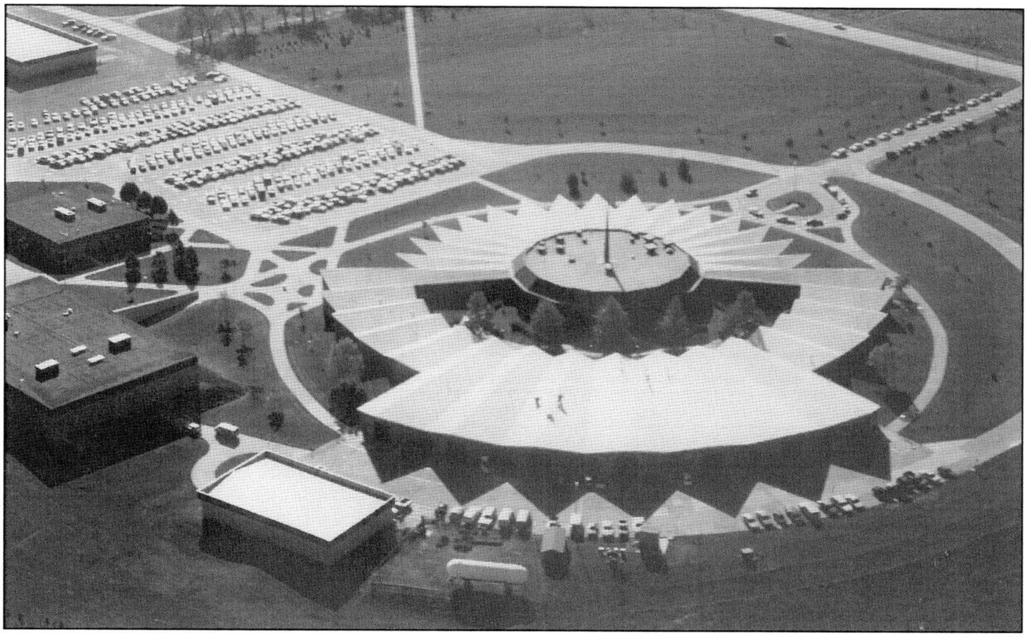

The first two-year college, Creston Junior College, opened its doors in 1926. In 1958, when the new junior high school opened, the junior college moved to the old junior high building, and its name was officially changed to Creston Community College in 1960. As part of the statewide college system, Southwestern Community College opened its campus in 1966, taking over the Creston Community College offices. The $2 million circular instructional center shown here was occupied in 1970. The state-of-the-art, vocationally focused facility has continued to expand into the new millennium, completing a new dormitory for resident students in 2010. (Southwestern Community College.)

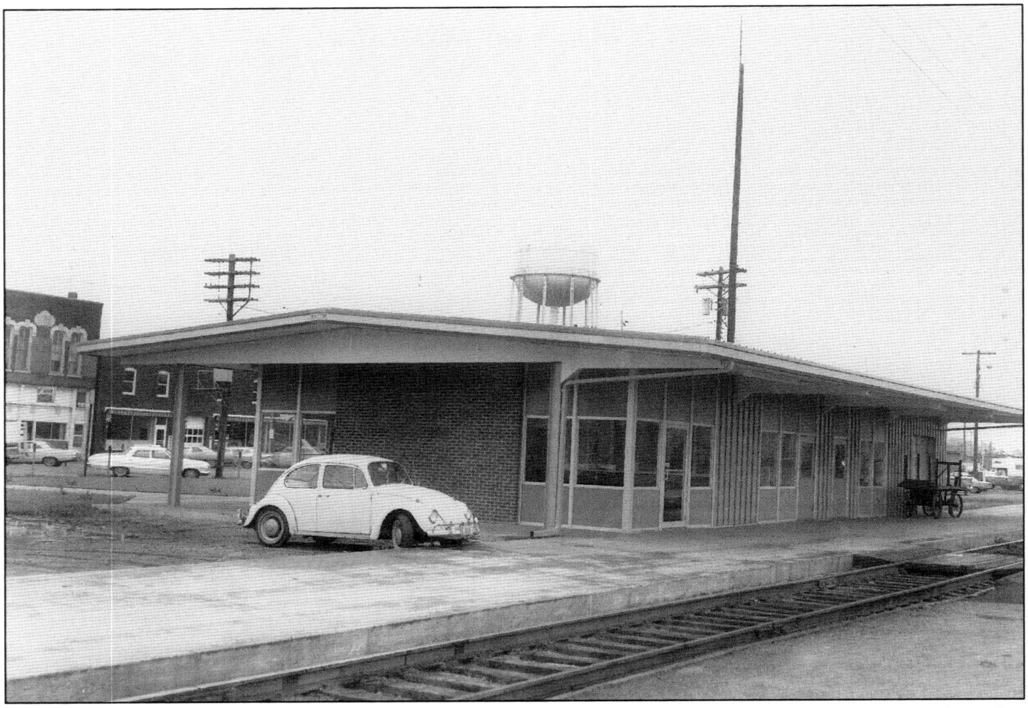

As passenger travel continued to decline into the 20th century, the railroad determined that the 1899 depot had outgrown its usefulness. This utilitarian brick-and-steel edifice was constructed in 1969 near the site of the original frame depot. Amtrak continues to offer passenger service through Creston on its California Zephyr as of 2011. (Corbin-Wagner Collection.)

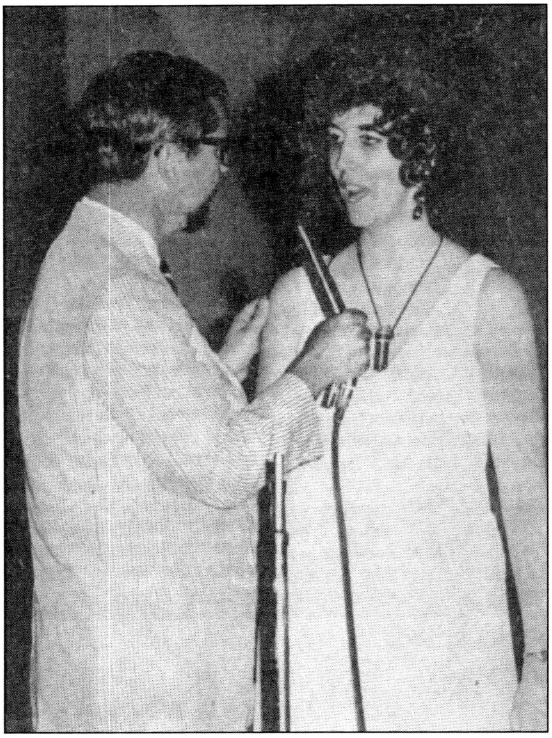

Marcia Wallace was born in Creston on November 1, 1942, and graduated high school in 1960. Her interest in drama took her to New York, where she held various jobs until her big break. She is best known for the role of Carol on the *Bob Newhart Show* and more recently as the voice of the teacher on the *The Simpsons*. She participated in the "Crestarama Performance" at Creston's centennial celebration in 1969. (*Creston News Advertiser*.)

Six

Honoring the Past

As Creston's centennial anniversary approached, a group of residents organized and incorporated the Union County Historical Society on October 25, 1966. Initially the group searched for a suitable building to house a museum. Not finding one, the group obtained land in McKinley Park to develop a museum complex. The first building brought to the center was Lincoln Township School No. 5, the last one-room county school. Over the next few years, the organization continued to add additional buildings. In 1979, a large steel building was erected to serve as a display area.

After the city's purchase of the old Burlington depot in early 1973, the building's destiny hung in limbo. Originally the city council had planned to raze the structure to make room for a parking lot; however, interested citizens launched the Save the Depot Committee, which presented city council with 700 letters supporting their position and raised funds to help finance an evaluation and renovation of the landmark. On August 15, 1973, the committee applied for and received National Register of Historic Places status. A June 4, 1974, bond election was a resounding victory for the depot. Renovation was delayed, however, until the Iowa Supreme Court intervened in favor of the depot. The newly refurbished depot was dedicated in December 1978 as the new city offices.

Since opening its doors on April 7, 1931, the Matilda J. Gibson Memorial Library has served Creston as its only public library. The structure was placed on the National Register of Historic Places in 1983. But, by the early 1980s, it became apparent that some much-needed improvements had to be made if the library were expected to continue in the current location. The lack of handicap accessibility was a major issue. After much discussion, several debates, evaluation, and a citywide vote, it was determined that the existing library would be remodeled. In February 1996, Creston Middle School students carried books from the library to a temporary location just up the street in uptown Creston for the duration of the remodeling. An open house in February 1999 displayed the $800,000 renovation.

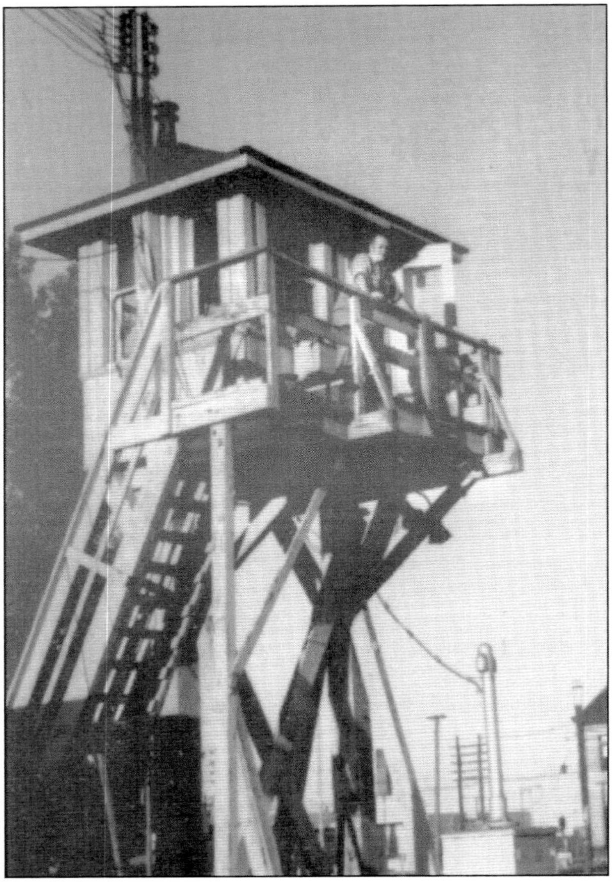

The earliest Elm Street crossing was undoubtedly like any other dirt road crossing over a railroad track, with "combatants" responsible for their own safety. As activity in the young town of Creston increased, safeguards became necessary. By 1894, railroad traffic experienced marked expansion, with 18 passenger trains passing each day in addition to the freight traffic and switching activities. (Lynne Schlaht.)

Sometime around 1900, gates were installed to guard the crossing along with a tower and watchman to control the gates. The 30-foot-tall tower contained levers and cables that controlled the gates. Around 1934, the gates were electrified, leading to the demise of the pesky cables that froze in the winter. The Elm Street crossing tower was retired in 1974, when automatic crossing gates were installed. The tower now resides in the historical complex at McKinley Park. (Lynne Schlaht.)

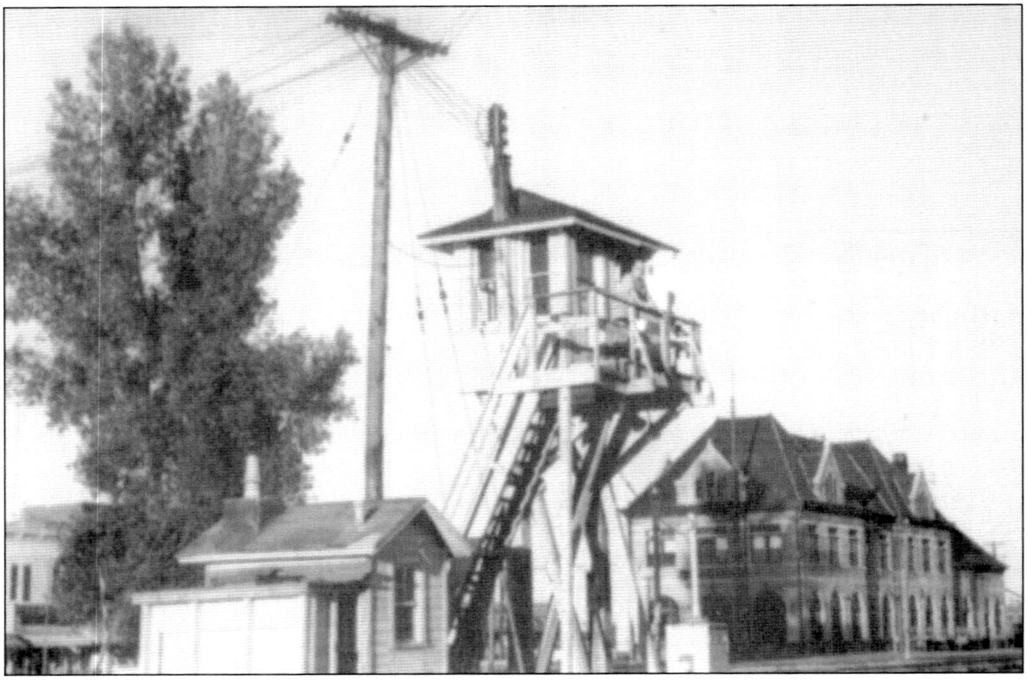

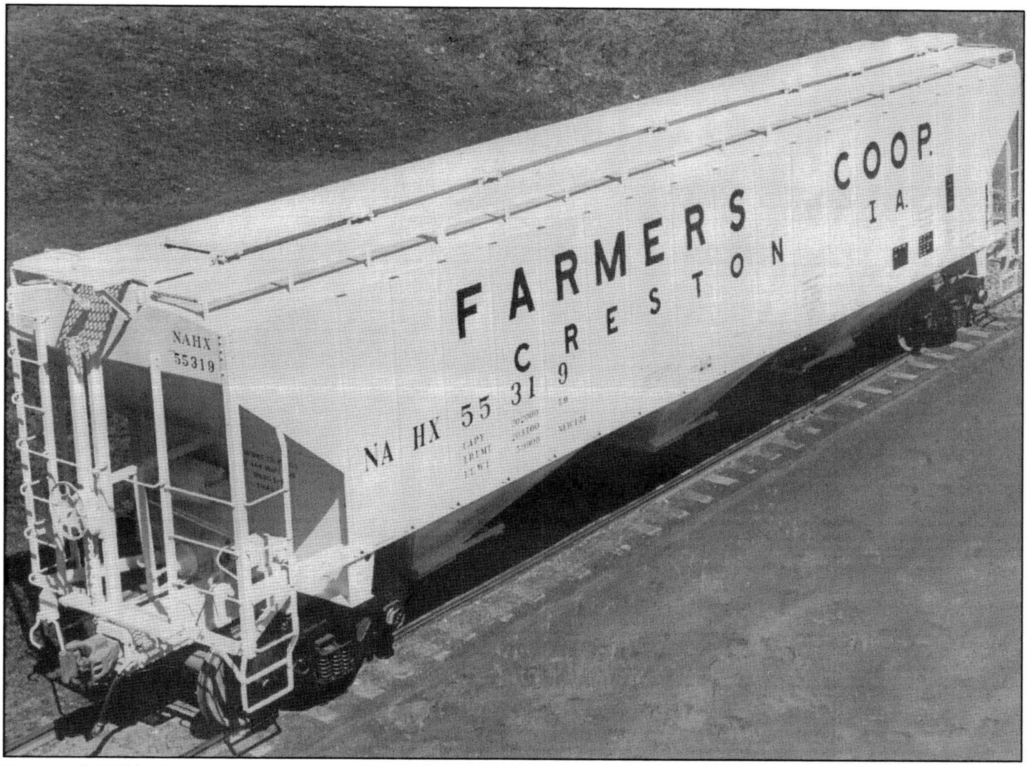

In April 1974, Creston citizens witnessed an astonishing sight: 54 pink hopper cars were delivered to the Farmers' Cooperative of Creston by the North American Car Company. Each car had a logo, which proclaimed it to be the rolling stock of the Farmers' Cooperative of Creston, Iowa. A similar group of another 54 cars, a "unit train," was purchased in 1976. (Rosalie Denton.)

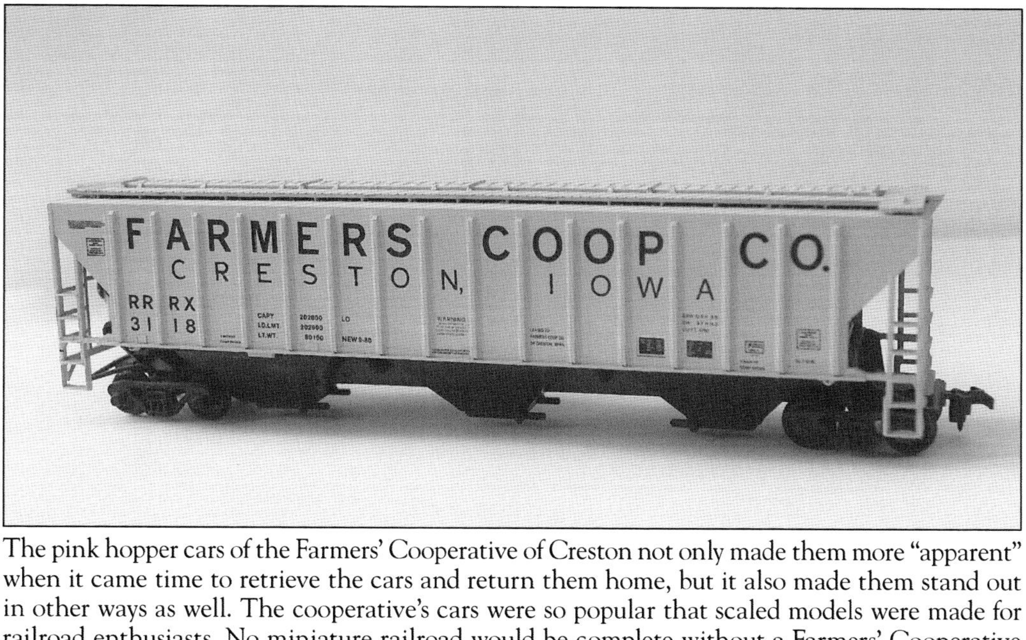

The pink hopper cars of the Farmers' Cooperative of Creston not only made them more "apparent" when it came time to retrieve the cars and return them home, but it also made them stand out in other ways as well. The cooperative's cars were so popular that scaled models were made for railroad enthusiasts. No miniature railroad would be complete without a Farmers' Cooperative of Creston pink hopper car. (Rosalie Denton.)

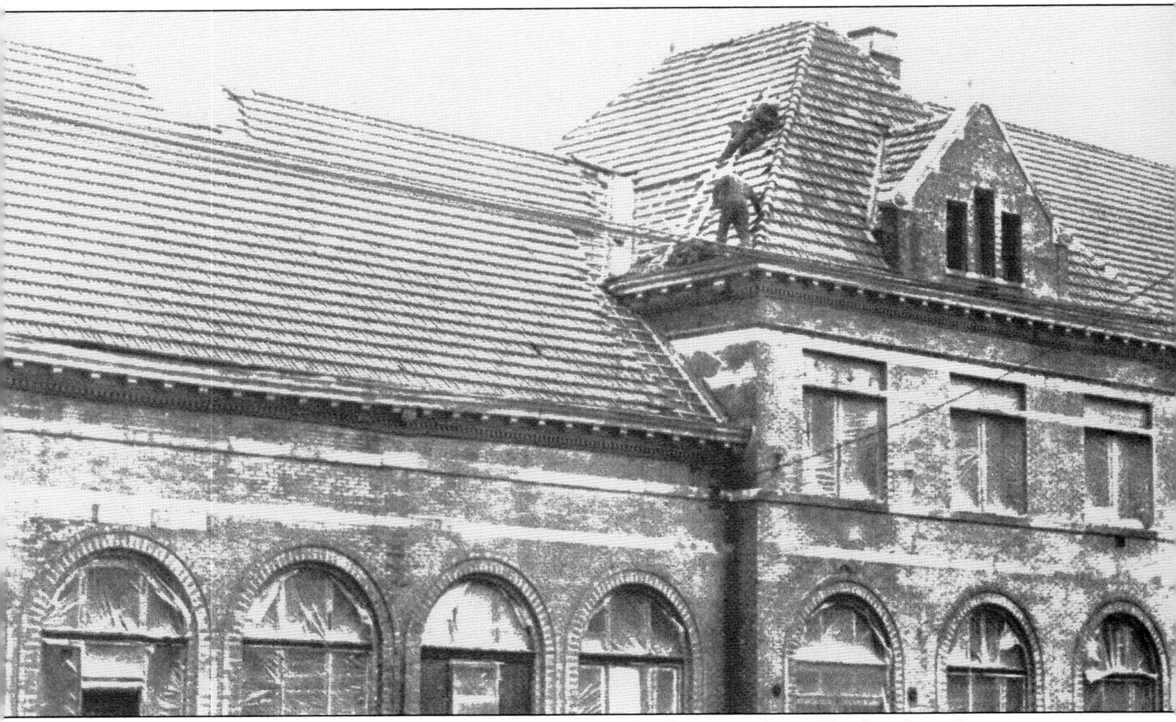

The 1899 depot was sold to the City of Creston for $1 in early 1973 after lengthy negotiations with the CB&Q and the city's repeal of its ordinance requiring a watchman at the Elm Street crossing (see page 112). The city initially planned to raze the structure to make room for a parking lot. Concerned citizens organized the Save the Depot Committee and presented the city council with 700 letters in support of saving the depot. The committee then applied for and received National Register of Historic Places status on August 15, 1973. A special bond election on June 4, 1974, was a resounding victory. A prolonged legal battle ensued, which took an Iowa Supreme Court decision to resolve. The depot prevailed and renovation was completed in 1978. Workmen are shown here restoring the tile roof. (*Creston News Advertiser.*)

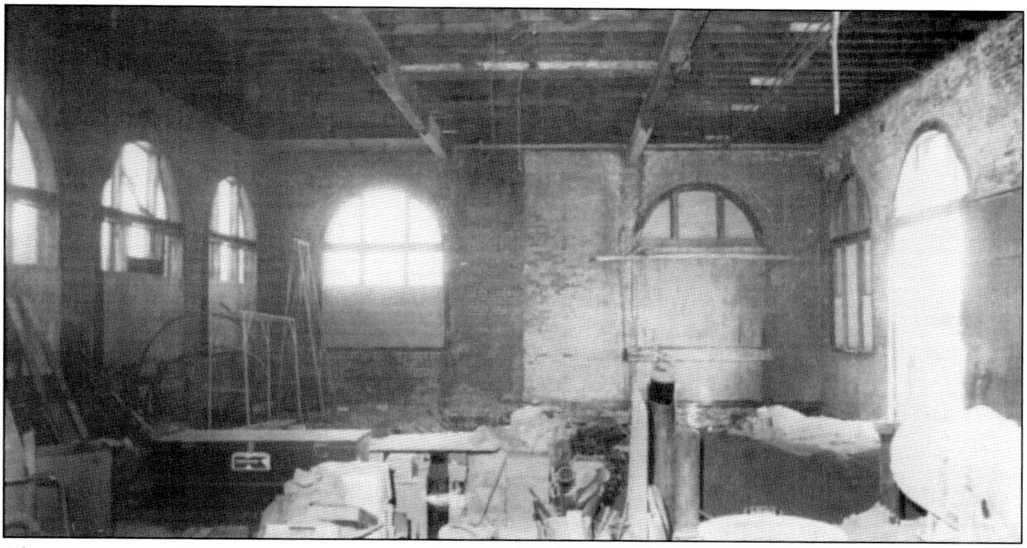

The structure underwent extensive renovation before being dedicated in ribbon-cutting ceremonies on December 3, 1978, as a city office building and meeting place. This view shows just a small amount of the work done to refurbish the historical structure. The efforts led to a special recognition award from the Iowa State Historical Department in 1980. (*Creston News Advertiser.*)

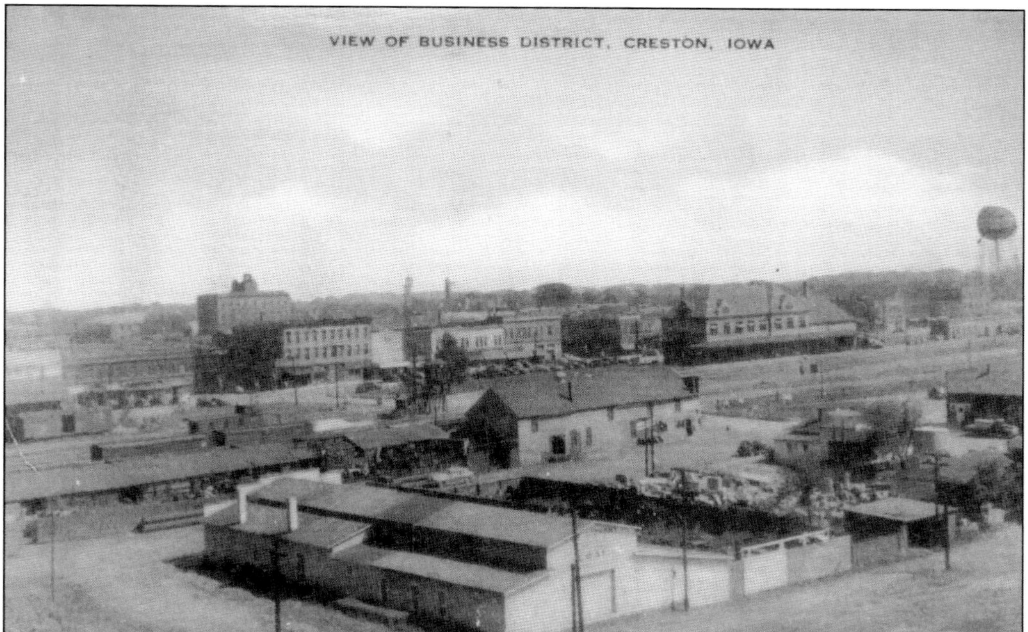

This view of the uptown business district was taken sometime in the early 1950s; the depot still has the copper canopies that were removed for a Korean War scrap drive. The tall building toward the center of the picture is the Iowana Hotel (see page 67). The large building in the center is the Farmers' Cooperative of Creston lumberyard. Also visible is the city water tower to the far right. (Lynne Schlaht.)

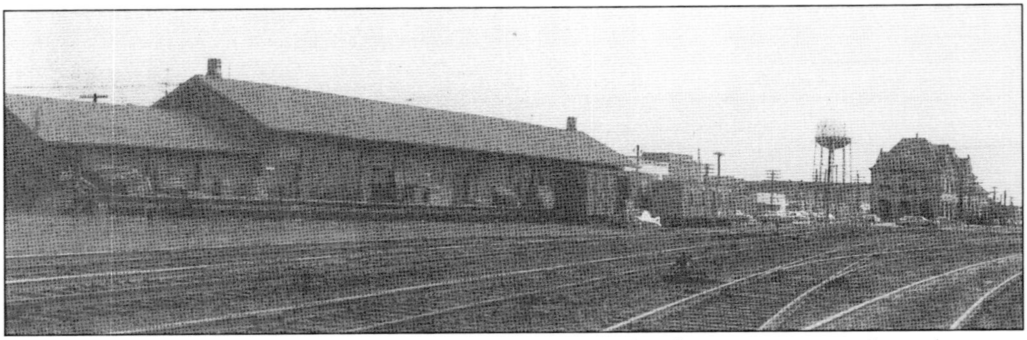

Taken in the mid-1970s, this track-level view of the 1899 freight station is seen from the grain elevator, looking toward the northeast. The addition on the left was added at a later date. Elm Street and the passenger depot, also built in 1899, are seen in the distance. The structure was razed shortly after this picture was taken. (*Creston News Advertiser.*)

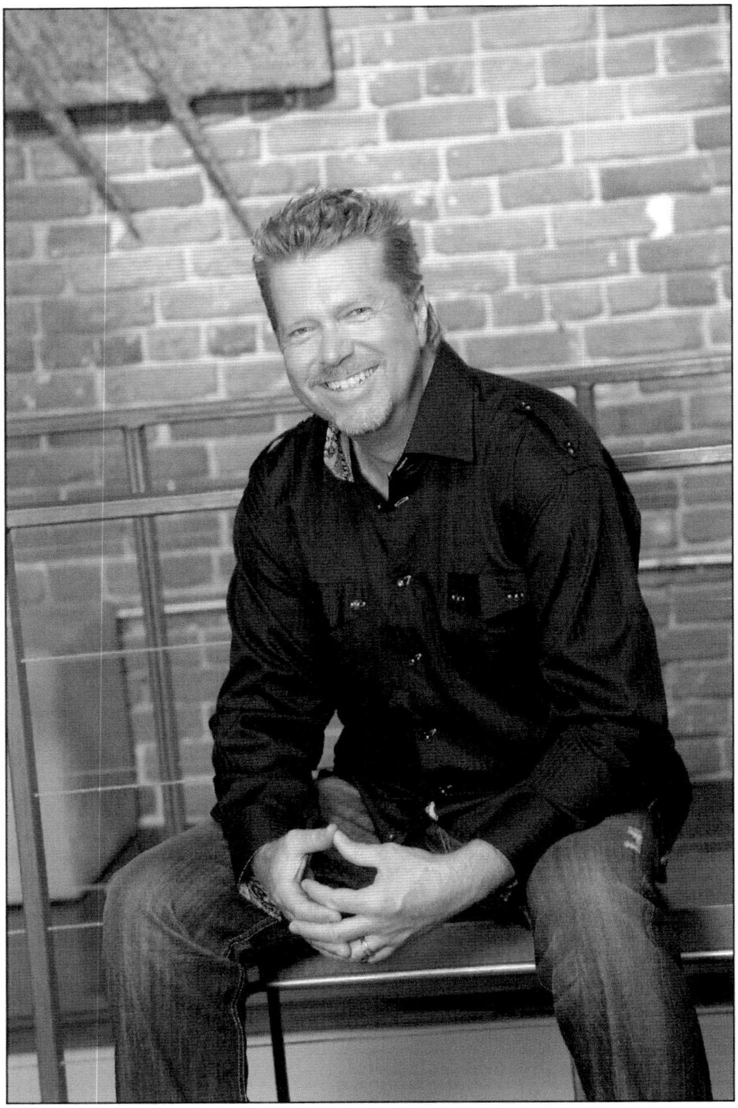

Hailed as the most recorded drummer in history, John Robinson was born in Creston on December 29, 1954. Starting his own band at the age of 10, music has always been a part of Robinson's life. His big break came in 1978, when Rufus and Chaka Khan came into the club where Robinson was playing. By the third set, the band Rufus was sitting in with Robinson. (John Robinson.)

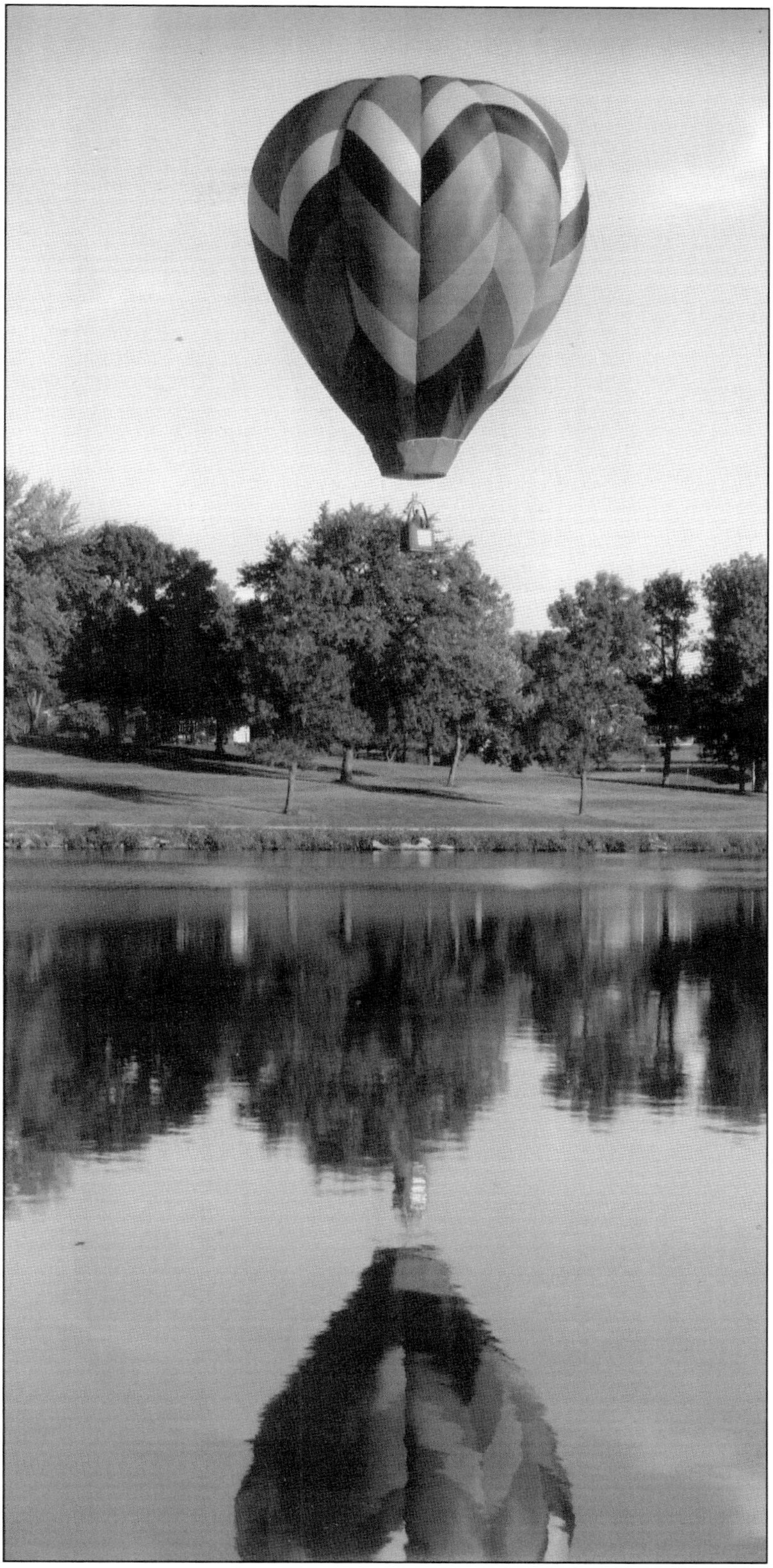

Held during the third weekend of September every year, the Balloon Days celebration began in 1978 with 22 participating balloonists. The event has grown to include a flea market, parade, craft fair, pet show, car show, dancers, and much more. Each year, more than 10,000 people flock to Creston to watch at least 55 balloonists participate in Iowa's second-largest balloon event. (Photograph by Barb Coenen.)

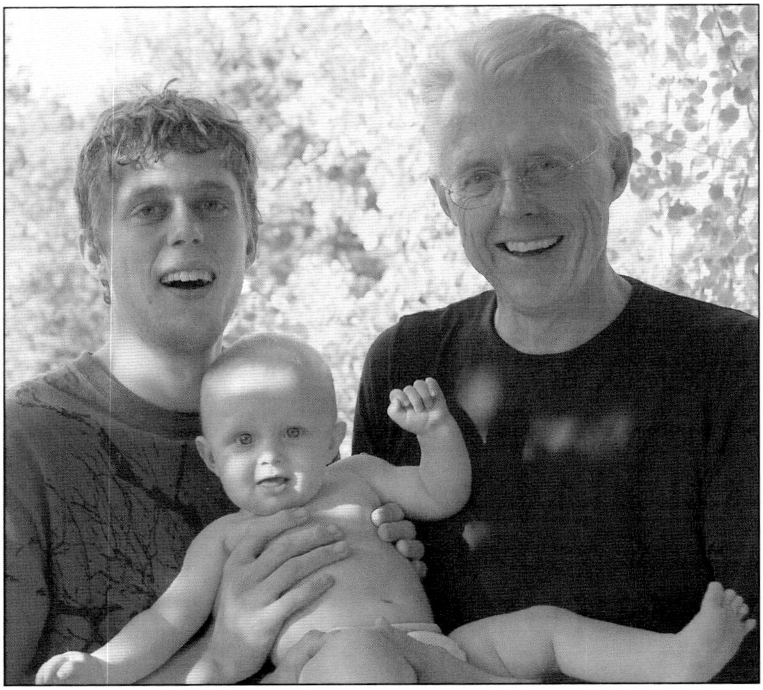

Dr. Larry Tilley, shown with his son and grandson, is a world-renowned specialist in canine and feline cardiology who was born and raised in Creston. He has written 12 textbooks and hundreds of articles related to veterinary medicine. He serves as the president and chief medical officer for VetMed Consultants in Santa Fe, New Mexico, where he resides with his wife, Jeri; son, Kyle; grandson, Tucker; and two dogs, Wendy and Zoe. (Dr. Larry Tilley.)

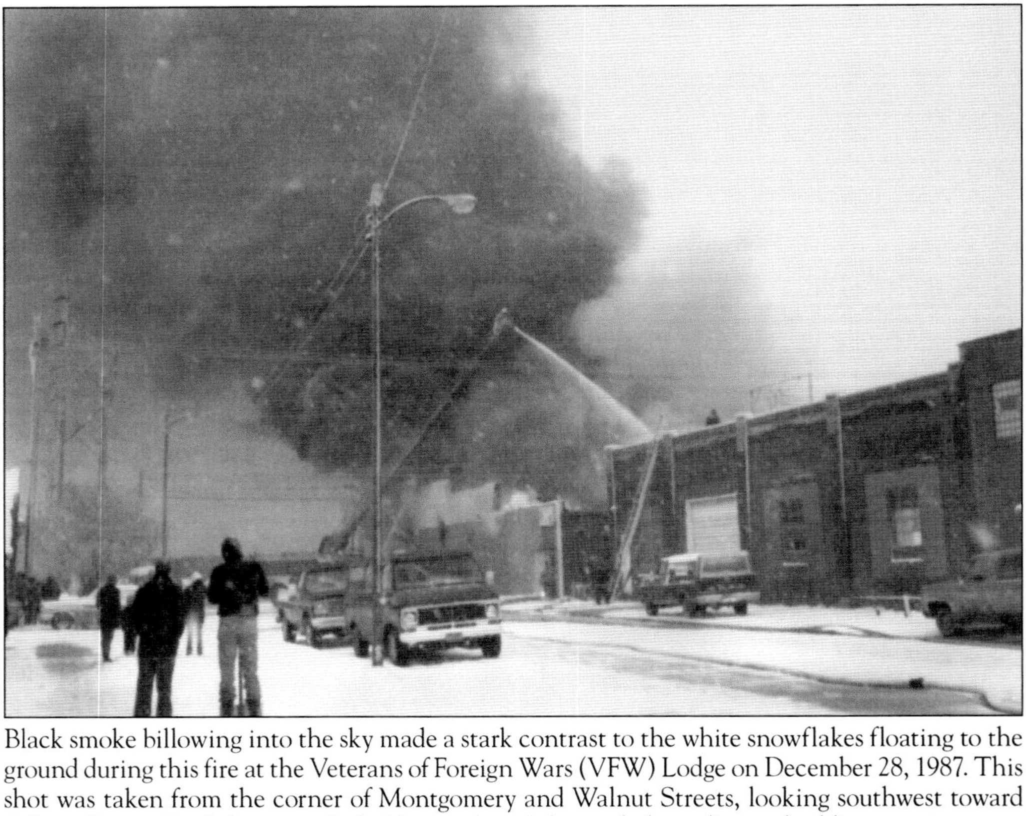

Black smoke billowing into the sky made a stark contrast to the white snowflakes floating to the ground during this fire at the Veterans of Foreign Wars (VFW) Lodge on December 28, 1987. This shot was taken from the corner of Montgomery and Walnut Streets, looking southwest toward Adams Street. Firefighters used a ladder truck and the roof of an adjacent building to gain access to the flames. (Roger Nurnberg.)

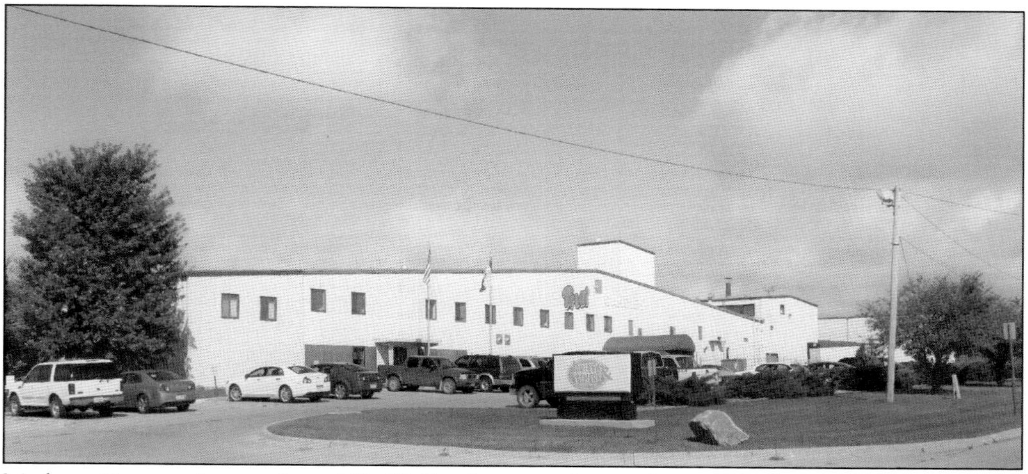

Mederer Corporation, maker of Trolli Candy, opened a production facility in Creston in 1987. Over the years, the company has changed hands and names several times. One thing that has remained constant is the Trolli Candy name and the production of an impressive variety of "gummi-style" candy. In 2011, the company is owned by Farley and Sather's Corporation. (Photograph by Warren Woods.)

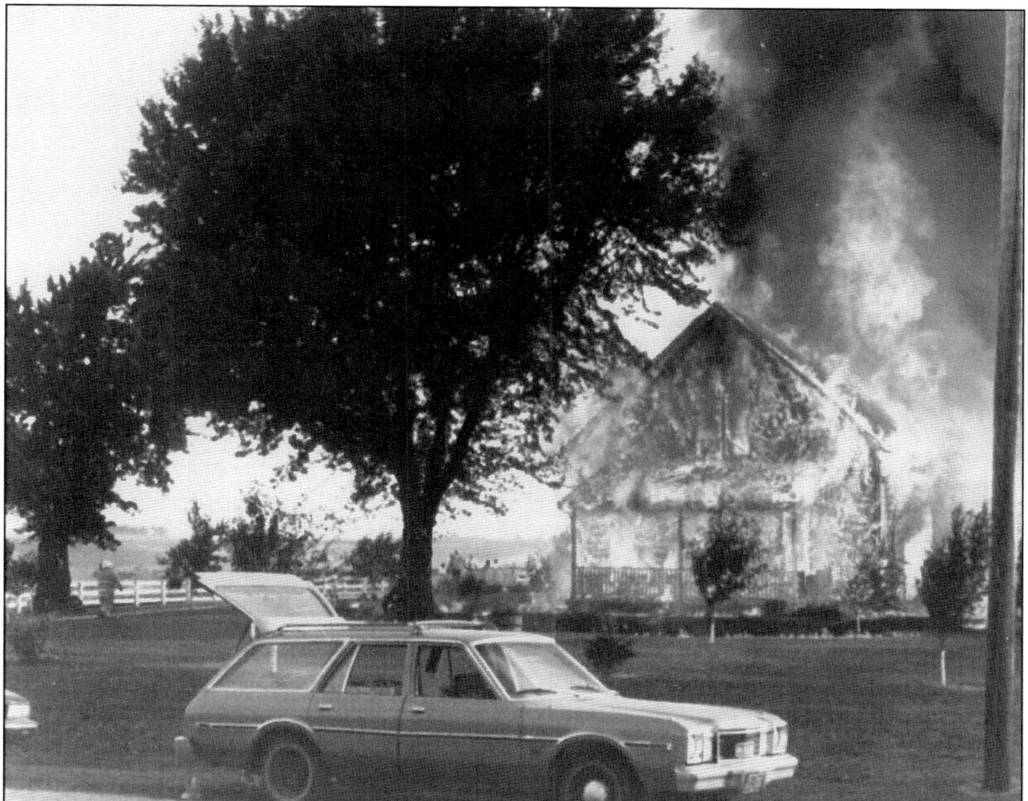

The most costly fire in Creston history occurred on July 4, 1991. It took place at the Kozerski residence, northwest of town. Anthony Kozerski was an avid hunter of big game. His extensive collection of trophies at his home were destroyed in the blaze. The loss was estimated at $150,000. (Roger Nurnberg.)

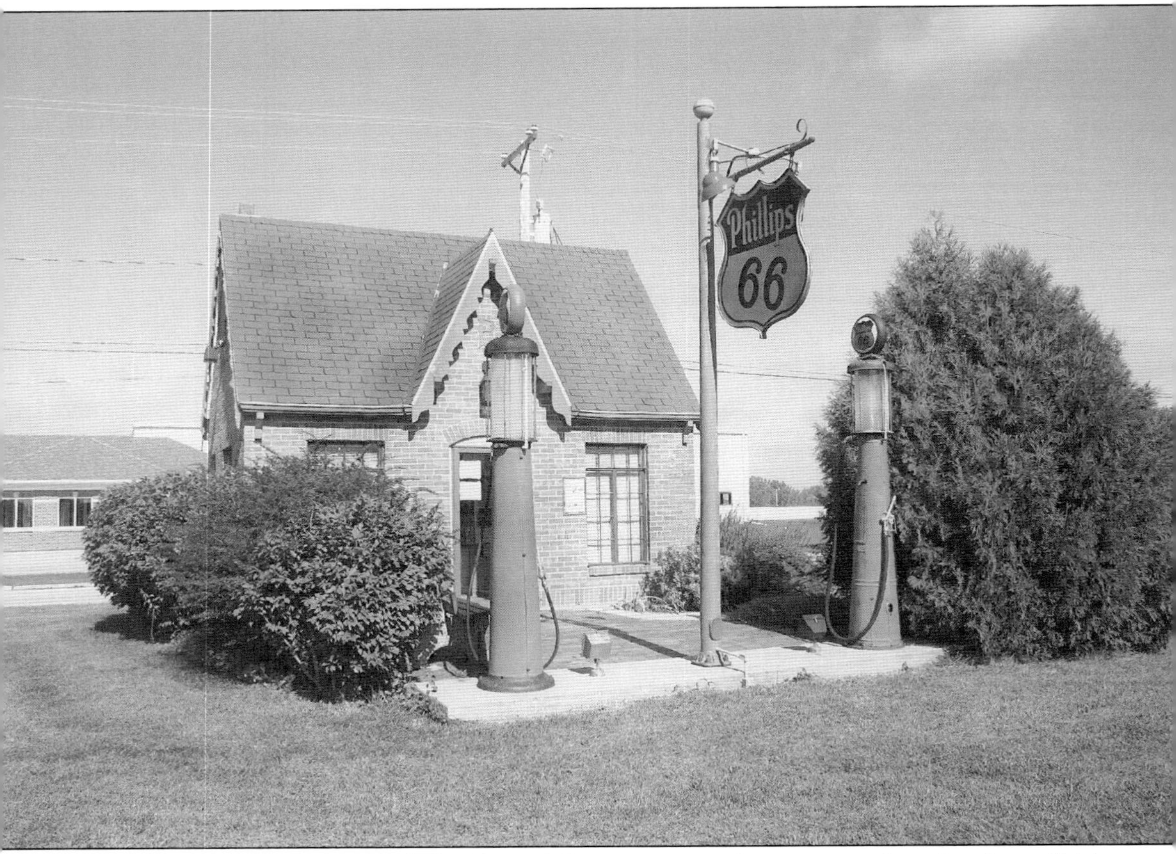

In 1994, Union County and the City of Creston received a generous donation from Shirley Lorimor in the form of one of the original c. 1931 Phillips 66 gasoline stations. A determined group of citizens worked diligently to restore the structure to its initial appearance, with the Phillips 66 trademark orange-and-green color scheme, and move it to its current location at New York Avenue and Park Street. Period signage and gasoline pumps add to the authenticity of the station. It now serves Union County and Creston as a visitor information center. (Photograph by Warren Woods.)

Seven

The Dawning of a New Millenium

As the new millennium emerges in Creston, the railroad still plays a vital role within the community. Though the beehive of activity of a century ago has waned, the railroad remains active. There is a new name, as the Burlington Northern and San Francisco Railroad now simply goes by the BNSF Railway Company, but the process is much the same. Freight trains pass through on their way to various markets. Crews continue to change out and passenger trains still stop.

The industrial park is home to a wide variety of businesses, many of which have resided in Creston for many years. The same attributes that initially attracted the companies—a vibrant work force, clean air, and exceptional transportation and shipping facilities—remain in place.

The area reservoirs that were once so vital to the survival of the city by providing water for use by the railroad and for consumption are now used for recreational activities. Three Mile Recreational Area, located just a few miles east of Creston, offers the area's largest recreation facilities, with boat ramps, a lodge, cabins, and a beach. Hunting and fishing enthusiasts find Union County and the Creston area an ideal destination. Green Valley State Park is home to Green Valley Lake, which was built in response to concerns of another devastating drought like the one suffered in the 1930s. Camping and boating fans enjoy the facilities in the state-run park. Summit Lake continues to offer fishing and other nature opportunities as well. The Creston Country Club, organized in 1908, remains in existence (see page 56), though the social aspect of the group has largely disappeared.

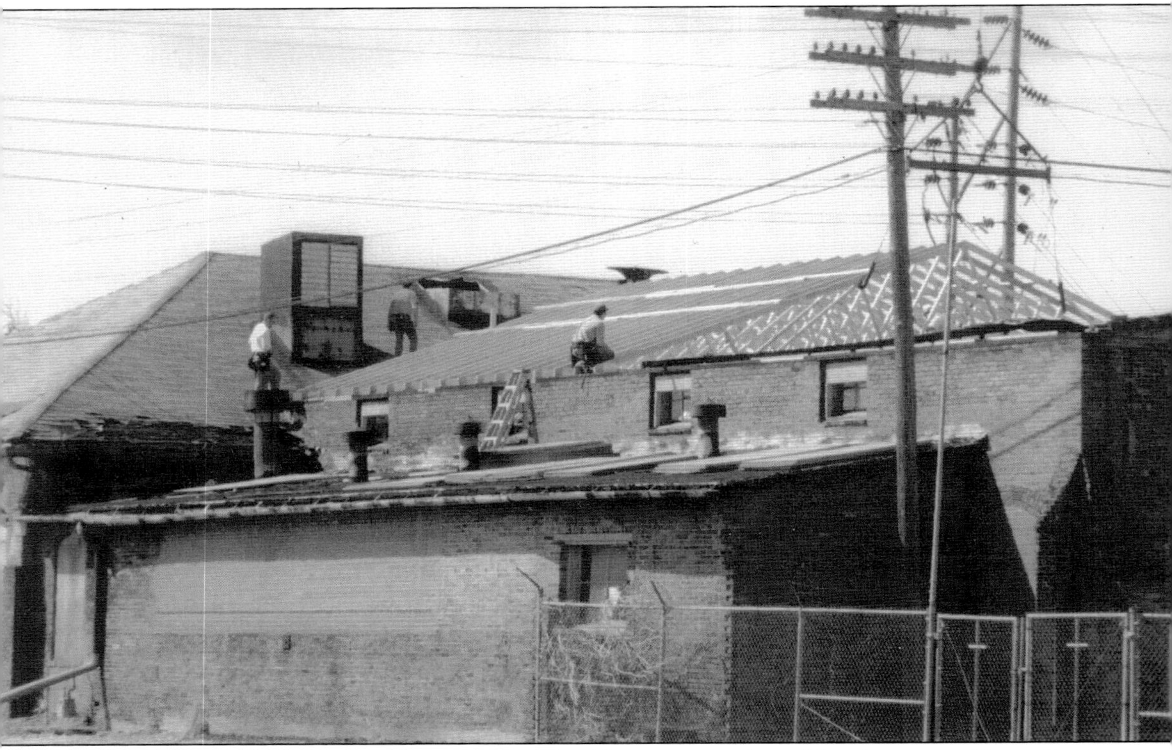

In 2000, the old Iowa Southern Utilities building was purchased by American Home Design Center/American Homes by Dave Long. After extensive renovation, which included restoring the arched windows to the facade and rebuilding the roof, Long moved both businesses into the building in 2003. (Dave Long.)

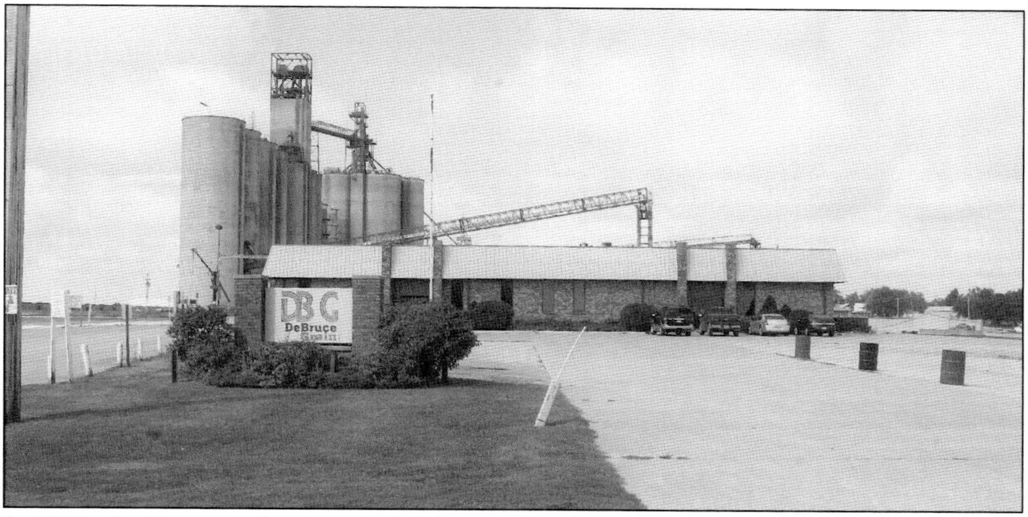

In 2002, the Farmers' Cooperative of Creston was bought out by the DeBruce Companies. Founded in 1978, DeBruce Companies is a growing $5 billion organization that ranked 56th on the Forbes 500 list of private companies in 2010. The DeBruce Companies operate high-speed grain-handling facilities located throughout the Midwest, a fertilizer distribution network, feed mills, a bean-crushing plant, and retail fertilizer operations. (Photograph by Warren Woods.)

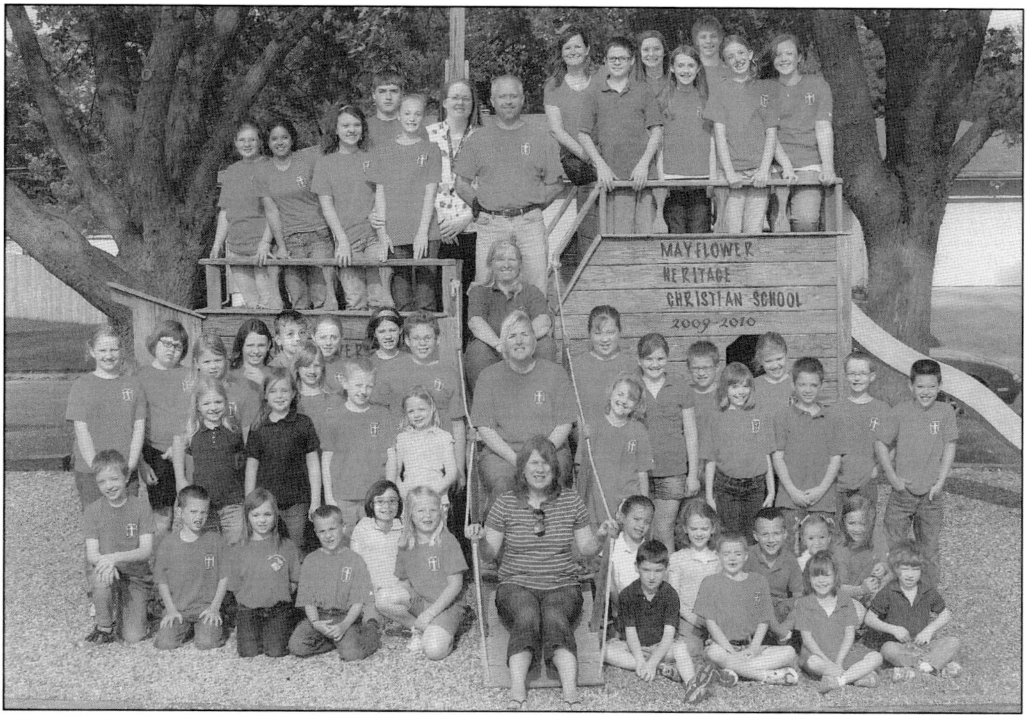

Creston's newest school is Mayflower Heritage Christian School, which is an interdenominational Christian school covering kindergarten through eighth grade. It was started in 2002 by four couples who were searching for a biblically based education for their children. Not finding what they were looking for, they took on the task of creating such a school. In 2010, Mayflower Heritage Christian School constructed a new school building on Townline Road, located with the Crest Baptist Church. (Mayflower Heritage Christian School.)

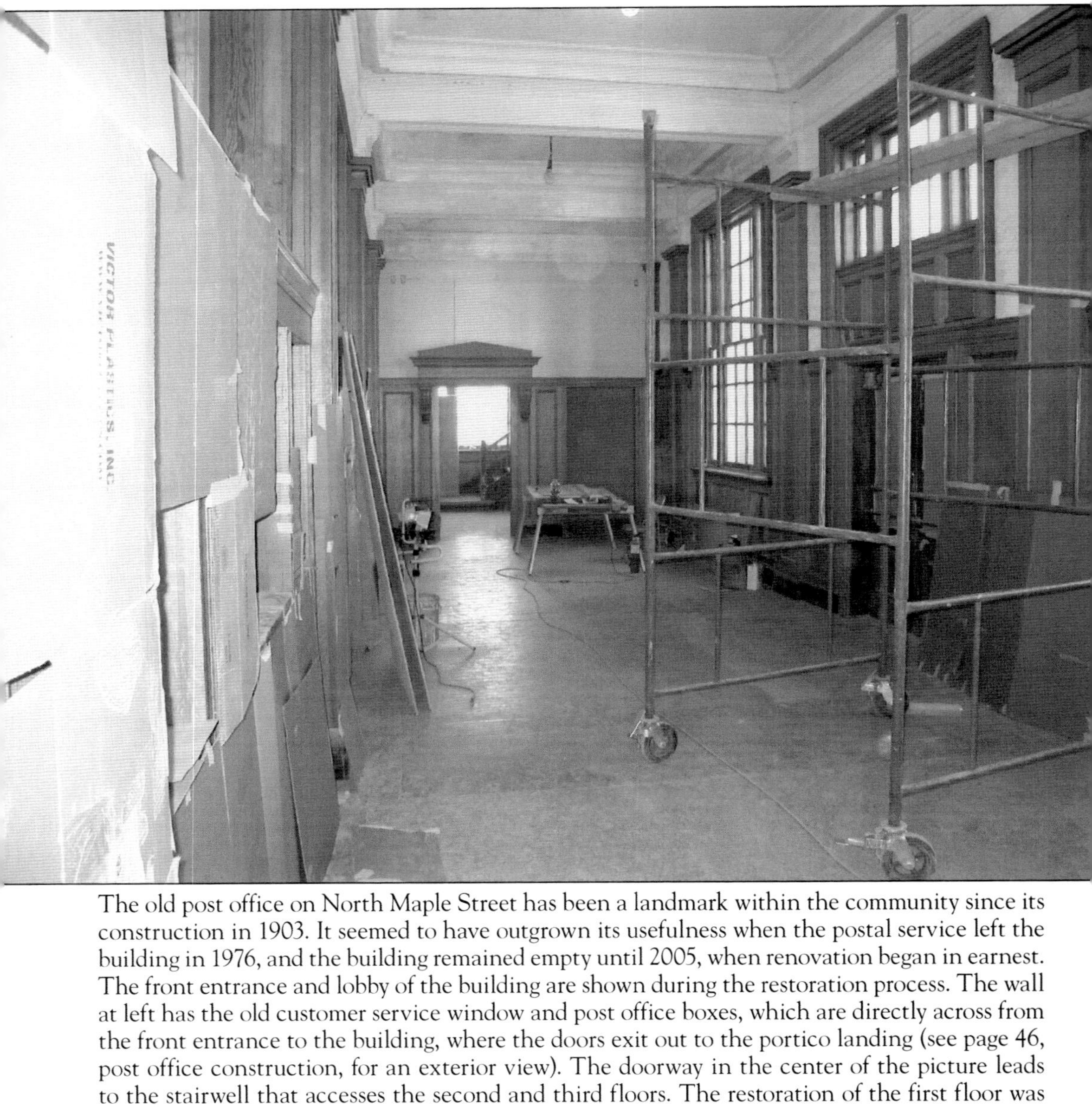

The old post office on North Maple Street has been a landmark within the community since its construction in 1903. It seemed to have outgrown its usefulness when the postal service left the building in 1976, and the building remained empty until 2005, when renovation began in earnest. The front entrance and lobby of the building are shown during the restoration process. The wall at left has the old customer service window and post office boxes, which are directly across from the front entrance to the building, where the doors exit out to the portico landing (see page 46, post office construction, for an exterior view). The doorway in the center of the picture leads to the stairwell that accesses the second and third floors. The restoration of the first floor was completed in June 2006, when it became the home of Maple Street Memories Scrapbook Store. Restoration work continues in 2011 on the second floor courtroom, judges' chambers, and offices. The third floor offices were completed for private offices for the owner. (P. F. Allen.)

After extensive renovation, the postal sorting room of the old post office became the Maple Street Memories Scrapbook Store in 2006. This view shows the restored post office boxes and customer service window from the opposite side of the previous picture. The dark box at the ceiling near the window was a peephole used by supervisors to monitor postal employees below. (P. F. Allen.)

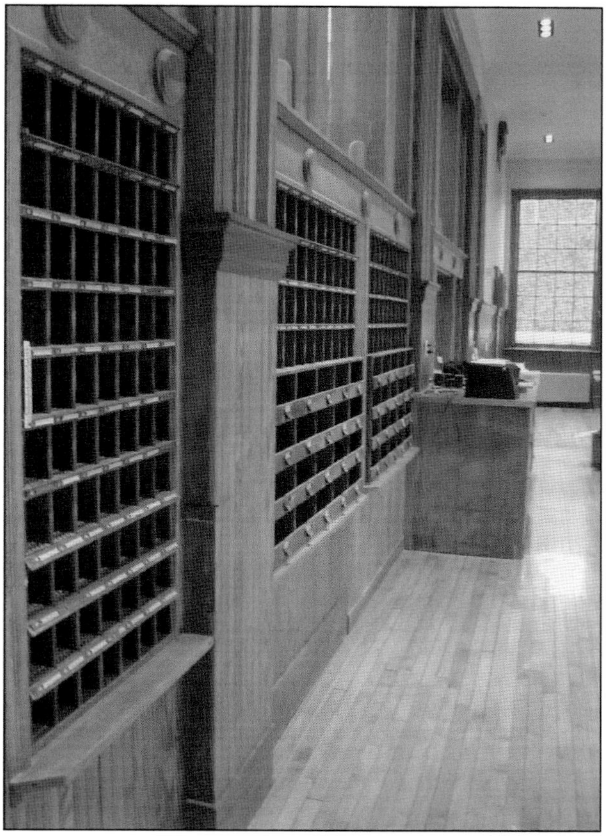

Summit Lake continues to be a source for city water consumption, but it also offers many recreational opportunities. A concrete boat ramp just off the Summit Lake Bridge on Highway 25 provides fishermen easy year-round access to prize catches of catfish, crappies, largemouth bass, and bluegill. An excellent waterfowl habitat at Mitchell Marsh supplies exceptional in-season hunting as well. (Photograph by Warren Woods.)

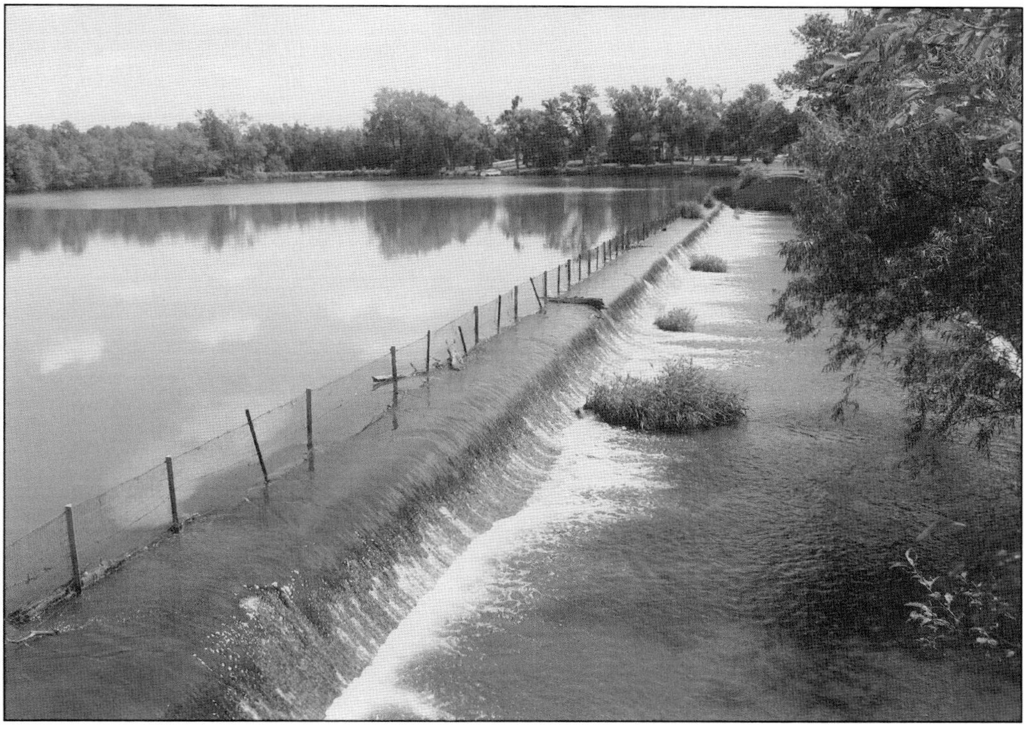

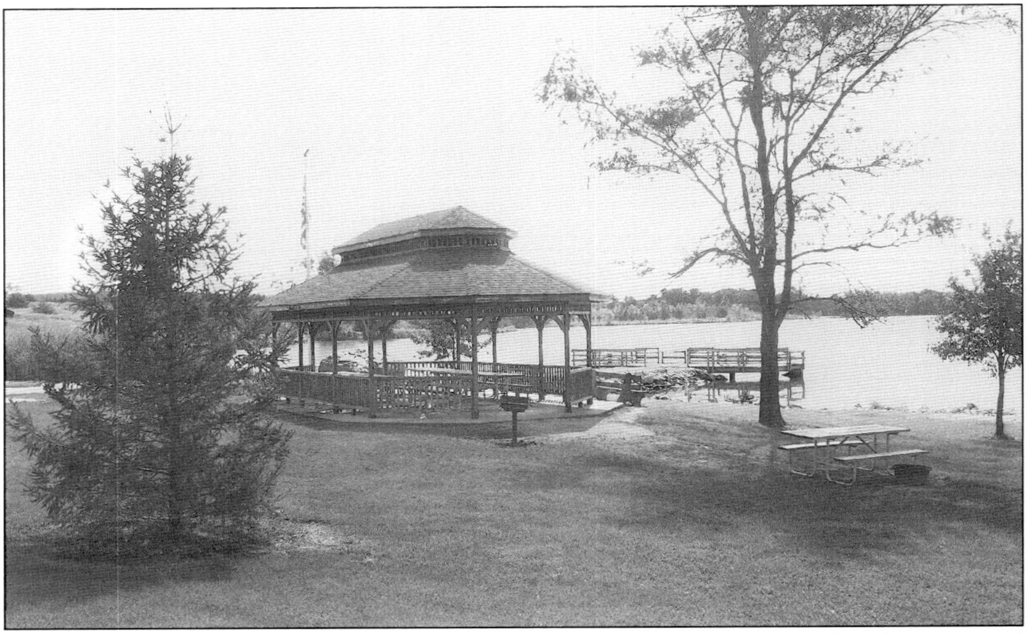

Three Mile Lake Recreation Area is Union County's largest recreational facility. Though constructed in 1995, the recreational opportunities only became a focus in the past decade. The area is a refuge for nature lovers, offering fishing, boating, swimming, camping, wildlife, cabins, and a lodge. The addition of this and the other reservoirs in the surrounding area have established Creston and Union County as a recreational destination and a leader in conservation practices. (Photograph by Warren Woods.)

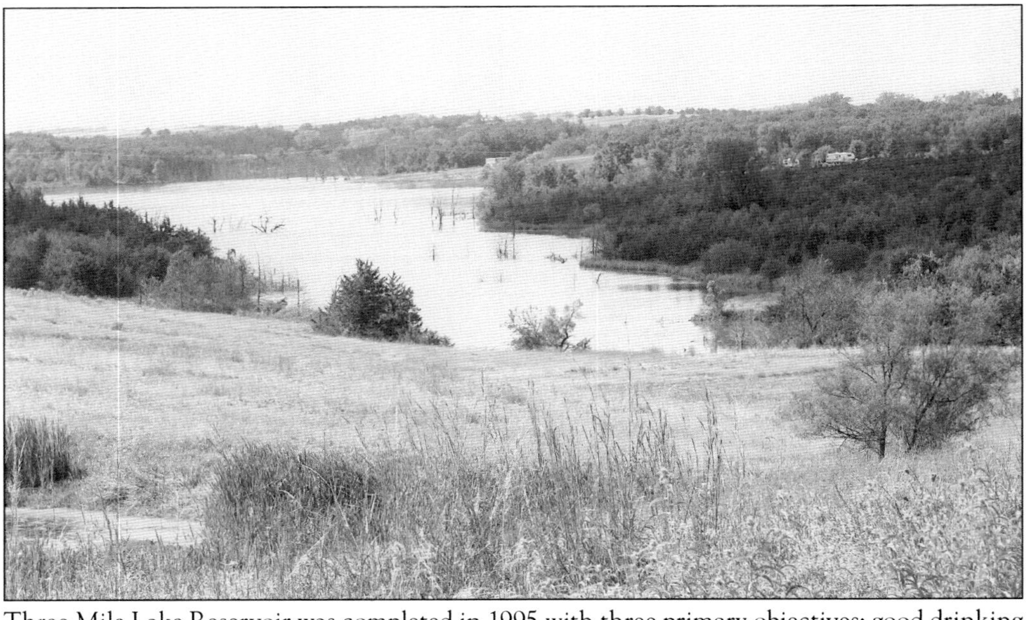

Three Mile Lake Reservoir was completed in 1995 with three primary objectives: good drinking water, flood control, and recreation. Long before the lake was constructed, a preventive approach to water protection was taken in the Three Mile Watershed Pollution Prevention Project that was initiated in 1991. It was one of the first projects of this type in the nation. (Photograph by Warren Woods.)

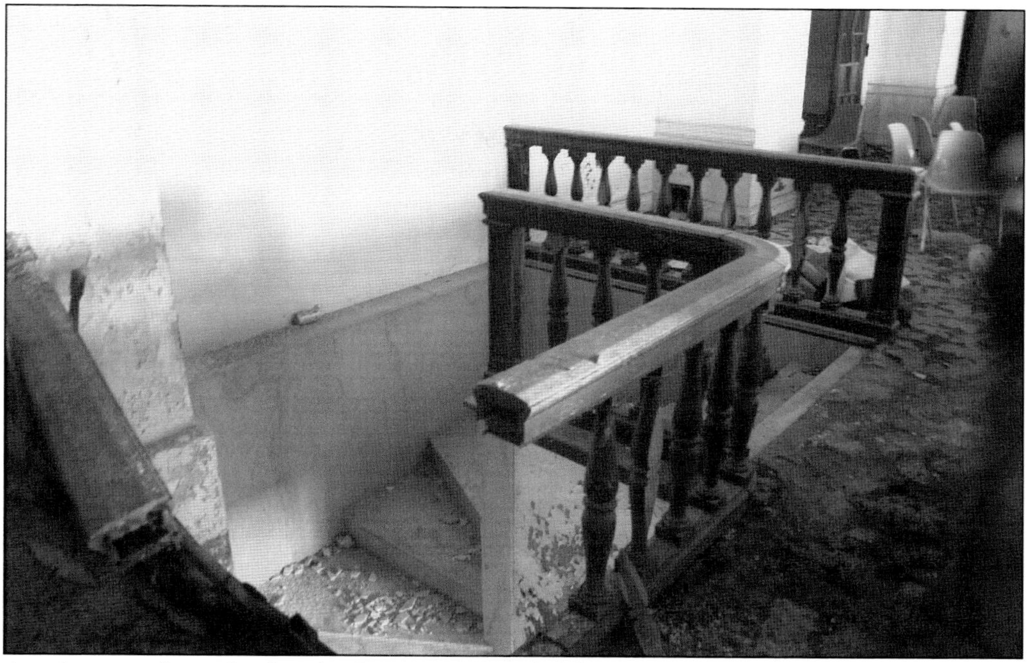

Another significant landmark, the Iowana Hotel, fell victim to abandonment and neglect in the early 1990s. Vandalism, Mother Nature, and pigeons left the once-beautiful structure with an uncertain future. In 2009, after obtaining ownership, the city began exploring options for its use. Renovation of the 90-year-old building into low-income housing began in November 2010. (Photograph by Warren Woods.)

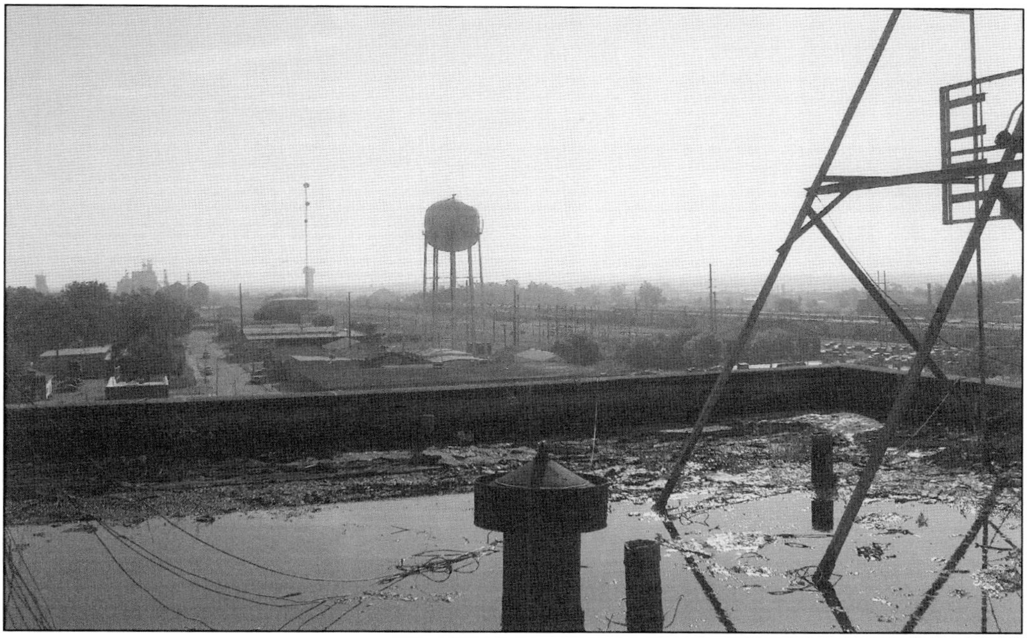

The extent of the renovation can be seen from this unique perspective taken from the roof of the former Iowana Hotel. The iconic Iowana Hotel sign still overlooks uptown Creston. Dirty water standing in pools on the roof are one of the first projects of the renovation. Plans also include restoration of the Iowana's sign. (Photograph by Warren Woods.)